SOCIOLOGY AND SOCIAL WELFARE SERIES

edited by Paul Halmos

The Personal Service Society

The Personal Service Society

Paul Halmos

Schocken Books · New York

Published in U.S.A. in 1970
by Schocken Books Inc.
67 Park Avenue
New York, N.Y. 10016
Copyright © 1970 by Paul Halmos
Library of Congress Catalog Card No. 75-114164

For Tom Marshall

Printed in Great Britain

Acknowledgements

The old sociological landscape seems to disclose less and less as time goes on. An effort of trying to look at it anew to espy a few more of its secrets will, almost certainly, turn out to be vain. Just the same, I am obstinate enough to strive on to see things from a new angle. Of course, in search of a new vista we must go off the beaten track. In doing so, we shall get our clothes torn, we may get lost, and we may be set upon by carnivorous reviewers. No matter: rather than stare at the same equivocal and dreary picture, I believe I can beat a path to a point of elevation, which people have tried to avoid because of its precarious foothold. I shall risk the hazards of the adventure in the hope that I can stand up long enough there to discern and survey a new landscape.

It is almost certain that my readers will regard my description of this landscape too optimistic. I must then challenge them to ask themselves what account of contemporary social changes other than mine might be given which was consistent with the expectation that humanity would still be creatively present in this universe in a couple of hundred years' time?

My first (advance) acknowledgement is to those readers who are willing to enter into compact with me to ask this question, and keep on asking it, every time when they feel that I am erring on the side of finding too many good auspices for mankind.

My second acknowledgement is to those handful who have been kind enough to read this book before publication, and have made helpful suggestions to improve it. I am happy to record my thanks to Irene Davies, Martin Albrow, Helmuth Heisler and Anthony Ashworth, for their valuable comments and criticisms. If I have not always acted on their advice it is because this would have lured me on to writing a second volume to this work.

Finally, I should like to thank the Editors of the Journal of *Ethics* and of the *British Journal of Sociology* for allowing me to reproduce some of the arguments I used in papers of mine which they have published, Messrs Allen & Unwin for permission to include the

v

diagram from P. J. G. Pulzer's *Political Representation and Elections in Britain*, Cambridge University Press for four tables from Deborah Paige's and Kit Jones' *Health and Welfare Services in Britain in 1975*, H.M.S.O. for material from *Health and Welfare, The Development of Community Care, England and Wales* (April 1963) and *The Demand and Supply of Teachers*, 1963–1986 (1965).

P.H.

Cardiff, 1969

Contents

Preface

'It is a mark of insincerity of purpose to spend one's
time in looking for the sacred Emperor in a low-class
tea-shop.' Alfred Emanuel Smith: *The Wallet of Kai Lung*

We are often warned that a society which has satisfied even the most
exacting material needs of man, the needs not only for survival but
for the most imaginatively varied comforts, will be a society emanci-
pated from want beyond endurance. A nightmare of a Brave New
World will have been called into being unless, of course, humanity
can find new wonders of the ineffable, mainly by contriving to develop
ever newly sensitised appetites for companionship, mutuality, and
love. Of course, as yet, we are far from the Utopian state of plenty
and safety which would justify spending time and labour speculating
on what kind of social system would make it possible for us to brave
the Brave New World. We shall be told without hesitation that, at
least today, there are more urgent matters near at hand demanding all
the attention of social scientists, and that speculation about improbable
and remote possibilities is a desertion of the social scientist's more
immediate duty, which is to help his fellow men here and now.

Yet certain facts in our contemporary situation make us pause to
consider whether there might not be strong and practical incentives
for us to identify and describe the germs of the better future in our
present society.

There are certain processes afoot in modern, reasonably affluent,
industrial societies which show a striking measure of consistency and
continuity, and which strongly invite extrapolation into the immediate
future. Science, technology, and economic growth have profoundly
changed the division of labour in society and the changes will continue
along lines which are not altogether unpredictable. One line, the
direction of which appears to be set for some time to come, points
towards a continuing growth in the proportion of those of the total

working population whose work is done in the personal services of health, welfare, and education. The measure of this growth seems dramatic when we observe that those in the personal service professions make their mark on the sentiments and values of several of the leading élites as a whole, and thus exert an influence on society which is in excess even of their already large numbers. Thus it is not at all the mirage of some remote future state of affairs, desirable or not, that has attracted my attention, but the orderly and linear development of certain characteristic facts of our social life. Of course, we do not yet live in a Personal Service Society; yet there is evidence to be found that we have begun to build such societies as this. Incipient though the evidence, and ambiguous though some of its indications for the future, I shall develop certain hypotheses about the social situation and endeavour to offer verification in their support. The whole of Chapter 1 is devoted to this theme.

Like everybody else, I too should like to know what happens next, and I refuse to pretend that we can say nothing valid about the future in the light of the present and the past. But, of course, we must face the fact that if in some measure our extrapolations become a part of our current social science, and humanity becomes aware of these extrapolations, then our status of 'social scientists' has been changed: we shall be unable to free ourselves of the stigma of being almost propagandists rather than merely assessors of an impending future. The contemporary sociologist is well acquainted with the proposition that the definition of a situation becomes part of the situation. The formulation by social science of a social fact becomes part of the fact and modifies it. Contemporary social science offers not only separate definitions but also *systems* of definitions, theories of society, 'scientific' as well as 'ideological' systems about social structure and social change. These have penetrated the social realities amidst which we live, and have themselves become powerful internal regulators or adaptors of the social process. Now, because an increasingly systematic tuition in the social sciences is regarded as essential in the training of professional workers in, among other things, health, welfare, and education, I will examine some of the implications of an exposure to sociological and social science teaching. Then, following this exploration, I shall pass on to show that a special stream of social science thinking, *largely originating from clinical and social psychological sources*, has been yielding a flow of theory and pragmatic guidance, which seems to have an effect rather different from that brought on by the social sciences in general. This special stream of ideas emerged from, and is applicable to, the intimate personal relationships which characterise professional work in health, welfare, and education. Such professional work is carried on to render some personal services to clients, patients, pupils, students, and so on.

Consequently, the two sections of Chapter 2 – one on the impact of social science on society in general, and the other on the impact of the social psychological science of the helping professions on society in particular – deal with ideas which seem to nudge society in different directions. Social science in general is manipulative, positivistic and impersonal; the social psychological science of the helping professions is lured away in the direction of the personal and the phenomenological. Yet the seemingly objective and impersonal standards of a general social science are themselves suspect: the first of these two sections will explain why the cultivation of social science can never be a 'pure science' activity, and why it is impossible to 'explain' society without changing it through the rendering of explanations. This section is included in this book to discourage people from pretending that teaching social science to the functionaries of modern society is anything less than a potent indoctrination. In their training a growing number of workers in the professions are put through social science courses and there is nothing to hold back this growth: by now we think we should be failing in our duty if we stressed the obligatoriness of a sociological tuition any less than the obligatory tuition in Latin, English language, or mathematics used to be stressed. Of course, whether we teach several of the social sciences, or only sociology, the instruction remains on an academic level, and its moral influence remains subtle, implicit, and almost entirely concealed. But when we teach a special social-psychological 'know-how' to the helping professions the interpretations offered are often thinly veiled precepts.

The age in which we live distrusts interpretations which are not tough-minded and even self-deprecating or sceptical. Any account which is not tough-minded is immediately suspected of being not only complacent but also deluded. Not surprisingly, the self-denigration of man brings with it the austere repudiation of moral hope or optimism. It is unconsciously assumed that if the social scientist is hopeful or optimistic he must be *eo ipso* complacent and, therefore, not rigorous enough methodologically to be trusted. The result is that in order to ensure a discipline of sound realism we must be compulsively sceptical about all encouraging versions of the social epic. Writing of autobiographies, Francis Hope recently noted in *The Observer* (13 April 1969), 'Since Rousseau, we expect confessions rather than memoirs: the test of self-description is honesty and the test of honesty is self-deprecation.' This austerity towards ourselves is a quality of the culture in which social science is being cultivated. Intellectual and aesthetic sensitivity is almost invariably associated with philosophical pessimism; as if sharpness without bitterness was not to be regarded as possible, and as if an experience without a tang was an experience without a taste. It is not only that sociologists often pursue truth with a jaundiced look or at least with a frown: the *Schöngeist*, and the avant-garde intellectual, seem to think that smiling is a sign of complacency and therefore a sign of having been deceived. In a harsh universe – objectively and truthfully viewed – optimism is a sure sign of credulity and naivety. Intellectual integrity demands that we should not only be vigilant in the face of our own tendencies to wishful thinking, but also that we should *a priori* distrust all comforting versions of man's prospects. We must for ever search for deliberate deceiving intent behind all promising lines of thought. It is thought effeminate, and in some ways discreditable, to spend one's time on extrapolations from the past and the present which tell us of desirable landscapes ahead. It is decidedly manlier to eschew this sort of speculation, and it has been taken to be a sign of intellectual virility to doubt, to disbelieve, and to be resigned to the worst. Of course, there is sociological writing in which these tendencies are not apparent, but mostly it is the spirit of the discipline – unsure of itself as yet – which seeks to discipline itself with much severity, partly to show that it is there and working.

The curiously one-sided evaluation of social science, the pessimistic sensing of danger, often elicits both a conservative and an avant-garde ideological bias: both see bias elucidation as profanation, conservative opposition to social science is frequently charged with anxiety and apprehension. The anxiety is about a loss of reverential feeling, and of innocence, which is taken to be a consequence of allowing social science to trespass everywhere. The conservative mind takes it as categorical that to understand is to lose all illusion. Almost as if the tag was now revised to read, *tout comprendre c'est tout con-*

damner. But the idiosyncratic aesthete too resents social science and its explanations for almost the same reason. The spelling-out of the ineffable, the jargon in lieu of the poetic language, the explanation of the joke, are all blasphemies in the aesthete's eyes. In the estimation of both conservatives and progressives social science is an ingrowing toenail of our cultural limb, not only causing pain but threatening to go septic.

Contrary to the views of both conservatives and avant-gardistes we must now consider the possibility that – far from profanation by discussion – a new ennoblement by discussion and insight may be heralded by the entry of social science into the causal order of social events. This entry may be direct so that the findings and operative principles of social science affect those who engage in these discussions. The result of the direct influence is not profanation but rather an elimination of pomposity. Nor is the outcome an idealisation or a fanciful ennoblement: rather it is growth in sobriety, and a reduction in the wasteful feelings of guilt, indignation, blame, and hatred.

Sociology is a critical science constantly embattled with the prevaricators of social truth. Here the built-in doubt and scepticism is a methodological necessity, and the exposing of disingenuousness a daily task. This habit of not believing is a factor of some ominous importance in our time, yet, of course, this campaign of pitiless disclosure had been and is still totally necessary. Without it, objectivity would not have been possible. Complacent misrepresentations about the springs of social change had to be discredited if social science was to develop. Indeed, even today, the methods of disclosure must be retained, and further refined, so that we remain undeceived by distortions introduced by wishful thinking.

And yet, objectivity will not be far advanced if in the pursuit of social truth we give credence only to what we can show to be a conscious or unconscious prevarication, or simply what we do not like in ourselves. If our search for more social intelligence will throw light only on the working of those motives which our cultures have branded as base or unattractive, and either ignore or underestimate the role played by other, less unseemly, motives, then our search for more social intelligence will begin to fail and our conclusions will become ideological in an unexpected manner. In the past we strove to secure objectivity by giving full publicity to our failings in virtue and we must now consider the possibility that, in the end, we may have failed to achieve objectivity because we have discounted virtue altogether.

I, as a sociologist, must confess to a not inconsiderable apprehension of the role I have assumed, the role of one who is to correct this pessimistically self-critical method. Being a part-time idealist, I am reminded of the saying that 'a man gazing on the stars is proverbially at the mercy of the puddles on the road'. And it may be said that I am certainly neglectful of the wisdom in Oscar Wilde's observation that 'it is safer to believe evil of everyone until people are found out to be good', but we might also remember Wilde's warning that that 'requires a great deal of investigation nowadays'. I am engaged in that sort of investigation, and expect to be called a sentimentalist, an enemy of clearsightedness, and even an ideologist of the declining bourgeoisie. Yet, what I have done may, I hope, claim the attention of those sociologists who are deeply concerned with anticipating social change in our time, and who desire to keep an open mind on what mixture of human qualities will eventually determine the nature of future human societies. Will the competitive, self-asserting and aggressively creative man always prevail over the co-operative, sympathetic, and gently imaginative man? Will the sustained advancement of our culture always and mainly depend on the first kind, or can this advancement be sustained mainly by the second kind?

Whilst propounding its hypotheses and to some extent testing them, the book that follows may also imply some tentative answers to these questions, and possibly to some others. In doing so, I am unrepentant about allowing such a prominent place in my study to anticipations of betterment. It would seem that description of disastrous contingencies is a better tolerated concern of our sociologists than the prediction of improvements in our lot. Nor is there half as much industry expanded on the incredulous scrutiny and questioning of the grounds upon which the dark apocalyptic prophecies rest as there is on the testing of the hopeful hypotheses of betterment. But whatever the discrimination between the treatment meted out to the two kinds of predictions, I anticipate the charge that my predictions are inadequately supported by evidence. Alas, in man's history no predictions can be *adequately* supported by evidence. All that I can hope for is that my account of what is likely to happen in some strictly specified aspects of our future social history will be taken not only as possibly but even as probably valid.

At any rate, the early stages of pregnancy are not visible to the naked eye, and special tests are required to ascertain it. I am engaged in the study of a social process which I freely and repeatedly describe to be embryonic, with perhaps no more than one 'period' missed, if as much. But as a healthy embryo irresistibly develops in a healthy maternal body – unless aborted – so, I believe, will the incipient process – to the study of which I devote the following pages – evolve into an identifiable part, and perhaps even a dominant part, of the social process.

Of course, it might be easy for the 'advocate' of, or the 'believer' in, some favoured outcome to be tempted to deceive himself. He may be enticed into singling out only the confirming testimonies and signs, and keep silent about the invalidating ones. And it would also be possible to contribute heavily to bringing about the outcome by persuading others that it was sure to occur. The influence of the sociological cognoscenti is somewhat underrated: they are no mean agents of social change themselves. How can I take out an insurance policy against being caught *in flagrante delicto* at the same game of trying 'to expertise' my fellow men into believing that *my* conception of *his* future is going to be his future and, therefore, he may as well stop resisting? The plain truth is that I cannot contract out of being responsible, in however minute a way, for a future which I estimate that the situation predicts, and which I then hawk around while trying to make as many people listen as I can. But then, I could join instead the ranks of those whose sociological consciousness is powered exclusively by three motives, by the motives of 'debunking, unrespectability and relativising'[1]*, and thus make my contribution to an already mountainous pile of evidence for the rationality of hopelessness. At any rate, a good deal of contemporary sociological literature is committed to distrust and to a sterilising scepticism. This follows from its methodological regimen and from its refusal to see sociological enquiry and communication themselves as major social actions and interventions.

I shall be presenting my case in the manner in which I have chosen, because plainly it is a case which has been grossly overshadowed by its 'anti-case' or 'anti-cases' in other sociological accounts. I shall be following an insistent quest, because I feel that without some deliberate emphasis on assets that always get written off the books will not be

* Notes and sources begin on p. 199.

sorted out, and the balance will not be clear. I am not going to relegate the negative testimonies to subordinate clauses and paragraphs either because I underrate their significance, or because I wish to deceive the reader and myself. I am going to review the prospects of impending social change with reference to certain potentials and qualities of man which have not yet had a dog's chance to attract sociological attention in our time. It is still the vast and brutal forces, or the small gnawing-disintegrating poisons which keep sociologists honourably occupied; for in the study of *social problems* these must be postulated, and in the study of *sociological theory* they must always and unsentimentally be given their plausible dominant place. Sociologists, like garage mechanics, are often less interested in the idea of a well-oiled and well-functioning machine than in the ever present question of 'what's wrong with it?' It is *a priori* that 'there is something wrong with it'. The theoreticians of social life also express their moral scepticism in the choice of their seemingly positive explanatory concepts; this is apparent in the two dominant groups of theories, the conflict-theories and the functionalist theories. One group explains all change in terms of conflict, strife, war, or competition, in which renewal takes place through the clash of opposing forces – these being the greed, desire for power and pleasures in dominantly egotistic men. The other group explains everything in terms of compromise, balance, contract, integration, between the forces of greed, desire for power and pleasures in dominantly egotistic men; the functionalist will add, 'so that society can continue to exist'. As we see, both the conflagrationist and the integrationist sociologies formed a sceptical view of man. This scepticism was at least partly an outcome of rigour: they were not going to be deceived by their own wishful thinking. No one considered that this rigour was a sign of intellectual honesty and of courage, two virtues which offer small grounds for moral scepticism: nor have man's creative imagination and his capacity for imaginative sympathy had a very prominent role to play in the dominant explanatory theories of society: theories have been mainly of two kinds, 'the head-on collision theories' and the 'heady collusion theories', of social change. In keeping with their philosophical dishonesty the totalitarian ideologies of the twentieth century – subscribers of one or the other of these two sceptical theories – go on to offer us a utopian human nobility with rugged workers seven feet tall and blond heroes. And the sentimental optimism is presented to us as 'realism'! No wonder that the intellectuals – to whom this glorious view of man is sickening – reject all optimism as the hackwork of propaganda ministries and commissariats.

But the objective, rigorous and utterly abstemious theoretical ordering of the social process which these intellectuals favour is rapidly becoming unobjective, superficial, and masochistically despairing, because it naively disregards or underrates the countervailing forces of a spontaneously unfolding humanity. It is oddly unobserved that this humanity is itself responsible for the self-denying scepticism of contemporary sociological thinking. My evidence for the presence of these forces, especially at times such as these, may seem somewhat diminutive. It might slightly amend this impression if we could reflect on the following: vast quantities of pitchblend yield only milligrams of radium, yet these minute amounts are sufficient to irradiate the vast quantities, and invest them all with their characteristically powerful charge. An analysis of the vast complexities of the ulterior motives of man will yield perhaps no more than one gram of luminosity; yet this book will try to furnish reasons why we might expect this minute quantity to irradiate the human enterprise in its entirety.

But even if this 'glowing' account of human motivation comes too early in this book it might at least be an occasion for an explanation, already at this stage, so that, in the manner of a 'trailer', a sample of the forthcoming argument should be offered.

One of the principal messages of D. C. McClelland's *The Achieving Society*[2] is that a culture which cultivates a high level of concern for achievement shows a more rapid rate of economic development. Ever since Max Weber – to say the least – the view that a cultural orientation might precipitate or reinforce an economic development has been well recognised. It is almost certainly true that economic growth is aided and abetted by a competitive, personal-success-oriented, and achievement-oriented culture. An all-out egotistic effort 'to win' in competition exacts maximal performance from all participants. *But now, another process comes into view.* The medium of achievement in an increasingly professionalised society is increasingly the 'services rendered' and decreasingly the 'goods provided'. In an increasingly affluent and technologically developed society the intelligent and educated manpower required to furnish the goods will be more and more rationalised and limited, while the manpower required to render *personal services* in health, welfare, and education need have no bounds. Moreover, the supreme and virtuoso efficiency with which man will provide the necessities and luxuries for man will become so automated that the personal creativity, responsibility, and corresponding prestige of the providers will become less and less glamorous in the public eye than those who serve persons and succeed in charging other persons', their clients', lives with health, meaning, and serenity. Achievement-orientation will continue, but it will now operate more and more prominently in the medium of personal services. Distinction and honour, social prestige and power will accrue to those whose ideas and performance in this sector of the world's work will be recognised as potent. And so, the very material-welfare-oriented and achievement-oriented culture will call into being the professionalisation of all intellectually demanding work, and the professionalisation of all intellectually demanding work will call into being the *personalisation* of much of the most respected professional work. Thus the desire for an enhancement of profit, of personal success and of power – or for that matter, of the gross national product – will lead to the concentration of thought and resources in the area of the personal services where the exclusively self-seeking achievement-orientation must now be modified so that a service-orientation should be able to develop at all. Thus, in spite of ourselves, the quality of our aspirations will have changed. Of course, it is not that there is less achievement-orientation in a personal service society, but that the terms and direction of achievement will have been changed. The achievers will have to draw upon sensitive, imaginative, and sympathetic proclivities even when seeking honour, or desirous of being loved or, indeed, of being paid. It is intriguing to reflect on what will happen when man, ambitious as he is, and perfectionist as he is, will make an end of the means by pursuing sensitivity, imaginativeness, and sympathy for their own sake. After all man has almost always sanctified the means he thought necessary for his ends! And in this case there is the strange and paradoxical extra incentive: personal service is so very much more successful when it is thoroughly sincere.

No doubt, it is rash to put this advance sample of my forthcoming reflections so curtly and hurriedly here. They will have to be fully argued later and judged in the light of all that there is yet to be said. All that I am anxious to do now is to warn the reader that the cultural-moral change elicited by our sheer material and industrial efficiency is likely to turn out unprecedentedly powerful, and that it is likely to act back on this industrial-technological base with an unprecedented force and decisiveness. There are many reasons for this new departure and I will certainly not be able to consider them all. Throughout, I will be committed to considering a few hypotheses from a comparatively limited point of view.

I do not claim to be able to include in this book a detailed documentation or even a substantial corroboration of all the hypotheses which will be put forward in the following chapters, though I shall endeavour to make at least a beginning in this task.

Some of the time – though by no means always – I adopt a method of corroborating my propositions by presenting representative testimonies from qualified, practising, and often prominent members of the professions as well as from psychologists and sociologists who have been engaged in a scholarly study of the professions. I call this method 'documentation'. Certainly, at its lowest estimate, this might prove no more than that my hypotheses are shared, and proferred by others, and that the views expressed by me are not isolated marginal views. Had I operationally defined what I meant by 'qualified, practising, and prominent professionals', had I counted them, and expressed them as a percentage of the total number in this category who write or otherwise communicate their views about the meaning of what they are doing, and had I subjected the results to sophisticated statistical checks of significance, my method would suddenly have been recognised as 'scientific', and my procedure as 'verification' or 'falsification', as the case might be. This, regrettably, I have not been able to do. Nevertheless, I am much tempted to believe that what I have done has gone some way towards strengthening the credibility of my hypotheses. Substantial corroboration, let alone verification, will have to follow from more detailed empirical studies yet to be undertaken. My task is to encourage both sociological interest and research in this area, and because of this, I shall devote my attention to the description of some of the social processes, which ought mainly to provoke sociological research, and of some of the processes of social change. The specific processes in which I am interested constitute a momentous trend in our times; they have not only made my reflections possible but irresistibly elicited them. This trend has brought to the fore the positive, humane, and altruistic concerns of mankind in a remarkably vivid way, and I shall have the temerity to argue that these concerns may henceforth influence the quality and direction of social change in a progressively more decisive manner than we have hitherto dared hope. A self-appointed task such as this is both ambitious in its aim and limited in its method. It will be for others to say whether it is discharged to any purpose.

1. The Personal Service Professions and the Counselling Ideology

A. THE COUNSELLING IDEOLOGY

Not unexpectedly this present work has evolved from the thoughts set out in my last book, *The Faith of the Counsellors*.[1] The present work, as it were, represents the next stage in my thinking, the stage which follows the conclusions of that book. These conclusions are that a group of professional workers, comprising psychiatrists, psychotherapists, social caseworkers, and some others, operate with a shared set of assumptions about the nature of man and of society. In the social status of the various branches of the counselling professions, there are, of course, differences in income, in professional aims and methods. But these differences do not conceal the fact – documented in my last book with some care – that they share a number of important assumptions both about the nature of man and about the methods and aims of their practice. In fact the hard core of their professional commitment can be shown, and was at length shown, to consist of the self-same set of ideas and values. Anticipating anxiety and defensive protestations both by some counsellors and by some others, I took the trouble to explain that I offered my concept of 'counsellors' as a new sociological category and that this category was analogous with already accepted categories such as, for example, the 'white collar' worker. If evidently multifarious groups of people can be subsumed under such categories as 'white collar', 'professional', 'middle class', 'intelligentsia', 'élite', or what you will, it is hardly necessary to carry out a public opinion poll to discover whether those who share certain operationally defined characteristics shall be called by the same collective epithet or no. It is therefore irrelevant whether some of the professions which I call counselling professions will be pleased to be classed with others who may more readily accept being so categorised. This needs to be said here, because the creation of a collective term to help establish a meaningful, useful, and therefore valid, category or group does not mean that there are no important and equally valid distinctions to be made within the groups for other equally valid reasons.

This group, the counsellors, administer help to others through the medium of intimate personal relationships and, although they rely extensively on knowledge of miscellaneous facts and techniques, they rely no less on certain metaphysical beliefs and moral affirmations which do not follow from their theoretical premises. The conclusion is reached in that book that these beliefs and affirmations add up to a creed, a faith, as well as an ideology, and that this ideology has played an important role in determining the moral orientation of our times. On the whole this ideology advocates concern, sympathy, and even affection for those who are to be helped by the professional practitioners. It also advocates the continued extension of knowledge and skill, yet it admits the central significance of concern and of personal involvement which it cannot explain in terms of its own positivistic theory of human behaviour.

I feel now that it is necessary to be explicit and specific about the minimum area of agreement embodied in what I call the counselling ideology.

Thomas Szász spoke of the 'hybridisation' of a variety of psychiatries and psychotherapies and of a 'psychiatrisation' of law, politics, and morality.[2] This is what I recognise when, as a sociologist, I speak of the emergence of the 'counselling ideology' as a socio-cultural phenomenon of our century. This ideology consists in a collection of tenets about the nature of man, which one might easily 'factor out' of the literature of counselling, no matter who the writer nor what theoretical branch of counselling he favours. Before presenting these tenets I should like to outline the kind of implicit agreement on human behaviour, that is on the psychology of man, which the counsellors generally observe.

The principal points of this agreement seem to be:

1. Human behaviour is a product of learning by an organism variously equipped by inheritance and acquired constitution to assimilate learning.

2. Learning is generally speaking of two kinds: in most species, including in man, there is a 'critical period' – usually the initial period of the organism's life – during which learning leaves behind a more decisive and more lasting 'imprint' than at any other later period of

that organism's life. In the case of man, learning during infancy and early childhood has some fundamentally predisposing consequences for later learning. Unlearning later what has been learnt initially is difficult – if not impossible – though the various theoreticians of counselling hold a wide variety of views on this matter.

3. The origin and circumstances of early learning and of some later learning are more often than not forgotten mainly because their conscious retention could threaten the social adaptation of the individual: they, and some other associated but forgotten learning too, are usually referred to as 'unconscious' material, which nevertheless retains a remarkably stubborn influence over the conscious behaviour of the individual.

4. To ensure that material which could threaten social adaptation remains unconscious the individual uses a network of so-called 'defences'. These are routinised social responses which, determining the individual's role-preferences in the course of his career, are the basis of his total role system, and what we recognise as his personality.

5. All socially relevant human conduct is classifiable into positive (loving) and negative (hating) kinds of response systems and roles, or fragments of roles. The labelling of these polarities may vary in the theories of counselling, but it is fair to say that a dualism of this kind is well-nigh generally assumed and very frequently openly professed. In these theories sexuality plays a more prominent part than the protestations of dissidence from Freud would allow.

There might be other propositions of psychology which could be identified as part of the assumptions which counsellors make. Marginal dissent is inevitable here, but this makes hardly any difference to the consensus, practice, and moral influence of the majority. Now, let us see whether we can sift out the ideological components of this consensus, that is those elements which lack the status of psychological propositions. I am using 'ideological' as a term meaning socially determined views about society.

1. It is of the greatest importance to note that all practising counsellors testify that the positive – loving, compassionate, sympathetic, co-operative, creative, or what you will – polarity has an edge over the negative polarity of our strivings. If nothing else, their having professionally committed themselves to counselling committed them to this belief.[3] In my opinion this belief is not based on a verifiable psychological proposition: it is a doctrine, an affirmation, without which

professional practice in counselling and in other personal service professions would not be possible. The professional role having been assumed, the doctrine arises from the role. It is 'situationally determined', and therefore, it is ideological. The so-called 'ambivalence' is, therefore, not equally poised, and man is fundamentally destined to keep in check his sado-masochism, or at least manage to rechannel its negative expressions into harmless or, at times, into creative directions.

2. The second ideological feature is rooted in psychological propositions which are in important respects valid, though this will not eliminate the ideological character of what issues from them. The propositions are, that (a) all socially relevant human behaviour is learnt in intimate social relationships and mostly so in the initial years of life; that (b) the only procedure through which this social learning can be effectively modified is in intimate social relationships in which the origin of the first learning can be retraced and, in the light of the day, examined, modified, or replaced. So far, so good. As the saying goes, 'insight' is obtained, and once in possession of it we can make *rational* choices, unencumbered by the dross of infantile and other residues. The choices are to be made nevertheless, and choices are not described by the label 'rational' for they will still represent aspirations, desires, and theories about the good life. To insist that the possession of 'insight' is somehow a potent antibiotic against the micro-organisms of faith and purpose is to attribute a decisive significance to one's professional ministrations to patients and clients in their search for insight. The expertise in decoding is, to some extent, an intellectual skill; the professional investment in this skill inevitably elevates the moral value of its product 'insight'. Here again the ideological element in the professional belief-system is evident.

3. It is professional to use tested science, and tried skill, and it is unprofessional to use the total, and certainly unmeasurable 'mix' of one's personality. Yet, to maintain his effectiveness the professional has not only tried to make use of his personality, but also explicitly prescribed to the acolytes its use as a professional resource of the greatest magnitude! The manuals of training invariably make a respectful bow towards the contribution which they expect the person of the professional will make to the pool of resources into which knowledge and skill have already been gathered. The position thus reached is paradoxical and to conceal its significance or to underplay

it, is in the interests of the professional practitioner; hence the ideological nature of this element.

4. In an era of liberalism, and in a civilisation which pays at least lip-service to the sanctity of the person and the inviolability of personal integrity, professional practitioners must often and publicly show that they don't go beyond the brief, either society or their clients have given them, and that they don't meddle with other people's lives. Counsellors claim that they are non-directive. Needless to say, their professional position would be at risk if they had to defend their prerogatives to tell other people what to do or think. They deny that they are engaged in doing just this, because denying it is in their interest. Hence the ideological quality of this particular strain.

5. Counsellors will construe their work as analogous to the healing work of medicine with clearly identifiable terminal cures as ends – a result less frequent in medicine itself than one would wish, and a result which – given mortality – is universally temporary, even in medicine. Nevertheless the language of ends and objectives must be maintained to serve the requirements of the social function which counsellors are discharging. They must appear to be 'delivering the goods' in at least the same sense in which other professional workers seem to be doing this. There must be operational goals and there must also be an admission that, really, there are no such things. The maintenance and simultaneous camouflage of this paradox is in the interests of the profession.

Here too there might be counsellors whose ideological orientation does not comprise all these features: there are bound to be variations of emphasis, but this will not alter the cultural significance of the broad stream of thought and professional performance exhibited to all and influencing all. Almost certainly there will be disputes – as there have been ever since my last book was published – whether all those who counsel will subscribe to all these points without protestations or demands for radical amendments. A careful analysis of the literature has already confirmed that there is a substantial consensus among the counsellors on these points and that, for the sociologist of culture in our time, this is already a momentous enough conclusion, entirely irrespective of a multitude of differences on finer points of detail or, indeed, irrespective of major disagreements on matters which fall outside the scope of what the five points cover. From the point of view of a sociological study of contemporary culture it is of only secondary importance whether the five psychological propositions and the five ideological features are universally – without exception – underwritten by all and professed by all.

Whereas the first five propositions do not differ from the five ideological features in language – they all use the positive language – there is a noticeable difference of emphasis. The first set merely tells us that such and such is the case with man – client or counsellor or anybody else. The resolve to act and the prescriptions to others to act in certain ways are embedded in the five features of the second set. The counsellors' invariable objective is to change the personality of the client or the patient of their ministrations. They wish to change the recipient of their services from condition 'a' to condition 'b', and openly profess that 'b' is preferable, better, or of greater value than 'a'.

The intention to achieve this and the process that takes place is usually described as 'therapeutic', whereas the intention to change the rules which regulate social relationships and the process evoked by the intention is 'reformistic'. Philip Rieff in his last book, *The Triumph of the Therapeutic*,[4] obliterates this distinction. He writes about 'the therapy of commitment' and suggests that even political ideologies, such as Marxism, for example, are 'therapies of commitment'. Of course, ideological commitments have always been occasions for self-transcendence, for conversion, for self-renewal. In this sense, the 'political' can become 'therapeutic'. But it is essential for the understanding of my 'counselling ideology', and of the larger complex, the 'personal service ideology', to keep the distinctions between the 'reformistic' and the 'therapeutic', for what I am trying to show is not that all commitments are by their nature therapeutic, but that the therapeutic mode of thought spreads from the counsellors to all others. Rieff in his most stimulating essays on *The Triumph of the Therapeutic* does not write about this spread.

There is a striking, though not altogether unexpected, congruence between the values of the five ideological features and the facts of five psychological propositions. These values, however, are not given in either of these sets, and they must now be spelt out:

(a) The notion of blameworthiness, of moral responsibility, of culpability, and the correlate sentiments of punitiveness, avengefulness, and the like are senseless, and, therefore, morally wrong in a universe in which we cannot control the most decisive phase of our learning. No choice is uncaused, and the *fiat* of the inherited constitution, as well as of the given environment, rules. Both the implied and, indeed, the openly professed value is forgiveness, a stoical tolerance, and patience. Mechanistic-behaviouristic psychologies encourage a sinister scepticism about responsibility without implying, let alone professing, these global values with which to retrieve a unified vision.

(b) If it is maintained that effective relearning is possible only in intimate social relationships, whether professional or not, which lead to a better informed reappraisal of the history of one's motives, then it would follow that intimate human relationships of a mutually interested, sympathetic, and concerned kind are, in fact, being pronounced as of central value. This conclusion of the counselling ideology is unlikely to be regarded as epoch-making: several of the greater world-religions and ethical systems have affirmed something of this nature. We have not been waiting with bated breath for the arrival of this 'revelation' all through the centuries of man's history. Just the same the modern version of the ancient truth is significant: for this reaffirmation takes place in the age of scepticism. Even this age finds the eternal verity irresistible and restates it in the characteristic clinical and purportedly scientific language of our time.

(c) Mischievous and self-defeating learning can be neutralised and discarded by turning the spotlight of conscious inspection on it: 'insight' into the origin and nature of this sort of learning is a powerful and beneficent antidote. 'Insight', a notion which is not far from the ancient virtue of 'self-knowledge' or, indeed, from the eternally utilitarian virtue of 'knowledge', adds the counsellor's testimonial to the twentieth-century opinion that *knowledge* is a supremely good thing, that *rationality* is a deeply desirable virtue, and that *understanding* is a core-value of humanity.

These three values – (a) abandonment of judgment and condemnation coupled with humility and stoical acceptance, (b) cultivation of the mutually honest and intimate 'I and Thou' relationship between man and man, and (c) the war on humbug, self-deception, false righteousness, angers or idolatries, and the correlate cultivation of clearsightedness and truthfulness – are all values at the centre of what I have been calling the counselling ideology or the psychotherapeutic ideology of the twentieth century.

But, yet again, why 'Ideology'?

This age is not only an age of objectivity, of scientific rigour and consequently of doubt; this age is also an age of the so-called secular sacraments. Social Justice, Human Rights, Freedom from Want, and other absolutes are fervently proclaimed and carved on the pedestals which the gods have deserted. For a while, practical and humanistic political ideologies have filled the vacuum of scepticism. But this *is* an age of science and the positivistic mood of science is an inhospitable climate for political ideologies. In recent years political ideologies have not had an easy time of it, at least with the intellectuals. The sensitive intellectuals of our western civilisation have progressively become more and more tired of ideological advocacies. Intellectual honesty, a categorical imperative of the age, simply does not get on with an attitude of unquestioning acceptance of political dogma. In writing about 'the discrediting of political solutions'[5] I put forward no surprising or unreasonable thesis: I was writing about the politically disillusioned yet socially still concerned intelligentsia, who have taken refuge in personal and intimate ministrations to others in their escape from the impersonal and generalised doctrines of social reform. I never argued that, as a matter of historical fact, political solutions were discredited. Such a development could not any more take place than a conversion of all politics into administration. Just the same, the misrepresentation of my position was tempting to those whose anxieties were aroused by the disclosure, and elaborate documentations, of their stark political disillusionment and scepticism. One or two politics dons also appeared to be disturbed by my notions, as if they had felt their livelihood threatened.

Nor did I propose that intellectual honesty of the counsellors was a cloak for indifference or even cynicism. On the contrary, intellectual honesty seemed to me to be allied with a scrupulous concern for a sense of integrity and truthfulness to ourselves as well as to others – whether we are counsellors or anybody else. I am still of the opinion that intellectual honesty is more likely than not to be in harmony with a respect for, and even a love of, our fellowmen. At any rate, there is no evidence to suggest that the volume of positive human sentiments of so many professionalised intellectuals has been diminished by political disillusionment, only that their compassion has now turned to new forms of expression. But again, in the age of science, sentimentalism had to be avoided at all costs. If they felt concern for others this concern must not be indulged; they must not contemplate their own kindly sentiments for this might cramp their very style of helping. They must be businesslike, and professional; they must be sensibly helpful or stand aside, though fully ready to intervene again when this is warranted. As a consequence of the disillusionment with the large-scale political solutions many intellectuals of our time sought refuge in a professionalised philanthropy, in a technology of personal helpfulness. But am I entitled to call this belief-system an ideology? If we mean by 'ideology' *a socially determined belief-system about the nature of human relationships*, then, I think, the contemporary belief-system of the counsellors is an ideology. I trace the social determination of this belief-system along the following paths: the contemporary intellectual élite seeks to combine its desire for leadership with an ageless desire for a sense of cosmic worth. Of course, it is both a native 'must', and a culturally given imperative, that he is impelled to search for significance, for a creative and restitutive soothing of his sense of loneliness, and for a triumph over his chronic alienation. After all, have not the political ideologies from Marxism to fascism striven to achieve this purpose, the overcoming of alienation, not only the alienation of the workers but also of the advocates themselves? And have these not been evolved from alienated social situations to meet fundamental human needs? Man, especially reflective man, is always impelled to search for significance; this is both an eternal native 'must' of his nature as well as a culturally fostered imperative. Whilst in the past he threw himself in the ideological movements and identified himself with the fervour of religious doctrine, or of party and movement, the current analytical and critical rigour has all but deprived him of the comforts of political righteousness. He still desperately craves for the radical and just political formula, but the formula fails to articulate itself let alone get itself transformed into intelligible political reform action. Now he often seeks his own salvation as well as the betterment of the condition of others through personal ministrations. If, for example, the capitalist ideology is taken to be determined by a design to protect class advantage then similarly, one might say, the counselling ideology is a smoke screen of the academically trained, professional intelligentsia to justify the advantages of the most important means of production, professional knowledge and skill. If the capitalists needed moral justifications, such as, for example, that they held property on trust for the welfare of all, so the intellectuals today need the justification that their personal professional services are for the good of their clients and of society.

B. THE CONCEPT OF THE 'PERSONAL SERVICE PROFESSIONS'

I need say no more than this about the counselling ideology except to refer to my insistent claim that the counsellors have exerted a very considerable moral influence on the so-called 'personal service professions'[6] of our time. Let me explain the meaning of this term. Consider first the professions of the clergy, doctors, nurses, teachers, social workers, to list only the largest groups, and compare these with the professions of lawyers, accountants, engineers, architects. Few are likely to be violently opposed to my proposal that the first group differs from the second in some important fundamentals: it will probably be possible to agree that the amount of self-denial, matter-of-fact self-effacing personal care, and even of human warmth and kindly solicitousness, required by the professionals in health, welfare, and education, is likely to be far more prominently in evidence than in the practice of law, accountancy, or architecture. Some fatherly lawyers may deplore that I have listed their profession with the engineers, and some severely academic and scrupulously impersonal teachers may resent being bracketed with the social workers and the clergy. Then let me further explain the rationale of this division. Professions whose principal function is to bring about changes in the body or personality of the client are the *personal service professions*, whilst all other professions which are not charged with responsibilities of this sort or, at any rate, which do not set themselves such tasks as these, are the *impersonal service professions.* It is my contention that this distinction has marked sociological significance and I hope to show that it is also strongly suggested by the facts and not merely by my desire to engage in sociological speculations. No doubt the two classes of the professions have certain basic allegiances in common but these allegiances are elaborated, enriched and refined only in the personal service professions and this is at the very root of the distinctions I am trying to make. To understand the ideological orientations of the personal service professions we must bear in mind that these professions are nowadays being trained in a socio-psychological theory, and indoctrinated by moral principles, which – in Western countries at least – are in spite of all protestations by the more rigorous scientists of behaviour, fundamentally Freudian in origin. Kindness, tolerance, acceptance, permissiveness, and a scepticism about strong loves and hates, have received a new lease of life in this psychoanalytical, social psychological, and sociological century. For better or for worse the psychoanalytic rationale for an enlightened education, for a humane penal system, for a better informed psychosomatic medicine, for a progressive management of human relations in our corporate enterprises, preceded the entirely legitimate scientific criticisms of that rationale. It is certainly easy to prove that, in all these areas of personal service, the counsellors' basically psychoanalytical and social psychological ideology conquered and converted. One may say that those in the personal service professions have been influenced by the counselling ideology even if they do no counselling themselves and even if they are unaware of this influence.

There are, in fact, other justifications than these notions of what I have called the counselling ideology for distinguishing the concept of the 'personal service professions'. They could be regarded as a distinct social entity because they share beliefs about the facts and values of social life which on any account amount to a large body of principles. These beliefs arise, first, from their being professions, so that their workers share the professionalism of their work-roles, and, second, from the personal service ideology of the culture in which they have come into being: this, in our western industrial culture, is a mixture of Hippocratic and Christian principles, wedded to the more contemporary standards of intellectual honesty and scientific empiricism applied to human behaviour. It is important that these reservations be noted, and that a reasonably close attention to my thesis be not denied by those who might regard my emphasis on the counselling ideology as too strong. Of course, the total belief-system of professional workers in the personal social services is also capable of being delineated: if there is a counselling ideology, perhaps there is also a distinctive ideology of personal social service, but the latter will surely include much of the former. After all, the counselling ideology itself has strong Christian and Hippocratic undertones, so it is likely to be found in the ideologies of professional workers in health, education and welfare, although of course each of these professions is separate and distinctive, and the shared ideology will inevitably be a smaller complex of thoughts and values than the whole ideology of each speciality.

It was the very recognition of this that has recently made instruction in social science, and especially in 'human relations', one of the requisites of good training in the professions of medicine, nursing, social work, teaching, and so on. It is now believed, by many earnest investigators of training problems in these fields, that an 'interprofessional rapprochement', and a co-ordination of effort might be most illuminating for all concerned. If the structure of 'service-action', and the structure of human relationships, in which these services operate are analogous, then, the understanding of the analogies will lead to a better understanding of what is required of the professionals in spite of their commitments to their respective specialities. In a report of an 'International and Interprofessional Study Group Convened by the World Federation of Mental Health'[7] we read that 'present conditions would be better served by less rather than more definition of professional frontiers, and by a freer passage of skills and insights from one profession to another'.[8] It would seem that the sharing of some important basic principles of thinking and working in all the personal service professions warrants that this sharing be recognised not only for purposes of training these professionals, and, indeed, for guiding their practice in greater co-operation with one another, than has hitherto been possible, but also, that we should recognise authoritative testimonies such as that of the World Federation of Mental Health as, in a way, anticipating and supporting the sociological diagnosis I am putting forward about the emerging distinctness, unitariness, and identity of the personal service professions. Recently Professor Titmuss added his support to this ecumenic idea when he referred to 'social service professionals with common objectives'.[9] In my previous book I proposed that the sociological category 'counsellors' be recognised and accepted in this way. This appeared to some as a cramping and limiting category. No doubt there will be reasons put forward why the present proposals too – about personal service professionals – be regarded as oversimplifications. At any rate, I have not been alone in looking upon this new generic role-concept as useful in practice and sociologically sound. Since 1958, I have been closely associated with many others in the advocacy of inter-professional training for the staff officers of the modern welfare state. This advocacy included a case made out for combining the generic elements of all personal service professions, the generic theoretical and practical contents of service in health, welfare and education.[10] It seems to me that, irrespective of the success or failure of these proposals, the presence of these generic psychological and sociological factors throughout the helping professions cannot be in question. And this would remain my hypothesis even if the counselling bias in personal service were to prove much less significant than I suspect.

After this preamble I can now formulate my hypotheses. *Firstly*, I believe that those professions which I have called the 'personal service professions', having already dramatically grown in numbers, will go on growing and proliferating in the coming decades. *Secondly*, I also believe that the paedagogical régime of these personal service professionals as well as their professional ethics are influencing the self-image of other professional workers whose calling is not in the area of the personal services. Engineers, architects, lawyers, and others like them, are trained in higher education institutions, which now include in these courses of impersonal technologies the sociological and social psychological tuition originally reserved for students of the personal service professions. And thus even the impersonal service professions are now brought within the orbit of the personal service ideologies. At the same time the traditional ideology of professionalism – originally evolved in medicine, the law, and the church – is in the process of merging with the ethics of the counselling ideology of the twentieth century. And *thirdly*, I should like to put forward the view that – mainly as an outcome of their growing numbers and social prestige as well as their participation in the actual leadership of society – the moral reformation of the professions brings with it the moral transformation of some influential leadership outside the personal service professions as well and, therefore, a major change in the moral climate of society as a whole.

C. PROFESSIONALISATION AND THE GROWTH OF THE PERSONAL SERVICE PROFESSIONS

When we look at the leadership of contemporary industrial societies we find that it consists mainly of people who are either members of a profession or are striving to be regarded as members of a profession. Even managers of society's productive enterprises either employ professional specialists and experts or themselves assume the role and stance of professional workers. At the same time, in the affluent welfare states at least, both the general staff and the rank and file in health, education, and welfare services consist almost entirely of professional experts of one kind or another. In fact, the leadership class in our modern industrial societies is increasingly dominated by

C

the professional worker, and the moral climate of the leadership class is permeated by the aspirations embodied in a code of behaviour which professional people tend to adopt. An ever increasing number of leaders are in the habit of matching their behaviour to a standard of professional conduct. It is a sociologically naive and parochial repartee to offer that 'I see no such influences in evidence in Messrs Johnson, Nixon, Wilson, Heath, de Gaulle, etc. etc. . . .' for the rising of an entirely fresh moral sap to the crown is slow and gradual, and it takes possibly longer than years, or even decades. *The sociologist must be able to view this hypothesis as pertaining to a long-term process in cultural change,* and therefore frivolous references to our politicians of the day become either entirely irrelevant or, at least, totally inconclusive.

The personnel of the ruling class of our industrial societies is undergoing this change of orientation both inside and outside the world of business, and the ramifications of this change are wider than may appear from what I have said so far. It is well enough appreciated that the growth of the middle class is by and large a growth in the number of educated people, people who are trained to perform the complex tasks of a scientific technological society. In fact, the occupation of these people is often a profession. To set aside and define the concept of 'profession' is not only semantically difficult but it is bound to be the subject of an endless contention between those who are included and those who are omitted by almost any definition. The difficulties in the way of defining the sociological concept of 'professions' are notorious, yet the existence, and indeed the importance, of the social category to which the concept relates has never been in question. Of course, there is nothing unusual in finding it difficult to define a social category; the most important of these, such as for example, class, power, religion, to mention only a few, have proved equally intractable. I agree with William Goode that though the multitude of definitions offered to us by various writers differ in all sorts of ways they do not contradict one another.[11] William Goode identifies two traits which seem to occur in all definitions; these are,

(1) prolonged specialised training in a body of abstract knowledge, and (2) a collectivity or service orientation.[12]

For the purpose of the ensuing discussion I will adopt these two criteria as the basis of the definition of the 'professions'. This, I believe, can be done without rashness, for Goode himself stresses that 'collectivity or service orientation' is not to be confused with individual altruism. This orientation means that the professional may, like others, seek his personal advantage but only on condition that he renders a service, his best service, to the advantage of others. Needless to say, this is an ideal standard, but the standard is a potent social reality. It is one of the hypotheses of this book that the advance of professionalisation enhances the power of this social reality. R. K. Merton lends his support to this view when, writing about the differential attitudes of the intellectual and of the businessman towards work, he says: 'However concerned the intellectual may be with bettering his own economic status, institutional controls require him to view this as a by-product rather than as the immediate purpose of his activity'.[13]

The process of professionalisation performs a function not only for the intellectual and the 'professional' individual but also for society. *For the individual* it helps to blend the anomalously contradictory standards of our culture, that is to say, standards which prescribe that we selfishly, self-assertively, and self-sufficiently prove our mettle by excelling in competition – at the same time – that we practise charity, fellowship, and render personal services. If one wanted to be cynical, one could say, that to be a professional is to have one's cake of virtuousness, and also enjoy one's feast of pride and social advantage. To be a professional is to have one's moral conflicts about one's duties and ambitions eased, and even solved, by a code of conduct which clothes the all-too-human self-seeking in the robes of self-denying dignity and nobility.

Professionalisation is not only a process which secures for some intellectuals a large share of the cake, and a more important place at the table, but it also allows the guest of honour to feel content in the knowledge that his presence is a source of inspiration and security to others around the table. In an age of reason and unbelief, professionalisation is a convenient secular answer to an age-old human need, the need to reconcile man's longing to break through the shell of his separate individuality with his wish to continue to glower self-assertiveness from the encapsulated security of the self. There are some vivid little models of this which are by no means exceptional; thus, the psychoanalyst regards his acceptance of not inconsiderable fees as a therapeutic device for the benefit of his patient, while the university don – cutting the time devoted to teaching, so that he can be more generously available to do research, and raise his own status as a scholar – regards his preoccupation with his discipline in this way as not only beneficial to his students but essential to good teaching.

Professionalisation seems to fulfil the intellectual's need for moral sustenance, especially when he is in doubt about entitlement to leadership. At a time of disenchantment with most kinds of moral inspiration, the pride of craftmanship, of esoteric knowledge, and professional dutifulness, all help to put one right with doubt. The intellectual prefers getting his inspiration in this way to getting it from some charismatic political or religious doctrine. Whilst engaging in 'service' of a personal kind he contrives to generate his own charisma from his role-image of being a professional and from society's respect and recognition. Professionals do not have to refer back to some party or church for justification and moral replenishment, though, of course, there are Christian-professionals, communist-professionals, and the like, who have undoubtedly arrived at a 'concordat' with the world and merged their professional avocations with their extra-professional loyalties. All I am saying is that the individual intellectual does not have to underwrite such a merger to function professionally.

For society, professionalisation does the job of socialising the privateering and potentially anarchical intellectuals. Instead of cultivating non-conformity for its own sake, the intellectual is made to cultivate his personal integrity in serving his fellowmen. In addition to this, by professionalising leadership we are introducing a new form of qualified and even licensed authority: it's not that all leaders are ex-teachers, doctors, engineers, lawyers, and so on already, but that it is becoming difficult for them not to have been recruited from the professions. Instead of the barons, the warriors, and later the industrial and commercial magnates, it is now the university trained, academically and professionally licensed intellectuals who rise to positions of leadership. And now, indeed, I will try to show that the personal service professionals are beginning to lead these intellectuals either in fact or through the influence of their ideas.

The aspirations of the professional workers are incorporated in the rules of professional associations, which have greatly grown in numbers during recent years. To protect their interests as well as those of the specialist services which they were rendering to society, professional workers have organised themselves in Britain into formally established 'qualifying associations' at the rate of a dozen per decade between 1870 and 1910 and two dozen per decade between 1910 and 1950.[14] This process of so-called professionalisation has served not only to protect the practitioners themselves and to afford them material advantages, nor merely to secure a competent service for the community, but also to inspire and confirm a sense of dedication and unselfishness in the professional worker.

In his analysis of 21 writers' definitions of the concept of 'profession' Millerson extracts 14 elements which these definitions use – in various combinations – from 'skill based on theoretical knowledge' to 'altruistic service', and from 'competence tested' to 'fiduciary client relationship'. Of these 14 criteria no fewer than 8 contain references to moral terms such as 'loyalty', 'impartiality', 'public service', 'code of conduct', 'relationship', 'application to the affairs of others'; as well as 'altruistic' and 'fiduciary', the terms already mentioned. No doubt the professional worker is out to earn a good living, secure a high status for himself, and is often even bent on assuming positions of power or importance – but it would be simply untrue to say that his occupational orientation consists solely or even predominantly of seeking, what are conventionally described as mercenary ends, at the expense of serving the moral purposes to which the professions are committed. It would seem that the awareness of service, of an impartial and other-regarding stance, is a psychologically essential requisite of effective performance.

Certainly, it would be a mistake to idealise simplemindedly the professional function which, after all, comprises as diverse activities as nursing in a hospital for infectious diseases, and designing pubs or petrol stations. Nor would it be very sensible of us to banish from our minds the not infrequent spectacles of mercenary and prestige-conscious professional behaviour. Nevertheless, in all professional avocation there is a commitment to conscientiousness of service, and to a standard of dependability, which is, of course, more vividly apparent in those professionals who render personal services to their clients than in those who are in impersonal professions. Yet it is in some measure present in all professionals. As Talcott Parsons observed, professional activities also have motives which are other than 'the enlightened self-interest of economic and utilitarian theory' and that 'the institutional pattern governing professional activity does not, in the same sense, sanction the pursuit of self-interest as the corresponding one does in the case of business'.[15]

Naturally, the altruistic and service element of the professional role comes in all measures and guises. There will be cultural differences: for example, the respective forms of medical public opinion in the British Medical Association and the American Medical Association are somewhat at variance, and no doubt this is, to some extent, reflected by the two different moral self-images of the practitioners themselves.

Notwithstanding these difficulties in justifying the unitary concept of 'professions' the general picture is one of considerable growth in the numbers of those who have identified themselves with a professional role and accepted the rules of professional ethics. No doubt these rules vary in stringency, in social importance, and in moral sincerity. This is well understood. But the spirit of the older model regulations in medicine, law and pastoral practice, as well as of the more modern counselling ideology, somehow percolates even to the remoter replicas of these ancient professions, and creates a moral atmosphere of consensus about what the professional attitude should be. Taking it indiscriminately, though by no means inaccurately, the total population of all the important professional practitioners contributes to social life a spectacle of service which, though not untarnished by the periodic haggling about payment and working conditions, does in fact create a constantly sustained climate of social service attitudes. Admittedly many, like Talcott Parsons for example, have rightly advised caution to those who would simply characterise the professions by disinterestedness and the entrepreneurial world of selfishness. This is an oversimplification which I, too, condemn.

Of course, the members of the professions are possibly no less ambitious and self-seeking than those who are not professionals. But they have to learn to confine their selfishness to certain areas of competition and explicitly renounce competition in some other areas. Furthermore, they have to resist temptation to discriminate between clients on grounds which are not relevant to the discharge of professional duty. This universalism of the professional is an especially important streak in the character of the role he is assuming. Talcott Parsons mentions this and also the rationality of the professional function which is distinct from the traditionalism of the business entrepreneur.

With all these reservations and qualifications, the definition provided for me by William Goode may have lost much of its usefulness; and indeed, after presenting some facts of social change, I shall have to amplify and add to these qualifications. But on the assumption that my progress will not be halted by the lack of a 'hard' definition of the concept of the 'professions', I shall now proceed to these facts of social change undeterred by these initial difficulties.

During recent decades, those who could claim to be called members of a profession have much increased in number. Using the 1901 and 1961 Censuses in England and Wales and overlooking the inevitable differences of classification, comparisons can be made which are set out in Figure I and Tables I–III.

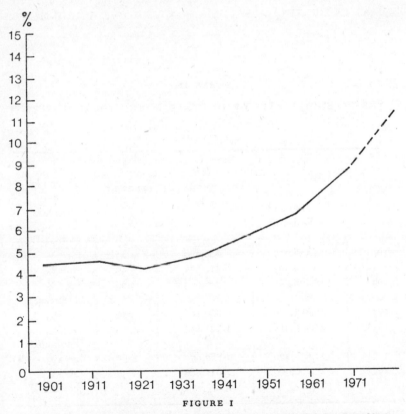

FIGURE I

Numbers of professional workers expressed as percentages of the total working population in England and Wales, 1901–61

TABLE I

THE NUMBER OF PEOPLE PER PROFESSIONAL WORKERS
IN ENGLAND AND WALES

	1901	1961
Total population	32,527,843	46,104,548
Professional and ancillary occupations	606,260	1,880,090
The number of people per professional worker	53·7	24·5

TABLE II

THE DECENNIAL RATE OF INCREASE IN THE TOTAL NUMBER
OF PROFESSIONAL WORKERS IN ENGLAND AND WALES
1901–61

Year	(1) Employed population of England and Wales	(2) Total number of professional workers	(2) as a % (1)	Decennial rate of increase
1901	14,328,727	606,260	4·23	—
1911	16,284,399	714,621	4·39	16·2%
1921	17,178,050	700,614	4·08	−2·0% (Decrease)
1931	18,853,376	860,108	4·56	22·8%
1951	20,336,418	1,341,133	6·60	28·0% (Estimated)
1961	21,694,470	1,880,090	8·67	40·2%
1971	23,200,000*	2,635,886*	11·37*	40·2% (Estimated)

*Increases estimated on the assumption that the 1951–61 rate of change is maintained during the decade 1961–71.

TABLE III

THE GROWTH OF THE PROFESSIONS IN ENGLAND
AND WALES, 1901–61

per thousand of the population 'occupied or economically active'

(a) *The personal service professions:*

	1901	1911	1921	1931	1951	1961
Clergy	3·92	3·56	2·97	2·80	2·52	2·51
Physicians-dentists	1·96	1·91	1·95	2·16	2·64	3·02
Nurses	4·77	5·22	7·15	8·16	11·58	13·43
Teachers	16·38	15·47	16·16	15·06	15·40	21·04
Social workers	—	—	0·17	0·38	1·09	1·76

(b) *The impersonal service professions:*

	1901	1911	1921	1931	1951	1961
Engineers-scientists	1·00	0·84	1·94	2·90	6·01	11·42
Accountants	—	—	0·42	0·74	1·59	4·46
Legal professions	1·47	1·31	1·05	1·00	1·15	1·35
Architects-surveyors	1·20	0·86	0·62	0·55	2·30	3·21
Veterinary surgeons	0·21	0·18	0·13	0·12	0·15	—

TABLE IV

NUMBERS IN THE PERSONAL AND IMPERSONAL SERVICE
PROFESSIONS IN ENGLAND

	1901	1961	Increase % in 60 years
Total number of professional workers	606,260	1,880,090	
Personal service professions	392,058	919,570	135
Impersonal service professions	214,202	960,520	349

Though the two Census categories are not described in identical terms both have in fact included all the occupations we normally describe as professional, such as, for example, legal, clerical, medical, paramedical, veterinary, teaching, engineering, surveying, architectural, scientific, social work, and some others, all of these falling within the British Census occupational categories of 760–819. By now the range of occupations desirous of being regarded as professional has become very large. Some people may include the members even of the Institute of Brewers and of the Institute of Meat, and of some others, mainly of lower middle and working class affiliation. Yet, in spite of this, the majority of professionals are in fact members of the leadership class. The overflow of this professionalisation into the lower middle and working class is merely an example of the difficulty all stratification theorists encounter in that there are always interstitial areas between strata which refuse to fit in with any scheme whatsoever. I should now like to present some facts about the growth of the professions in England and Wales, facts which, to my knowledge, have so far gone unmentioned. These facts are clearly brought out in Table IV as shown on previous page and Figures II, III, and IV.

These tables and figures show that all the professions, with the exception of the clergy, have grown, not only in absolute numbers but also in numbers per 1000 of the working population. The current acceleration of growth in the impersonal service professions far outstrips the advance of the personal service professions and there are certain observations which it would be a mistake to omit about this marked discrepancy in development. The *first* is this: we are now coming into an automated and computerised phase of technology. It is not unlikely that the demand for technologically trained manpower for routine operational requirements, and for administratively trained manpower to discharge routine control or supervision functions, will decline. Naturally, this need not lead to a reduction in the numbers of impersonal service professionals, for manpower could always be transferred to research and development tasks. Anticipating this, one might say that there need be no halt in the growth of the impersonal service professions and that the present rate of growth may well continue. However, on the assumption that the moral priorities of health, welfare, and education will win out, when the minimum requirements of peace and physical subsistence for most or all have been met, it seems to me inevitable that the present trend of diverting

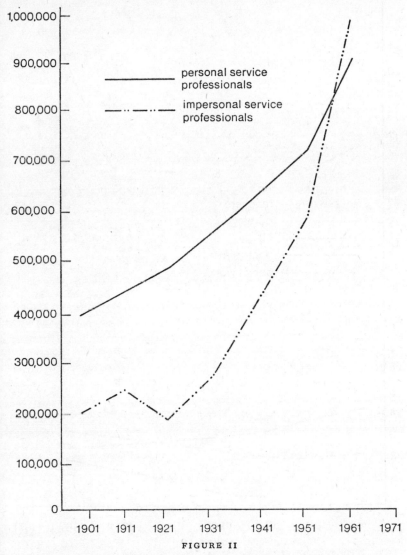

FIGURE II

Numbers of personal and impersonal service professionals in England and Wales, 1901–61

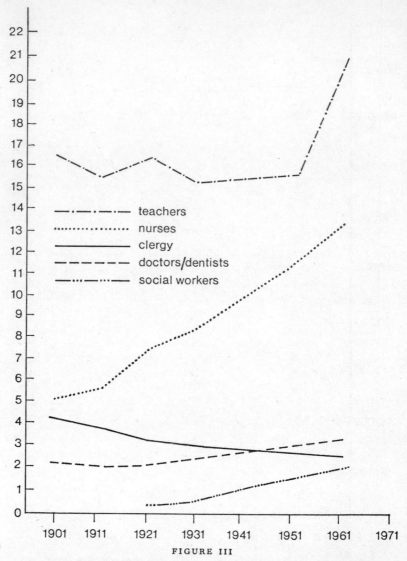

FIGURE III

Numbers of professional workers per 1000 of the working population in England and Wales, 1901–61 (Personal service professionals)

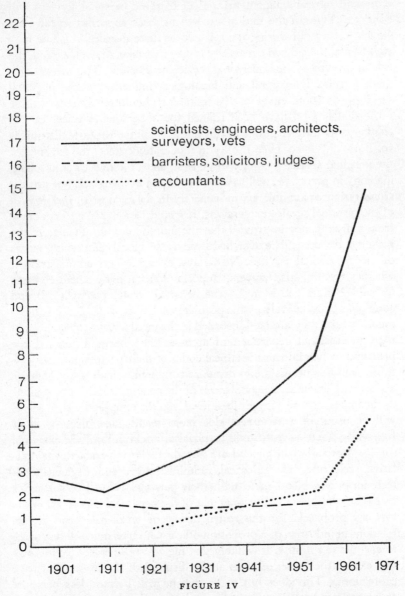

FIGURE IV

Numbers of professional workers per 1000 of the working population in England and Wales 1901–61 (Impersonal service professionals)

more and more intelligent manpower to these personal services will continue. Though the rate of growth in these areas has so far been slower, at any rate during the last two or three decades, this rate may well be maintained and eventually it may overtake, or even exceed, the rate of growth of the impersonal service professions. The *second* comment is this: The moral and ideological influence of the personal service professions envelops the training and cultural context of these professionals who have been trained for impersonal service. In this chapter, and at other points in this book, I will try to show that this is so. But if this is so, even if only in moderate degrees, the advance of the personal service ideology in general, and of a kind of counselling ideology in particular, will have to be viewed in the context of professionalisation as a whole and not merely in the context of the growth of the personal service professions. It would be a mistake to conclude from a discrepancy in growth that the moral-cultural influence of the personal services will be overshadowed by the moral-cultural influences of the impersonal services. Nowadays, even business administrators, whether accountants, lawyers, or technologists, allow themselves to be guided more and more by the personal service professionals and certainly not exclusively by the pecuniary calculus of classical business-men. At least they are half-absorbed in the intellectual problematics of their professional expertise and at most they have assimilated the principles which inform the ethical codes of their professional associations. And this brings me to my *third* comment, which is that there is also a complementary *rapprochement* of the personal service professions to the impersonal service professions. Even the counsellors themselves will be using pharmaceutical aids more readily and abandon their frequently doctrinaire attitude to physical intervention. The personal service professions in general are already using impersonal, manipulative, scientific, technological, administrative, and organisational techniques and blend these with their personal help. The surgeon's case is an obvious one; but so is that of the personnel officer who puts forward proposals for the restructuring of work-roles and work-relations in industry, or a probation officer who uses material resources to encourage a hobby. It is likely that the advancement of technology will extend the *cachet* of arms at the disposal of the personal service professional. This does not mean that he will become less personal and more manipulative. He will merely fuse the devoted attention to a person with devoted attention to detail. To quote T. S. Eliot:

The wounded surgeon plies the steel
That questions the distempered part;
Beneath the bleeding hands we feel
The sharp compassion of the healer's art
Resolving the enigma of the fever chart.

In the ultimate resort more knowledge and more skill *needs* to be fused with more concern because knowledge and skill will themselves have testified to their own inadequacy when used in the vacuum of a personal absence.

At the other extreme we have the impersonal service professionals. Of course, one must always remember that the impersonal service professionals may be impersonal but they are still professional. They come from the same higher education institutions which not only produce the personal service professionals, but which are themselves institutions for a personal service, that is to say the service of education. Even when they are trained for an impersonal service, the ethics of personal service are exhibited to those who are trained by the personal service institution, such as a university. The novelty in the present social situation is this: the professional associations which embrace these impersonal professionals enjoin their members to emulate the sentiments of professional responsibility and dignity cultivated by the older personal service professions and thus a new moral climate is engendered and perpetuated.

There are numerous examples of this and they are getting more and more frequent. One of the original aims, stated in the preamble of the American Association of Engineers, is 'the profession's obligation to serve society'.[16] Assuredly, a non-technological ideal to be cherished by the practitioners of technology! But being trained in technology or engineering does not automatically include being trained in 'serving society': if this objective is not to be regarded as a disingenuously pious gesture, a deliberate intervention in the training programme of engineers must be its consequence. Many will dismiss stipulations of this kind as about as sincere as a mechanically mumbled grace before a gluttonous meal. This book was written to show that this is not an objective account of the social change that is taking place in our industrial societies today.

But my main concern is with the 'bearers and renewers of the message', the personal service professionals. That they have multiplied is now understood. Will they continue to increase?

It is necessary to consider my prediction of growth in the light of authoritative predictions and estimates offered by sources unaware of and certainly uninfluenced by my predictions. Tables V–XI will repay examination: the growth in these personal service areas is moderately but firmly predicted by British Government publications so that governmental and local authority planning should be able to take these anticipations into account. Of course, similar extrapolations, perhaps even more sanguine, have been made in respect of the impersonal service professions. 'We need more scientists, technologists, accountants, solicitors, and so on', one hears, and there are confident predictions that the numbers trained in these and similar services will increase. The two comments I made above will, I believe, qualify these predictions no less than they qualified the record of growth in the impersonal services to date.

I think we can hazard the prediction that, in spite of their slower rate of growth in numbers, moral leadership will remain in the hands of those who lead the personal social services. Their interpretation of social realities and their formulation of social standards will continue to remain the authoritative and obvious guide of social reappraisal and social change for all, and especially for the professionals in the impersonal services. These have been trained in science even more rigorously than the personal service professionals, and they have been persuaded

TABLE V

COMMUNITY CARE WORKERS IN ENGLAND AND WALES
(the numbers per 1000 population are given in brackets)

Staff Whole-time equivalent	31.3.1962	31.3.1967	31.3.1972
Health visitors	5,269 (0·11)	6,698 (0·14)	7,607 (0·15)
Home helps	25,478 (0·55)	32,250 (0·66)	37,083 (0·73)
Home nurses	7,704 (0·17)	8,854 (0·18)	9,970 (0·19)
Midwives	5,261 (0·11)	6,232 (0·13)	6,509 (0·13)
Social workers*	2,943 (0·06)	4,265 (0·09)	4,879 (0·10)

*Local Authority only.
From *Health and Welfare, The Development of Community Care, England and Wales* (H.M.S.O., April 1963), p. 367, Table 11.

TABLE VI

ESTIMATED NUMBER OF FULL-TIME EQUIVALENT TEACHERS IN SERVICE, 1963–86
(in thousands) *(Secondary and Trust School Maintained)*

Year (March)	Men			Women			Total		
	Non. Gr.	Gr.	Total	Non. Gr.	Gr.	Total	Non. Gr.	Gr.	Total
1963 actual	79	36	115	142	23	155	221	59	280
1968	97	44	141	158	25	133	255	69	324
1972	119	55	174	177	29	206	296	84	380
1976	148	65	213	196	31	227	344	96	440
1981	193	82	275	228	37	265	421	119	540
1986	234	105	339	251	46	297	485	151	636

From *The Demand and Supply of Teachers 1963–1986* (H.M.S.O., 1965), p. 66, Table 35.

TABLE VII

FULL-TIME TEACHERS OUTSIDE MAINTAINED PRIMARY
AND SECONDARY SCHOOLS, 1963–73
(*in thousands*)

	Number in service 1963	Numbers needed 1973	Increase
Universities	15	23	8
Colleges of education			
Graduates	3	6	3
Non-graduates	2	4	2
Further education			
For the 19's and over	16	26	10
For under 19's	14	26	12
Independent schools	22	25	3
Government grant schools	5	7	2
Special schools	6	8	2
Total	83	125	42

From *The Demand for and Supply of Teachers, 1963–1986* (H.M.S.O., 1965),
p. 73, Table A1.

TABLE VIII

ESTIMATED SUPPLY OF DOCTORS IN GREAT BRITAIN,
1955–85
(*in thousands*)

	1955–60	1961–5	1965–70	1971–5	1975–80	1981–5
Number of active doctors, beginning of period	56·3	58·3	59·9	62·4	66·3	73·2
Population per doctor, end of period	877	888	887	869	818	787

From Paige, D., and Jones, K., *Health and Welfare Services in Britain in 1975*
(National Institute of Economic and Social Research, Cambridge University
Press, 1966).

TABLE IX

NURSING AND ATTENDANT STAFF IN HOSPITALS AND
RESIDENTIAL HOMES, ENGLAND AND WALES, 1951–75

	General hospitals	Hospitals and homes for		Welfare homes
		mental illness	mental subnormality	
1951				
Nurses/attendants (ooos)	122·4	22·6	6·8	—
Patients/residents (ooos)	215·4	141·1	50·2	—
Ratio	1·8	6·2	7·4	—
1960				
Nurses/attendants (ooos)	146·9	27·6	9·9	12·1
Patients/residents (ooos)	217·8	136·8	55·7	84·5
Ratio	1·5	5·0	5·6	7·0
1975				
Nurses/attendants (ooos)	203·0	26·2	24·8	34·4
Patients/residents (ooos)	234·0	87·3	89·3	148·0
Ratio	1·15	3·3	3·6	4·3

From Paige, D., and Jones, K., *Health and Welfare Services in Britain in 1975*
(National Institute of Economic and Social Research, Cambridge University
Press, 1966).

always to turn to the expert or the specialist. In matters affecting
human relationships the personal service professionals are the experts –
or so the others are persuaded to believe – and hence the traffic of
ideas as well as of aspirations flows in this one direction: from the
personal service professionals to the impersonal service professionals.
Naturally, the attitude of the technologists to social science may vary
and it may be ambivalent or confused. But certain changes have
already been achieved. This is partly due to the Western fashion of
crediting sociology, and the Eastern fashion of crediting Marxism-
Leninism, with the authority of science. This has suborned the
technologist's scepticism and he is now reluctantly yielding to the

TABLE X

DOCTORS IN THE HOSPITAL AND GENERAL PRACTITIONER
SERVICES IN GREAT BRITAIN, 1949–80

	1949	1953	1959	1962	1980
1. Hospital doctors Rate of increase (per cent per annum)	15,950	18,500 3·8	20,950 2·1	22,700 2·7	32,400 2·0
2. General practitioners Total number of doctors Patients per doctor	— —	23,677 2,054	25,026 2,005	125,183 2,047	33,700 1,775

From Paige, D., and Jones, K., *Health and Welfare Services in Britain in 1975*
(National Institute of Economic and Social Research, Cambridge University
Press, 1966).

point of view that there is such a thing as a 'science of society'. Consequently, the technologist has been made susceptible, and even readily
receptive, to ideas coming from the experts of applied social science,
the personal service professionals. In the next chapter, I shall offer
some evidence in support of this.

However, the concerns of those in the personal services are predominantly social concerns, and their roles, always set in close human
relationships, are such that these concerns and the opinions about
them are constantly and inevitably communicated. In fact, one ought
to say that it is often a part of the personal service professional's duty
to communicate on matters concerning human relationships, whereas,
by the nature of their special training, this is rarely the case among
those whose speciality lies elsewhere. Though both groups are professional and share the discipline of a professional ethic, it is the personal
service professionals whose statement of much of this ethic will be
the more authentic one.

The personal service professionals themselves are inheritors of two
main streams of value orientation. *On the one hand*, they are the
receivers of a code, which is a fusion of the classical Hippocratic and
Christian 'Samaritan' attitudes to service and helping. *On the other
hand*, they are the eager students of the counsellors, those twentieth-

TABLE XI

SELECTED PROFESSIONAL STAFF OF THE FAMILY SERVICES, ENGLAND AND WALES, 1962–75

	Numbers employed				Per 100,000 population	
	1962 actual	1972 Local authority plans	1972 NIESR estimates	1975 estimates	1962	1975
Social workers						
Hospital medical social workers	1,020	—	—	1,300	2·1	2·5
Hospital psychiatric social workers	470	—	—	700	1·0	1·3
Other university trained	280	790	7,200	1,200	0·6	2·3
General	430	1,570		3,800	0·9	7·3
Other	2,230	2,520		2,600	4·8	5·0
Subtotal	4,430			9,600	9·5	18·4
Welfare assistants	250	745	850	900	0·5	1·7
Health visitors	5,270	7,610	9,900	10,500	11·3	20·2
Home nurses	7,700	9,745	13,100	13,900	16·5	26·7
Other nurses	890	1,235	1,350	1,400	1·9	2·7
Total	18,540			36,300	39·7	69·7

From Paige, D., and Jones, K., *Health and Welfare Services in Britain in 1975* (National Institute of Economic and Social Research, Cambridge University Press, 1966).

century secularisers of philanthropy. The personal service professionals are also 'appliers' of two kinds of social science. They are
supposed to be appliers of a general social science intelligence, though,
in the course of their training, they are increasingly being given
academic instruction in one or two specific social sciences. In the
event, they rather aspire to be the appliers of that specific social
science which derives mainly from clinical psychology, social psychology, and small group sociology. Of course, these two areas, the general
and the specific, are not strictly separable, but there is no doubt that
in the social science instruction of the personal service professionals
emphasis on clinical and social psychology has far exceeded that
placed on the other social sciences, even on economics! The influences
of preoccupation with these two kinds of social science on the value-
orientations of the personal service professionals will be considered
at length in the next chapter.

Here I will merely reiterate that the new era of social responsibility
and care in our societies no longer draws its inspiration exclusively
from religious and politico-ideological sources. Of course, even now,
the loudest references to these old sources of moral inspiration conceal
the other and incipient contributions of which I speak. The proclama-
tions, the demonstrations, and the marches are still under the banners
and insignia of theological and ideological doctrine, and for this
reason it will seem incredible that, even in the twentieth century, the
so-called counselling ideology could have become a seminal agent of
moral renewal.

The counsellors have acted as moral tutors to all the other personal
service professions. These personal service professions, merging their
traditional and Christian professional principles with what they could
learn from the counsellors, have in their turn primed and guided other
professional workers as well. And the total professional complement
of society, vastly increased in number and influence, is now in the
process of slowly renewing society itself. Indeed, the message I shall
be trying to convey is that the process of professionalisation is the
widest single avenue along which moral change in our Western
industrial communities is being guided today, and will be guided
during the coming decades.

Whether it is mainly the counselling ideology which fills out the
thinking and aspirations of the personal service professionals is a
question which many may answer in the negative. Some will say that

the so-called counselling ideology contributes only a small part to the premises of professional personal service; others may even add that this contribution is only a temporary one, and that it is being made at the present time only – possibly as temporary aberration – and that it will soon be superseded by something else. This book does not concede these points, but, even if it did, it would still argue that there is a reasonably discernible complex of ideas about facts, and values, which practising members and theoreticians of the personal service professions share, and which not only informs their professional conduct but which, because of their social prominence, also colours the general cultural tone of the societies in which these professional workers operate.

Now it is this latter claim which would lack all semblance of credibility unless certain facts about recent social changes were cited. Tables XII and XIII introduce some of these facts. These tables focus on the growing participation of the personal service professionals in the supreme legislative body of Britain, the House of Commons. The 630 members' first or formative occupation was regrettably not classified in the two tables by the same researcher and, therefore, continuity and comparability of the two tables may not be perfect. Just the same, the discrepancies, if any, are not likely to be substantial enough to stop us from linking the two tables into a continuous account. This account tells us about the doubling of the number of personal service professionals in the Labour parliaments of 1945, and a recurrence of this in 1964 and 1966. It also tells us about the same trend disclosing itself in the Conservative parliaments from 1951 to 1958. Both the Socialist and the Tory histories present an increase of this kind over the interwar average. It is true that this growth is recorded to have taken place entirely in the recruitment of teachers and lecturers, but those who read Chapter 2 of this book will be in a position to form an idea of how these paedagogically trained people can become at least the unconscious carriers and disseminators of values which originate in the counselling ideology of the twentieth century. There are invariably a good deal more of these professionals in the Labour Party than in the Conservative Party, and, should there be a Conservative come-back in the next election, the present total may fall again. But it is by no means certain that this fall would reduce the total numbers of these professionals to the 1951–1959 level.

Before I go on, I must note that Tables XII and XIII may well

TABLE XII

PERSONAL SERVICE PROFESSIONALS IN THE BRITISH HOUSE OF COMMONS, 1918–66

	Interwar average				1945				1950				1951			
	Lab.	Con.	Others	Total	Lab.	Con.	Others	Total	Lab.	Con.	Others	Total	Lab.	Con.	Others	Total
Doctors	3	6	3	12	10	3	1	14	6	4	—	10	6	4	—	10
Teachers, lecturers	10	7	5	22	49	5	2	56	39	4	—	43	39	4	—	43
Ministers of religion and social workers	2	—	2	4	—	4	1	5	4	—	3	7	3	—	4	7
Totals	15	13	10	38	59	12	4	75	49	8	3	60	48	8	4	60

Collated from Ross, J. F. S., *Elections and Electors* (London, 1955), p. 433.

TABLE XIII

PERSONAL SERVICE PROFESSIONALS IN THE BRITISH HOUSE OF COMMONS, 1918–66
(continued)

	1951			1955			1959			1964			1966		
	Lab.	Con.	Total	Lab.	Con.	Total	Lab.	Con.	Total	Lab.	Con.	Total	Lab.	Con.	Total
Doctors	9	4	13	8	2	10	10	5	15	9	3	12	9	2	11
Teachers, lecturers	42	5	47	39	4	43	37	5	42	51	5	56	72	4	76
Totals	51	9	60	47	6	53	47	10	57	60	8	68	81	6	87

Collated from Butler, D.E., *The British General Election of 1951* (London, 1952), p. 41; Butler, D. E., and Rose, R., *The British General Election of 1955* (London, 1955), p. 43; Butler D. E., and Rose, R., *The British General Election of 1959* (London, 1960), p. 127; Butler, D. E., and King, A., *The British General Election of 1964* (London, 1965), p. 238; Butler, D. E., and King, A., *The British General Election of 1966* (London, 1966), p. 208.

The Personal Service Society

underestimate the real extent to which the personal service professions have penetrated Parliament. In another recent publication[17] the figures relating to three categories are as shown in Table XIV opposite.

Even more suggestive is the comparison between actual numbers and new intake. This is vividly shown by P. G. J. Pulzer in respect of all professional workers (not only personal service):

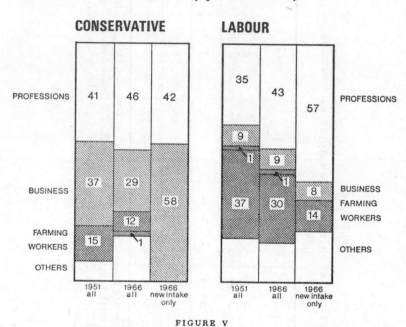

FIGURE V

From Pulzer, P. J. G., *Political Representation and Elections in Britain* (London, 1967), p. 68

The point to remember is that in legislation on moral issues which daily concern the counsellors, and most of the personal service profession also, issues such as those discussed in Bills on artificial termination of pregnancy, on sexual offences, and on the death penalty, the large Labour support of reform would not have materialised but for the strong advocacies by these professional elements in the Labour Party. Of course, some Conservative personal service professionals appear to be impervious to the influences of the counselling ideology for not one of them voted in favour of reform in two of these three

TABLE XIV

PERSONAL SERVICE PROFESSIONALS IN THE BRITISH HOUSE OF COMMONS, 1962–7

	1962–3				1964–5				1966–7			
	Con.	Lib.	Lab.	Total	Con.	Lib.	Lab.	Total	Con.	Lib.	Lab.	Total
Doctors	3	0	6	9	3	0	8	11	2	1	9	12
Teachers	17	0	62	79	40	2	55	97	16	1	99	116
Charities and co-operatives*	12	0	2	14	17	0	17	34	14	2	21	37
Taking only ⅓ of 'Charities and Co-operatives' as trained in one of the personal service professions, in all:				93				119				140
Expressed as % of 630, the total no. of members of parliament:				14·1				17·3				22·2

cases. But the point is that the Conservative Party has so far failed to secure a more enthusiastic support of its ideology and policies by the personal service professionals of Britain, and fewer personal service professionals aspire to be Tory MPs. Clearly these professionals are by definition middle class and, on a class basis, they ought to be either bourgeois-liberal or conservative. It would appear, then, that it was not their class but their professional ideological orientation which had to be the decisive factor for them to back the party of the working class, the party with the more explicit commitments to policies of welfare, and to rendering compassionate assistance to the weak, than to sturdy Adam-Smithian (or Enoch-Powellian?) policies of 'the devil take the hindmost!'

This prominent participation in politics, after a career choice pointing to personal service, may seem unexpected if we take the suggestion seriously that the contemporary professionalised intellectual is disillusioned by political solutions of man's problems.[18] I see no inconsistency here: I did argue in my last book that the proliferation of the so-called counselling professions was helped by the scepticism of the intellectuals of our time about ideological solutions; but I also explained in that same work that,

> Though I have shown that the counsellor is the product of a politically disillusioned century, the counsellor may not be forever trying to find private solutions for public evils or persuading others of the futility of political solutions. After all, the counsellor is a 'betterer', and, as such, he will have become alert to the political avenues of betterment, as soon as he can come round to thinking that in a 'personal service society' there will be more scope for counselling activities. . . . There are already signs that the initially apolitical counsellor can and will reawaken his political conscience after a period of counselling in the field. This seems to be a case of *reculer pour mieux sauter*.[19]

Though I shall argue that our paedagogues do receive indoctrination of a 'counselling' type, they are *not* counsellors and, therefore, their 'return' to politics is far less unexpected after their erstwhile professional orientation in education, than that of the counsellors themselves. The commitment of the teaching profession to a non-specific and indeed global task of 'education', its *in loco parentis* comprehensive care for children and adolescents, its respectability, derived both from presumed learning, and from the presumed integrity of those who are trusted with our younger generation leave the profession's ideological investments conveniently vague. But certain values of some moment, and certain assumptions about human nature, do sink in in the course of training to make their influence felt when it comes to decision-making and the use of power in at least some areas of ordering human relationships in our society.

This process began with the introduction of universal compulsory education. C. F. G. Masterman wrote of the English teaching profession in 1909 that they were

> everywhere taking the lead in public and quasi-public activities. They appear as the mainstay of the political machine in suburban districts, serving upon municipal bodies, in work, clear-headed and efficient; the leaders in churches and chapels, and their various social organisations. They are taking up the position in the urban districts which for many generations was occupied by the country clergy in the rural districts.[20]

It is not only in the national government that professionals have gained ground, in local government the advance in this way has been even more marked. In a recent British Government publication it is observed that 'Councillors had a substantially higher proportion with some form of qualification than electors . . .'[21] One can only guess at the portion of this large percentage which is taken up by the personal service professions. These are, of course, local authority councillors whose deliberations are strongly influenced by a professionalised local government bureaucracy. It is of great importance to bear in mind that in four departments, that is health, welfare, education and children, administrative leadership in British local government is in the hands of the personal service professions. The senior department heads sit on their respective committees, and by their expertise, their status, and often superior general education, exert pressure on the committee's lay members. This is comparable with the recognised and constantly discussed initiative taken by a professionalised civil service even at the level of political leaders in central government, but at local government level the professionalised bureaucrat penetrates the legislative enclosure as well. Of this J. M. Lee remarked that: 'Government by professional administrators had come to stay and come to change the function of the elected representatives'.[22] It seems to me that the influence on legislation of local government officers, such as for example the medical officer of health, who cannot be dismissed by the council without government agreement, and who is a member of, and usually dominates, the health committee, is likely to be greater than that of the permanent civil service, which cannot directly address itself to parliament. It is also interesting to note that, apart from the clerk of the council in some (but not all) cases, no other officer is likely to exceed in social status and popular prestige the medical officer of health, the director of education, and also perhaps the children's officer. The officer responsible for the welfare department is as yet too often inadequately trained, but the present trend is to heighten the professional standing of all social welfare departments, and sooner or later this officer too will everywhere join the ranks of the influential personal service officers whose opinion and orientation will guide others. A department such as housing may eventually become the fifth personal service department. In addition the expansion of the health services inside the health department is already leading to the creation of new senior appointments of influence such as, for example, mental health officers.

Of course, there are solicitors, accountants, and other impersonal service professionals serving as officers of the council and heading their respective departments. I suspect that the climate of leadership is coloured by the standards of expectation formulated by the personal service officers, who are the council's expert advisers on people's needs and on what current public demand should be met with a new appropriation, or how individual citizens will react in their several private lives to a measure contemplated by the council. Naturally, in many councils, all these professional communications will flow through political channels and will have tactical and strategic references; yet the hard information, the anticipated private response of people will remain the speciality of the personal service officers.

The slow but substantial penetration of the organs of national and local government by the personal social service professionals is clear. There are several other influential factors which affect society in this way. I shall now single out one entirely new factor of this kind, which seems to be the more effective as it is comparatively little known: important compromises and concessions are quietly being made by the entrenched professions, thus widening the scope of professionalisation.

These recent developments which have been taking place in the United States have brought to the forefront an unexpected extension of professionalisation. Under the vast pressure of racial discontent and civil strife, US social scientists have been enlisted to explore the various problems which arise in planning general social and specific remedial measures. One of the major matters of concern met at this stage has been the professional manpower shortage, already in evidence for some time, and showing every sign of becoming more acute with every extension of service in the areas of health, welfare, and education. By 1970 the US anticipate a deficit of half a million teachers in the public elementary and secondary school system.[23] Martin Luther King's book, *Where Do We Go From Here?*, is quoted as saying that the expansion of human service industry is going to be the 'missing industry' which will 'soak up the unemployment that persists in the US'.[24]

The concept of 'New Careers' was introduced by Arthur Pearl and Frank Riessman in *New Careers for the Poor* (New York, 1965). They propose 'that human service occupations can be re-organized to produce better services by allowing disadvantaged, undereducated people to perform useful work at new entry-level jobs with training and education built-in to allow advancement on the organizational hierarchy'.[25] There is no doubt that the urgent demands stress the need for new professional career systems, multi-entry provisions for professional auxiliaries who through in-service training, and in other ways, could even catch up with the more conventionally trained personal service professionals. The idea is not new, and was first applied extensively after the second world war, even in Britain. The emergency teachers' training schemes, and the Younghusband social work training programme in Britain have certainly been devices of this kind. What seems to be new in the work of the New York University 'New Careers Development Center' is that they propose to convert 'former welfare recipients' into aides, auxiliaries, and trainee dispensers of 'welfare' and eventually into professionals. Patricia Elston sets out the basic components of the new career models and mentions, among others,

> creating new entry level jobs, staffing these positions with non-professionals, developing a career ladder in which entry level jobs are linked to jobs higher up the line restructuring the professional positions. . . .[26]

The counselling orientation of this new para-professional cadre of workers is often inevitable, for the proposals make it clear that their induction shall take place under the wings of fully trained social case-workers, and other fully trained personal service professionals. This orientation is especially in evidence in the document *The Indigenous Nonprofessional*, issued by the American National Institute of Labor Education Mental Health Program. This document regards these new personal service para-professionals as 'bridgement' between the professional worker and low income people.[27] They talk of 'sub-professionals', 'informal leaders', 'indigenous organizers', 'mental health aides', and maintain that these recruits would not only enrich the effectiveness of the established personal service professions but evolve new types of personal service professionals. As yet, at any rate at the present stage of the programme, they suggest that,

> The indigenous non-professional *is* poor, *is* from the neighbour-hood, *is* often a member of a minority group. His family *is* poor. He *is* a peer of the client and shares a common background, language, ethnic origin, style and group of interests which it would be impossible and perhaps even undesirable for most professionals to maintain.[28]

The cause which is being advanced here is not unexpected: both the values and the techniques of the professional personal service partake of the values and techniques of co-operative, symbiotic, and mentally supportive primary group relationships. But whereas in the past, the ideological framework within these spontaneous, self-helping com-munity relationships operated was mainly religious and to a smaller extent political (e.g. trade unions, party organisations, etc.) *they are now being brought under the control and ideological patronage of the modern personal service professions.*

Even the spirit of discontent and of the 'class war' is translating itself into a new idiom while the 'exploiter – exploited' stratification is mellowed and is increasingly displayed by 'professionally qualified – unqualified' stratification. Naturally, the moving of the clash from one arena to another does not mean that privilege and deprivation or envy and rebellion have come to an end. The fact that even the language of discontent is acquiring references to professionalisation shows the strong presence of professionalisation in our culture today. The professionally unqualified raise the cry of 'credentialism', a fascinatingly new charge of selfish exclusiveness, for it both recognises the value of *and* undermines the respect for training, learning, and special knowledge. Yet the attack on 'professional élitism' – another telling phrase – is, on balance, salutary. There have been some constructive reviews in the selection and training of professionals, and professional careers in the personal services have been opened to people who lacked entry-qualifications and who eventually showed equal or even superior ability to perform.

These political undertones and conflicts have been created mainly by those who were as yet outside the professions. They do not in any way weaken my hypothesis that professionalisation is the contemporary vehicle of integration in society and of moral renewal.

The cultural impact of professionalisation is thus vividly illustrated both through the measures which are either already being adopted by the 'New Careers' movement and by the new language of covetousness as well as of legitimate ambition. If evidence is required to show the 'professionalisation of leadership ethics' in our time, surely these particular developments must be cited and taken into account.

At the end of the day, the growth, the differentiation of services, and of the available expertise, will depend on how much money is there to spend on health, welfare, education, and the like. The process of extensive growth in the personal services is a function of material enrichment and only indirectly of the advancement of science, in the fields imminently concerned with health, welfare, and education. In fact, our know-how to assist others paedagogically, clinically, and personally has outstripped our material resources in spite of our relative affluence.

But is the process of professionalisation an outcome of western capitalist affluence only? Recently, a good deal has been written about the alleged or real convergence of development in the industrial societies of the capitalist and communist worlds.[29] The thesis has been emerging that industrial societies, both capitalist and communist, are obliged to fit their social system into a technologically given framework which tends to be the same for all systems, whether communist or capitalist.

I believe that professionalisation in the capitalist west inevitably introduces more and more collectivistic and other-regarding considerations into the social functioning of individuals, and weakens the *laissez faire* licence of a free enterprise, the *rapacity* of penal justice, the

E

TABLE XV

THE GROWTH OF MEDICAL, PARAMEDICAL, AND
PAEDAGOGICAL PERSONNEL IN HUNGARY, 1930–60

	1930	1949	1960
(1) Population	8,685,109	9,204,799	9,961,044
(2) Medical, paramedical, and paedagogical personnel	53,634	68,790	154,676
(3) (2) Expressed as a % of (1)	0·62	0·75	1·55

Compiled from *Központi Statisztikai Hivatal 1960 Évi Népszámlálási 'Össze-foglaló Adatok'*, Vol. 13. Census (Budapest, 1964), p. 77, and *'Demographiai Adatok'*, Vol. 5 (Budapest, 1962), p. 9.

TABLE XVI

THE GROWTH IN THE NUMBER OF TEACHERS IN HUNGARY,
1937–64

	1937–8	1953–4	1960–1	1963–4
(1) Population	(appr.) 9,000,000	(appr.) 9,300,000	9,961,044	10,104,179
(2) Teachers (kindergarten, primary, secondary, university)	32,838	59,918	79,423	88,872
(3) (2) Expressed as a % of (1)	0·36	0·64	0·80	0·88

Compiled from *Hungarian Central Statistical Office, Statistical Yearbook 1963* (Budapest, 1965), pp. 4 and 337.

TABLE XVII

THE GROWTH IN THE NUMBER OF PHYSICIANS IN HUNGARY
1930–63

	1930	1949	1960	1963
(1) Population	8,685,109	9,204,799	9,961,044	10,104,179
(2) Physicians	8,285	9,909	15,698	17,865
(3) (2) Expressed as a % of (1)	0·095	0·107	0·157	0·177

Compiled from *Hungarian Central Statistical Office, Statistical Yearbook, 1963* (Budapest, 1965), pp. 4 and 309.

TABLE XVIII

SOME PERSONAL SERVICE PROFESSIONALS IN
CZECHOSLOVAKIA, 1950–65

(a) *Health personnel**

	1950	1955	1960	1965
Physicians	12,580	18,322	23,997	29,150
Pharmacists	3,728	4,217	4,848	5,291
Dentists	3,331	2,588	2,303	2,074
Professional nurses	20,374	29,391	31,982	36,244
Pediatric nurses	1,429	10,195	15,089	19,252
Obstetrical nurses	5,253	5,274	4,751	4,658
Total	46,695	69,927	82,970	96,959
Other auxiliary medical workers – with high school education	7,350	14,909	14,176	18,550
Total	54,045	84,836	97,146	115,509

*Source: Vladimír Srb, *Demografická příručka* (Prague, 1967), p. 178.

TABLE XVIII (*cont.*)
(b) *Teaching personnel*†

	1948	1955	1960	1965
Teachers in –				
kindergartens	—	14,694	17,529	23,467
– elementary schools	54,569	66,416	92,918	95,950
– high school	9,314	13,343	10,218	20,488
– university level	5,925	7,143	10,504	15,388
Total	69,808	101,596	131,169	155,293

†Source: *Statistická ročenka ČSSR* (*The Statistical Yearbook of Czechoslovakia* Prague, 1967), p. 44.

(c) *Total personal service professionals*

	1950	1955	1960	1965
‡ Total population of Czechoslovakia	12,338,450	13,092,570	13,654,088	14,158,697
Total health and teaching personnel	123,853	186,432	228,315	270,802
Total health and teaching personnel as a % of total population	1·00	1·33	1·67	1·91

‡Source: Vladimír Srb, *Demografická příručka* (*Demographic Handbook*) (Prague, 1967), p. 21, 40.

harshness of educational discipline and the *mercenariness* of 'marketable' doctoring. At the same time the increasing efficiency and affluence of the communist countries will extend their capacity to pay for more and more personal social services in their communities and multiply the numbers of leading intellectuals whose concern will be with personal services and personal ministrations of help and not with the grand strategies and actuarial realities of the state or the party. And when both systems have eventually overcome the difficulties of

TABLE XIX

GROWTH IN THE NUMBER OF SOME OF THE PERSONAL SERVICE PROFESSIONAL WORKERS
IN THE U.S.A., 1900–50

(in thousands)

	(1) Physicians and surgeons	(2) Nurses	(3) Dentists	(4) School teachers	(5) University teachers	(6) Social welfare, and religious workers*	(7) Total population	(8) Total no. of personal service professionals	(9) Column (8) expressed as a % of column (7)
1900	131	12	30	436	7	—	76,094	616	0·81
1910	152	82	40	595	16	19	92,407	904	0·98
1920	146	149	56	752	33	46	106,466	1,182	1·11
1930	157	294	71	1,044	62	71	123,077	1,699	1·39
1940	168	377	71	1,086	77	119	131,954	1,898	1·43
1950	195	491	76	1,149	127	137	151,234	2,175	1·44

* Not including clergy.
From *Historical Statistics of the United States* (U.S. Bureau of Census, Washington, D.C., 1960), pp. 7 and 75.

meeting all their material requirements beyond the dreams of avarice they will increasingly give themselves over to planning, organising and rendering personal services to the individual. And eventually, if sanity prevails, the two systems will converge towards what I call a *personal service society*.

TABLE XX

THE GROWTH IN THE NUMBERS OF PERSONAL SERVICE
PROFESSIONALS IN THE USSR

(a) *Teachers (in thousands)*

	1930	1940	1950	1960
(1) Total population	179,000	194,000	179,000	212,000
(2) No. of *all* teachers	548	1,237	1,475	3,000
(3) (2) expressed as % of (1)	0·31	0·64	0·82	1·42

(b) *Medical and paramedical personnel (in thousands)*,

	1940	1950	1960	1965
(1) Total population	194,000	179,000	212,000	229,000
(2) Doctors	1,349	2,369	3,854	4,850
Dental surgeons and dentists	204	281	463	692
Middle grade medical personnel including nurses	4,720	7,190	13,880	16,920
Total of (2)	6,273	9,840	18,197	22,462
(3) (2) expressed as % of (1)	0·32	0·55	0·86	0·98

Compiled from the following sources:
(a) *Narodnoye Khozyaistvo, SSSR, 1956*, as quoted in Counts' *The Challenge of Soviet Education*, from *Narodnoye Khozyastvo, SSSR., 1965*, as kindly translated for me and made available to me by Mr T. M. Ryan of the University College, Swansea. (b) *World Survey of Education* Vol. IV (Unesco, 1966), pp. 1144–45. (c) *Demographic Yearbook of the United Nations* (1965), p. 103.

2. Social Thought and Social Action

All personal service professionals are either already interested in social science or are becoming interested in it. Whether they are social workers, doctors, nurses, or teachers, they are concerned to find out about the social background and history of their clients. They are also increasingly conscious of the fact that their own relationship with their clients is complex, and that social science has a good many useful observations to make about that relationship. Indeed they recognise that rendering effective help to their clients, while remaining only intuitively sensible of social realities, is no longer thought satisfactory in social work, and is rapidly becoming regarded as amounting to incompetence also in all the other branches of the personal service professions. Today, sociological, psychological, economic, and even anthropological tuition, that is to say, tuition in the major social sciences, is progressively promoted in the training courses for personal service professionals. The Todd Report in Britain recommends the normalisation of social science instruction to medical students, and nowadays it would be difficult to find a teachers' training institution which did not stipulate some familiarity with the findings and the mode of thought characteristic of the contemporary sociology and psychology of education, as a condition of qualification. And so, the social sciences have become the foundation disciplines upon which the conceptual structures necessary to think about, and perform in, a personal service role are expected to rest.

But the impact of the formalised social thought on social action is in evidence in *all* sectors of society, and not only in the personal social services. Yet whatever general conclusions I shall be able to reach in this respect will, of necessity, more markedly apply to the personal service professionals. After all, apart from academic social scientists and research workers in the social sciences, these professionals are the only educated people who receive systematic instruction in the social sciences already, or are soon to be exposed to such instruction as this in their usual training programmes. Indeed, the social science instruction of the personal service professionals inevitably carries with it the implication that what they learn from the social sciences they will be expected to apply in the course of their professional work, rather as engineers will be expected to apply the physics and chemistry they study in the course of their training. No matter how theoretical, and even abstruse, the social sciences may appear, they tend to be taken to have an important bearing on the practicalities to which the personal service professionals are attending.

And for this reason, in the *first* section of this chapter I shall make some general observations on this larger on-going process, on the process of the overall moral influence of social science on social change. The reflections which follow in this first section are mainly about the 'social scientist'. If the personal service professional is nowadays trained in 'social science', the moral climate which his leadership calls into being will be affected by the principles of his thinking. In addition to this, the social scientist, either as teacher in a university or college, or as a consultant, or some other practitioner, is himself a practising personal service professional. But this is not what brings his intellectual wares under our scrutiny here. The reason for this exploration lies in a fundamental objection to my theory of the counselling ideology. This objection consists in the argument that the personal service professionals, if they are intellectually honest and dependable people – and we should like at least to give them the benefit of the doubt that they are honest and dependable – are called upon to do no more or less than *apply social science*. 'Practice' consists in applying social science, and if it consists in other things as well, we must guard against saying anything definite about them until science succeeds in bringing those things within its orbit.

The discussion which follows shall first show that social science, or rather the *acts of communicating* social science, are themselves a *practice* of a special kind, and that social science has not been able to say anything very substantial as yet about this area of human activity. At some length and, I hope, with some care, I set out to prove that cultivating social science is a species of practice amounting to social action and intervention and that it is the beginning to acts of social betterment. Following this, I shall explain that – though the practitioners of personal service are inevitably guided by social science – they set up insurmountable barriers to being taken over by social science by virtue of the subjectivity and personal involvement in their practice, a condition in which they invariably find themselves.

And so, in the second section of this chapter I shall enquire into the nature of the influence exerted by the mixture of a specific and narrower social-psychological science and of the counselling ideology on the thinking of professional workers. In my last book I explored this very influence on the professionals in social work, psychiatry, and medicine. Here, I will go further afield and subject the literature of the professions of teaching and business management to the same kind of treatment I applied to the literature of counselling in my last book.

A. SOCIAL SCIENCE AND SOCIAL CHANGE

The interest even when amounting to a vogue, or even to an obsession, in the Sociology of Knowledge, tends to be the product of a self-searching age, an age preoccupied with its motives. In this so-called 'scientific era' our chief concern has been with the distortions and distorters of positive and empirical truths, with the ideological influences of a thinker's position on his thinking about social matters. We have persistently scratched about to show the ways in which social position determined 'thinking', and especially 'thinking about society'. Today, many of us feel obliged to ask, 'How, and to what extent, does this "thinking about society" change society?' or a little more specifically, 'What does this scientific approach to social matters do to society?' This is a question which the Marxist-Leninist either does not ask, or if he does raise it, he prejudges it by relegating all ideas into the realm of mere superstructures. Of course, one can never be sure how weighty these superstructures are in the Marxist's estimation. If one suggests that historical-materialism has reserved all potency to change society to the technological-economic sphere of life one is likely to be tabbed a 'vulgariser' of the materialist scriptures. It is usually Engels' 'heads you lose, tails I win' corrective which is quoted for the edification of the naively incredulous outsider:

> According to the materialist conception of history, the *ultimately* determining element in history is the production and reproduction of real life. More than this neither Marx nor I have ever asserted. Hence if somebody twists this into saying that the economic element is the *only* determining one, he transforms that proposition into a meaningless, abstract, senseless phrase. The economic situation is the basis, but the various elements of the superstructure . . .

and Engels enumerates among others, 'Political, juristic, philosophical theories, religious views', and so on, 'exercise their influence upon the course of the historical struggles and in many cases preponderate in determining their *form*.'[1]

Alas, Engels does not tell us how to distinguish between *form* and *substance*, nor does he explain what he means by the 'production and reproduction of real life' being the 'ultimately' determining element of history. To begin with, the 'production and reproduction of real life' is a poetic phrase, the meaning of which goes far beyond the 'production and reproduction of the material wherewithal of life' – which is, presumably, the honest pivot of the historical-materialist theory. And also, the device of 'ultimately' makes the theory as an explanatory instrument all but useless. We may equally fairly produce theories such as 'the nutritional theory of health', and use Engels' explanation to justify this manifestly trumped-up theory (I mean, of course, the 'nutritional theory') in the following way, 'according to the nutritional theory of health the *ultimately* determining element of health is the quality and quantity of food we consume.' I don't think that, even with the Engels kind of reservation, we could entertain the theory of historical materialism any more readily than we could seriously consider my improvised dietetic theory. 'Marx and I' wrote Engels in one of his letters of the nineties,

> are partly responsible for the fact that at times our disciples have laid more weight upon the economic factor than belongs to it. We were compelled to emphasise its character in opposition to our opponents who denied it, and there wasn't always time, place and occasion to do justice to the other factors in the reciprocal interactions of the historical process.[2]

This is a reasonable explanation resembling the one about making crooked sticks straight by bending them the opposite way. The trouble is that historical materialism explicitly and unqualifiedly appoints the technical-economic factor the *sole* determinant of social change. All other facts of social existence are derived from it and are secondary to it. This *is* the theory, and if it is not the theory, then there is no theory left! Or, at least, the theory must undergo considerable amendment to incorporate the qualifications clearly conceded by Engels. Those who complain that some stupid and insensitive communists put forward a 'vulgar' version of historical materialism say, in fact, that they put forward an unqualified and unconditional theory of historical materialism, and that such an unqualified and unconditional theory is a vulgar simplification, that is to say untrue or invalid. They never explain what qualifications and what conditions must be explicitly and clearly stipulated so that the main substance of the theory is preserved, and the so-called 'vulgar' interpretations are firmly put beyond the pale. We are never told what propositions of the theory are still explicitly affirmed, with what explicit qualifications. We are told merely, time and again, that the theory is sacrosanct, an immutable historical truth, yet one which, when taken literally, is to be condemned as a vulgarity.

Marx in the Preface to his *Capital*'s first edition betrays his own secret admiration for the humanistic influence and unexplained anticapitalistic independence of the personal service professional. Here is a testimony that could not have been published in a more prominent place! Marx writes, that the Germans would be

> appalled at the state of things at home if, as in England, our governments and parliaments appointed commissions of enquiry into economic conditions; if these commissions were armed with the same plenary powers to get at the truth; if it were possible to find for this purpose men as competent, as free from partisanship and respect of persons as are the English factory inspectors, her medical reporters on public health, her commissioners of enquiry into the exploitation of women and children, into housing and food.[3]

Presumably the honest and objective empiricism of these mid-nineteenth-century British health and welfare workers and officials was the social intelligence of the day and, therefore, its social science. Also, presumably, as they were 'free from partisanship' so they were no mere ideologists of the system. Did their ideas 'roll down the back' of the system? Marx answers that himself when he says that the Germans would be 'appalled' if they were treated to social science of this kind. People who are 'appalled' are hardly unmoved and unlikely to be entirely unchanged!

It is not my wish to emulate those for whom the most important causal process in the poultry yard is the one in which eggs cause hens to be made whilst thoroughly neglecting that other causal process in which hens cause eggs to be made. Unlike the historical materialist I do not attribute all power to the superstructure in the manner they attribute all power to the substructure. It is obvious that the potency of the presence of social science information in our contemporary societies would have to be regarded as zero if we accepted a consistent – even if somewhat 'vulgar' – notion of historical materialism. The purpose of my citing Engels is to show that the so-called 'not-vulgar' historical materialist is, in fact, not a historical materialist (except in name) and that, therefore, we need expect no logically coherent opposition from that quarter.

Today, the accumulated social science intelligence is beginning to act back upon the source from which it has originated, and the feedback appoints social science as a pervading factor in the social process. Hitherto the main concern of the Sociology of Knowledge has been the social determination of mental contents; we must now enquire a little more insistently into the mental determination of social facts. An important branch of this enquiry will be that which deals with the dissemination of social science intelligence as a factor of social change. '. . . Sociological investigation discovers', writes Znaniecki,

> that there are two kinds of connection between knowledge and social life. On the one hand, upon men's participation in a certain system of knowledge often depends their participation in some social system and their conduct within the limits of the latter. . . . On the other hand, the participation of men in certain social systems often determines (though perhaps not entirely or exclusively) in what systems of knowledge they will participate, and how.[4]

This is an apt description of the two-way relationship between sociological awareness and social existence. Here I am chiefly concerned with the first half of their cycle, with the social impact of sociology and of social science in general.

There is, of course, dissemination of information or opinion about society by other than accredited scientific sources, recognised social science publications and authoritative pronouncements. These are the frankly ideological and often dilettante transmissions usually through the media of mass-communication. Whereas these, too, are obviously factors of social change, they are not to be confused with my present concerns; here I am interested in social scientific communications. The influence of these is growing *pari passu* with the general public's thriving trust in the social scientists, the social science experts, and in the 'appliers' of social science, the personal service professionals.

My general thesis in this chapter is that all sociological communications to people modify their behaviour as well as their moral valuations. In a paper entitled 'Can Men change Laws of Social Science?'[5] Alan Gewirth calls attention to the need for separating the influence of social science on social conditions from its influence on the so-called social laws, which are thought to be operative in society. Whereas the first is comparatively easy to account for, the second calls forth serious difficulties. Nonetheless he concludes that even there changes are effected: man, through his social science, intervenes and removes certain laws from operation altogether. Now here I do not propose to re-examine the logical predicament of the so-called 'social law' and its vicissitudes in the glare of social science. I am reasonably certain that human society from time to time overhauls the laws of its own functioning.

Clearly, as Herbert Marcuse put it, if the social laws were unalterable, society would be 'throttled by the inexorable'.[6] Surely, these laws cannot escape the consequences of our discovering them: Shakespeare's rhetorical question in *All's Well That Ends Well* (Act IV, scene 1, line 43) ought to be constantly before the eyes of the working social scientist: 'Is it possible he should know what he is, and be that he is?'

My present task follows from these conclusions and aims at opening up a new issue. If we must concede that both social laws and social conditions are verifiably affected, influenced, and modified by social science communications, is not the logical status of these communications radically changed? The social scientist who conveys social science propositions must concede that the act of 'conveying' is also an act of 'persuading'. Then how can he preserve the logical status of his propositions? It is sometimes suggested that social scientists need not worry about the influence their writings and pronouncements may exert, for the intellectuals, the eggheads, have little or no power anyway.[7] Power is wielded by the aggressive, cleverly manipulative individuals in business and politics whose resourcefulness is an intuitive skill, a charismatic talent, not a social science expertise. Indeed, they are not given to a reflective appraisal of social matters, for this would merely squander their energy and diffuse their one-pointedness. Yet, I think that these men of action send their sons to the universities where they assimilate methods and acquire knowledge. Eventually, these men of the 'educated generation', mostly professional workers, replace the 'men of action' of the previous generation, and make use of what they have learnt. This is a process which is now greatly accelerated by the extensive professionalisation of modern society in which an increasingly large proportion of the managers and leaders achieve their status through excellence in academic performance or, at least, through academic qualifications. Though the graduates in the social sciences have to share leadership with graduates in the experimental sciences, the social science graduate will continue to dominate, for he is the 'social science expert', and, therefore, he is the trained staff officer! Moreover, the culture of the experimental scientist will always exact the experimental scientist's respect for the expert in a social science speciality, even if this respect may be reserved for those social scientists whose strictly quantitative methods are more like those of the experimental scientist.

All these speculations about the influence of social science on society would be scorned by those who think with William Graham Sumner that 'the great stream of time and earthly things will sweep on just the same in spite of us'.[8] But even Sumner had to admit that 'if we puny men by our arts can do anything at all . . . it will only be by modifying the tendencies of some of the forces at work, so that, after a sufficient time, their action may be changed a little, and slowly the lines of movement may be modified. This effort, however, can at most be only slight, and it will take a long time.'[9] But we have all the time in the world – unless mankind commits suicide – and we do not require very much more than 'modifying the tendencies' to self-destruction. It is interesting to note Myrdal's comment on Sumner's fatalistic musings:

> Sumner could not fail to have a particularly strong influence on social science thinking about the problems of the South and, specifically, about the Negro problem. The theory of folkways and mores has diffused from the scientists, and has in the educated classes of the South become a sort of regional credo. The characterisation of something as 'folkways' or 'mores' on the stereotype that 'stateways cannot change folkways' – which under no circumstances can be more than a relative truth – is used in the literature on the South and on the Negro as a general formula of mystical significance.[10]

In other words, Sumner was *not* an insignificant factor in 'modifying the tendency' to racial equalisation by equipping reaction with a sociological formula![11]

In the past, the question of the responsibility of the social scientist was closely linked with the issue of bias and motive in his thinking. The social scientist had a responsibility because he could not help being biased. Such was the view expressed by Gunnar Myrdal in the oft-quoted Second Appendix of *An American Dilemma*. He asked us to make our bias explicit; this would not only help us to approach objectivity, but it is also a moral responsibility of the social scientist.

Certainly, making an effort to disclose his bias to himself and to others is the social scientist's responsibility. But this is not his whole responsibility. He must also realise that even when he can find no bias his role as an opinion-forming agent makes him, in fact, the cause of change and so responsible for it in some degree.

Then there were those who simply declared that 'knowledge brings responsibility'. Robert Lynd's *Knowledge for What?*[12] argued spiritedly that the initial interests in social problems lay at the root of all social science enquiry and that these interests continued to inform the work of the social scientist throughout his career no matter how much he denied it. It was moral responsibility which brought them to social science and they were not to deny this responsibility as they went along. Here the argument ran that all social science interest is preceded by a feeling of responsibility and commitment. The social scientist would be deceiving himself and others if he tried to live this down or somehow wished it away.

Gwynne Nettler called the sociologist siding with these two views 'evaluationist' and 'responsibility' methodologists and repudiated them both.[13] Now here I propose to raise the question of responsibility in a new form and, shifting the emphasis from motive, bias, or commitment, offer another conception. It is not the inevitable bias or the inevitable reformism in social science which primarily gives rise to serious apprehensions about the moral responsibility inherent in social science communications, but their inevitable persuasiveness and, therefore, their actual and verifiable consequences. It is the business of social science to examine the propagandistic, educational, and social control functions of social science; I shall try to deal with some aspects of that business.

In talking about 'social science communications' I propose to adopt the following definition of communication: it is a ' . . . process by which an individual (the communicator) transmits stimuli (usually verbal) to modify the behaviour of other individuals (the audience).[14] This definition was designed in connection with some researches into the persuasive power of some communications and not with a view to a linguistic analysis of the term. Now the communications there examined were explicitly and frankly attitude-moulding; they were primarily persuasive and only secondarily and incidentally instructive. It is my contention that, notwithstanding these qualifications, the above definition will be valid and accurately applicable to all communications about human social behaviour, even though they are ostensibly not persuasive, but informative and instructive. I propose to analyse a few communications of a simple kind before I venture any further.

Consider, for instance, 'This table is white', a proposition of no great complexity and one not much suspected of emotive undertones. Let us see what situations would call forth propositions of this kind.

Someone may have remarked that 'I place the book on this yellow table', and we may have replied by way of correction that 'This table is white!' In this case, we imply that we wish him to say 'white' and not 'yellow' when referring to the colour of this table on future occasions. Indeed we must have intended to convey this element of persuasion and of suggestion, otherwise we would not have spoken.

Then again, we may be explaining to a child while pointing, 'This table is green', and 'this table is white'. What we mean here is undoubtedly this: 'You, my child, should take note that, whenever you refer to the colour of this table or that table, you must call them green or white respectively. You should call them so; you must call them so; we have enjoined you to call them so.'

Is the situation different when the proposition is less trivial? For example, 'Light travels at the speed of 186,000 miles per second'. Now, what is intended by communicating this piece of information? Surely it must be something like this: 'If in the future you think of the source and perception of light, you must not think that there is an instantaneous link! Light is transmitted! You must accept the idea that it travels and that its speed is measurable . . .', and so on. In other words, the proposition proselytises on behalf of a specific metaphysical orientation towards the universe.

No matter what the positive statement conveys, it is simultaneously both information and injunction. All information is fused with the injunction that 'henceforth, such and such a proposition shall be thought true or untrue,' or even that 'henceforth, such and such behaviour shall be regarded as consistent with the facts or inconsistent with them.' And when the proposition is about people, the persuasive or even constraining impact of the proposition is even more in evidence. Indeed – unless the propositions of soliloquy are to be included – strip any communicative proposition of all its injunctive-normative content and the proposition's meaning will be hopelessly crippled.

Let us now enter the other side of the forest. Here one is on well-trodden paths. Take an obviously normative statement with unashamed emotive tones, e.g. 'Thou shalt not steal!' The positive content of such communication as this has often been laid bare and I do not claim to be adding to the stock of knowledge on these matters by defining that content. Yet, I wish to repeat the gist of what is known, for, if my remarks are joined to the foregoing observations, the outcome may turn out to be helpful.

The positive content of this last example is easily identifiable; firstly, I tell you that I do not want you to steal; secondly, I tell you that you would violate your nature or be inconsistent with certain principal features of it if you stole. In brief, I convey information on my psychology as well as on yours. All this is well known and has been frequently stated.

Thus, first we say that a proposition carried with it strong injunctive-normative elements. And now we are reminded that normative statements carry with them information of a positive character. Indeed I claim that both of these elements are present in all communications! Thus one is impelled to ask: 'Is not the sharp grammatical separation between the indicative and the imperative somewhat arbitrary?' We may say that the grammatical mood emphasises either the injunctive or the informative side of a communication; yet what we utter is a communication the substance of which is inseparably both. Now this is not to say that the informative should be converted into the injunctive, or the other way round, but rather to recognise that in an imperative the injunction is explicit and information is implicit, and that, in an indicative, information is explicit and injunction is implicit. Thus – with apologies to George Orwell – I would say that 'all propositions are injunctive but some are more injunctive than others',

F

and conversely 'all injunctions are informative but some are more informative than others'.

One comment I recall having been made on this is that I prove too much by claiming that all propositions are injunctive, for this would undermine the validity of the claim itself. This, however, is not so. No matter how injunctive a proposition is it cannot affect the categorical structure of the universe or of mathematical-logic and, therefore, it cannot affect the logical status of what I am saying. If all propositions are injunctive, it is true that they all enjoin us to think of objects or of people in a special way – in the non-social sciences (including logic and mathematics) and in the social sciences respectively. But, whereas in the non-social sciences the objects or their laws are not affected by our thinking about them in a special way, in the social sciences they are thus affected – if and when we tell the objects what we think of them. Also, whilst a social science proposition influences the conduct of those to whom it is communicated – because their newly acquired knowledge about their conduct evokes new motives for action – an electron, unlike an individual or a social group, does not change its characteristics, because it is not able to acquire its own knowledge of those characteristics as an outcome of our having disclosed them to it.[15]

In this present context, I should like to put special emphasis on the following: I do not wish to deny that there is a marked difference in the general tone of the two kinds of communications (informative and injunctive communications), nor do I intend to reduce one to the other. I am merely trying to show that all communications have an injunctive element in them and, therefore, as a matter of fact, are equipped to mould, to change, and to influence those to whom they are addressed. All the difficulties in the way of our deeply comprehending this nature of all human communications are caused by arbitrary convention and usage which, by now, have created the illusion of pure and absolute, as well as incommensurable, indicatives and imperatives.

This linguistic argument is offered as only the *first* of several in support of the thesis that social science is a factor of social change. The *second* argument owes its life to the great prestige of science in the culture of modern industrial societies.

It will be said that linguistic speculations about the nature of a proposition may, at best, prove that every time we say something, we are in fact trying to influence somebody. Should we allow this objection? Our experience tells of the presence of some other circumstances which we must now describe. As a matter of ascertainable social fact there is a widespread expectation present in society which is inspired by the belief that science will deliver not only the goods but also the solutions of problems, and the definitions of goals-states. The plausibility of this rash expectation is much strengthened by the dramatic achievements of the physical sciences and is not conspicuously weakened by the protestations of social scientists. And this expectation is not a symptom of ignorance, for the educated élite fosters it in every way.

> Not only neophyte graduate students, both governmental and private, but sponsors of research enterprises tend to seek solutions to such problems as world government, morality in public life, legislative-executive relations, efficiency in business or government organisation, freedom of the press, labour-management relations, responsible party organisations, regulation of monopoly, conservation and development of natural resources, and so on. In the planning movement we find deliberate advocacy of research to clarify goals, to explore the total problem situation, select and weigh the consequences of alternative courses of action, and to determine the appropriate aims of policy. There is more than a trace of this orientation in the developing 'science of human relations' and in proposals for 'institutes of behavioural sciences'. . . .[16]

Simply, the position is this: those to whom social science propositions are communicated are not only persuaded that the propositions are true, or at least, that the hypotheses are reasonable, they also feel entitled to take these communications as warrants to regard certain courses of action as morally worthier than others. In this scientific–technological culture the 'consumers' of social science communications find it convenient not to scrutinise the credentials of the social science expert to ascertain whether he also possesses some special moral authority (whatever that may mean in this context), to guide decisions, and suggest policies. After all, the scientific-technological culture has snuffed out the life of all other candidates for moral authority, and the social science expert might be used to fill the vacuum. The *second* argument explains why social science is expected, on a scale far beyond any help it has been known to give in solving social problems, to decide issues and guide policy. That this expectation is mistaken, and that it springs from a misunderstanding of the nature of a scientific discipline in general and of social science in particular, is not relevant to the point with which I am dealing here, which is that the culture of the age has set up the social science experts, and the practitioners of the expertise, the personal service professionals, as moral authorities even when they have no desire to assume that authority.

This second argument, let us call it the 'science-prestige argument', together with the linguistic argument form a strong alliance. What is common to these two is that the social scientist is not really responsible for the influence of the facts to which my present arguments relate. He did not endow propositions with injunctive power and he did not endow science with prestige. But his responsibility for the facts to which the *third* argument relates is clear. I am here thinking of the social scientist's authorship of the idea that social science can be cultivated by using the method of 'action research'. By using this method, the social scientist recognises his own intervention in the social process. In a hand-to-mouth fashion, he translates information into policy, into social action, into social change, with the excuse that the purpose of the operation is either to serve the preconceived policy decisions of others or to use acts of choice experimentally in the hope of obtaining more information. The posture struck by the operators of action research suggests that somehow they believe they have managed to transfer the rationality of their means to the ends which they have chosen to serve. There are signs of this 'transference of rationality' both in action research on the factory shop floor and in 'action research' in state finance! 'Not only has economic science changed its object and its nature,' writes Jacques Ellul, 'but it has produced a technique which is simultaneously a method of knowledge and a method of action. Political economy has not renounced its claim to being normative. It seeks not only to grasp reality but also to modify it.'[16A] In a perfectly good and strong sense all social science is action research, no matter how etherealised, abstract, and dispassionately academic it is. Naturally, when the personal service professional 'applies' social science he invariably blends his knowledge with decisions, no matter how much he protests that he is 'non-judgmental'. At the other extreme, the so-called theoretician can't escape the charge either: in fact, Marx was wrong to separate 'interpretation' from 'intervention' when he wrote the oft-quoted challenge, 'the philosophers have only interpreted the world in different ways; the point is to change it!'[17] My point is that *by interpreting* the world the philosophers – and the social scientists – *have in fact changed it!* The monumental greatness of Marx and Lenin consists precisely in this. Were it not so, they would have been mere spectators – not even linesmen – mere epiphenomena, mere leaves on a torrent. Instead of which – we know only too well – they were the very tornado which whipped up the torrent!

Much unlike the Marxists, many social scientists will repudiate responsibility for history by saying, 'but I had absolutely no intention of influencing anybody or of changing anything! I studied X, and published my findings about X, without the slightest desire to modify X!' Coming from a social scientist, as it sometimes does, this is a remarkably naive plea. To say the very least, the sociologist, by virtue of his special knowledge of social causation, and of social change, can no more rule out the possibility of influencing a social situation by publicly stating something about it, than a motorist soberly joining a drinking party can rule out the possibility of eventually killing somebody. It would not be to the credit of contemporary sociology to ignore or misjudge the scope of its own influence. In fact, instead of protestations of innocence, all too many sociologists in their prefatory remarks to their books and treatises say they hope for, and even expect change as a result of their reports about facts. Indeed, they are in the habit of justifying their labour, the expense to society of their activities as well as of their own subsistence, by claiming that the policy-makers and administrators will do their jobs so much better since they will be able to avail themselves of the intelligence the sociologist has contrived to collect. It is about time that we made explicit the prevarication which lurks in the prefaces and premises of so many erudite sociological treatises. There a paragraph often begins with 'my concern is with facts only' and ends wistfully with 'I hope that those who are responsible for legislating in respect of X, or for the administration of Y, or for the management of Z, will do their jobs much better than they would have done without my study and publication of these facts.'

At times, there is even detectable a characteristic gusto with which the social scientist hurls his facts at us, rubs our noses into his interpretations, and rips off our rose-tinted glasses. 'In their sometimes

ruthless and cynical criticism of other elements in our culture,' writes
Charles Dollard, 'social scientists have often failed to reflect the
anthropologist's discovery that a society, like a shirt, can split at the
seams if it is handled too roughly; nor have they factored out their
own deep aggression in analysing and reporting their data, on social
and economic problems.'[18] Of course, one of the academic speculator's
few chances of an experience of wielding power is through the perspic-
acity and provocativeness of his mind. It is sound sociology to
remember this, and give it its due, when assessing the factors of social
change in our times. 'Power?' asks Philip Toynbee. 'Few writers
want the direct kind which is exercised by generals and tycoons, but
to publish anything anywhere is certainly an act of aggression against
the public. "Now listen to *me*! I want you to be influenced by what I
have to tell you!" '[19] Psychologists are more often reminded of their
unsolicited and aggressive informativeness and so-called 'insight-
giving'. Social scientists, especially sociologists, have so far rarely
been reproached for gratuitous truth-telling.

The social scientist's self-image certainly includes a nagging belief
that what he knows and what he tells are of moment. Other people
would be less well informed if he remained silent. But the belief that
his discernment and perspicuity *make a difference* to others, is also a
testimony of the social scientists: it is derived from the empirical
observation of the social scientist that what he says and communicates
will not only inform, and enlighten, but will also sort people out and
therefore *change* them. This *fourth* argument, 'the unintended testimony of the social scientist that he is an agent of change', is freely
furnished by the social scientists themselves.

Those who have been able to preserve a naive faith in the immaculate positiveness of propositions in the social sciences may have
a second excuse for pleading innocence: they may exclaim with
incredulity or even with annoyance, 'In what sense is it proposed that
a chapter on Social Science and Social Change published in this book
can possibly have an influence on society?' And with all the out-of-
the-way and sometimes even obscure and exotic subjects sociologists
write about, they may ask, for example, 'What is the impact on society
of a paper, say, on some demographical data on marriage in Sweden,
and published in the *Revista Mexicana de Sociologia*?' These questions
suggest that positive social science statements are often either too
esoteric or are published in far-from-the-centre places to have any

influence on social change. One may as well argue that, as one cannot live in a brick, so single bricks have no significance to housing. The influence of social science on society is piecemeal, slow, and, in its phases, mostly indistinguishable to the naked eye. This influence is exerted through the cumulative weight of a multitude of propositions and hypotheses. It is, therefore, no excuse to say that what is being said here and there is so negligible that it can be ignored as a factor of social change.

The *fifth* argument springs from the inevitable respect the individual pays to majorities. In our culture with its emphasis on the democratic counting of heads, majority opinion and behaviour or even opinion and behaviour of sizeable minorities, or of mere large numbers, have an aura of rightness and virtuousness about them. This is probably truer of our Western culture, of Western mass society, than it has been of others since the time of the precultural herd. It is inescapable that social science communication about practices and views of majorities or multitudes has an influence on those to whom the communications are addressed and, furthermore, that this fact is known to the sociologist, of all people!

If, for instance, the treasurer of a sociological association were to announce that about three-quarters of the members had not paid up their fees and if he were to follow up this communication with a request for prompt remittances he would be singularly lacking in wisdom. (Of course, I am not suggesting that such a state of affairs has ever obtained in a sociological association. I have only tried to offer my sociologist readers a homely illustration.) For, if he made the fact known some members might find that the urgency of the matter no longer pressed on them with the onus of an uneasy conscience. The communication of the true state of affairs may either delay or accelerate consequent changing or preserving of that state of affairs – an anomaly known to moral philosophers for a long time. To illustrate further, should it be possible to assess the impact of the Kinsey Reports on the sexual behaviour of our time and should this influence prove to be of some magnitude, we should have an example of social science communication creating social change at least partly through the influence of revealing what 'lots of people' do. It is my *fifth* argument that if the sociologist is interested in the society's contemporary qualities, in the contemporary behaviour of people, he will inevitably find himself reporting either on majority behaviour, or substantial minority behaviour which may have been thought to be far less substantial. The built-in 'band-wagon-effect' of this kind of reporting is, by now, a commonplace. But the familiarity of the conclusion does not dispose of the *fifth* argument, the 'band-wagon argument', which joins an already formidable list of reasons for scepticism about the positive nature of social science.

The *sixth* argument arises from the social scientist's very defensiveness about his moral responsibility and from his very efforts to shake himself free of involvement. Naturally, he is not unmindful of the hazards of moral involvement and he will strive to 'immunise' himself against the bug of values. The esoteric, highly speculative and often incomprehensible conceptual systems, the frantic search for specially coined terms free from associated 'value-dross', the tendency towards explicit neutralism, and the pretence that scientific honesty and loyalty do not belong to a wider context of values – all these and some other aspirations will not stop the positive social sciences from their fact-moulding and object-altering function, a function which the non-social sciences do not possess.

Let me add to this one of David Riesman's reflections which aptly expresses my own sentiments:

Some social scientists have sought to escape from terms which common usage has loaded with values, escape into manufactured symbolism so lacking in overtones as to avoid connotations of praise or blame. In the spirit of certain schools of logical positivism, they want to make only 'meaningful' statements and only purely denotative ones. But, in my opinion, the relation of social science to its subjects, who are also its audience, forbids any such easy undialetical answer to the problem of the researchers' ethical judgments. Terminological opacity will itself be taken as a judgment upon the world, perhaps a manipulative, frightened, or unsympathetic one. Deadpan symbols may symbolize deadly determinism in the researcher. Literate peoples are going to read what is said about them, no matter how many verbal formulae are set up as barriers, and what they cannot understand they may aggressively misunderstand. Communication involves 'noise', redundancy and overtones.[20]

The elaborate prophylactic measures against being contaminated by values are themselves the carriers of values, vivid testimonies to aspirations and distastes, and thus 'defences' become, if not counter-attacks, at least active initiatives to entice.

The *seventh* argument has the same origin as the band-wagon argument: not only unexpected majorities and substantial minorities are facts but also certain budding beginnings, mere suggestions, and potentials.

In any and every social situation we may see the promise or threat of more than one other situation emerging. One may say that any and every social circumstance has the potentiality of becoming another kind of circumstance, with the passing of time. To recognise, identify and define these potentialities is a legitimate scientific activity. The sociologist looking at any particular social situation to form an opinion of the facts in that situation will of necessity include among the facts potentialities, beginnings, and what appear to him signs of potentialities and beginnings. These are just as much facts of the situation as the full-blown, unmistakable and undisputed realities of the situation are facts. In diagnosing the causes of the present features, in describing them and their structure as they are today, he will – if he is to do a thorough empirical job – examine the signs and pointers of what may emerge from the present. 'Estimating' the possible in a hard-headed and calculating way is inextricably intermeshed with 'imagining' the possible, and, indeed, with creatively hypothesising the possible. This activity cannot be hermetically sealed against some elements of aspiration mingling with creative imagination, for should such a sealing-off be totally successful it would stifle the very creative imagination upon which the thorough exploration of a maximum area of the future depends. If politics is the art of the possible, social science in general, and sociology in particular, include *the science of the possible*. But in cultivating this science, an inspired selectivity is utterly inevitable, indeed cultivating a rigid abstinence from selectivity would preclude cultivating the science of the possible. Naturally, these remarks are applicable in the currently fashionable 'futuristics' or '*futuribles*' as well.

It is for these reasons, at least, that the positivistic critic of Marxism will do well to observe some caution. The point that has occupied my mind for some time now is that the contemporary social scientist's criticism of the Marxist failure to discriminate between prediction and advocacy is not an altogether fair criticism. No social scientist can claim to be immaculately free from a similar failure. Certainly, the activity of formulating propositions about society and the activities of judging and choosing are not as strictly and reliably separable activities as we have been accustomed to think. 'By searching out origins,' wrote Nietzsche, 'one becomes a crab. The historian looks backward, eventually he also *believes* backward.'[21] Unlike the historian, the sociologist is not incarcerated in the past. If he were, he would be failing in his job. The study of the potentialities and exigencies of the present are – or should be – as much the sociologist's *métier* as analyses of origins, and of the present state of play. The notion of 'believing backwards' is no mere existentialist double-talk, for this kind of fixation of the eyes is inherent in the hideboundness of a historical orientation. A free passage from 'What happened, and why?' to 'What can we do now?' is, at most, only implicit in historical thinking. The discovery of the whole range of present possibilities is inhibited by the very objectivity required, to find out precisely what has happened. The discipline of a historical enquiry demands that our imagination be mainly confined by those facts which had a bearing on what happened and not so much on others which could have evoked different outcomes. When historians sometimes speculate on what might have happened, they include among the facts the recognisable potentialities of a situation.

When the historian digresses to speculate on what might have happened, what potentialities were present which were, in the event, not used, and so on, his digression is not history but sociology. What the historian describes as 'might have or could have happened', didn't happen, and cannot now happen, and – so far as the historian, an accountant of unique facts, is concerned – is derived from using general psychological and sociological principles, and not exclusively from the record. But, of course, when the sociologist studies the potentialities and exigencies of the past or the present it is proper for him to deal with generic facts, classes of facts, of which the unique, which in fact occurred, is only one instance. It is proper for him to estimate the outcome had some other unique fact occurred. Should he let others silence his extrapolations into the future, should they subject him to censorship, this would totally vitiate his role as a free and objective scientist of society. This freedom to calculate objectively from the past into the future will not only distinguish him from the historian but it will also set him apart from others who engage in the practice of anticipating the future: he will be 'believing forward' in a more deliberate, self-aware, rational, and, therefore, intelligent manner than a mere ideological-utopian advocate or a religious prophet would. On the other hand, of course, this orientation will also somewhat lessen the charges of indifferentism, moral relativism, and scepticism which, from time to time, are made against sociology.

These seven arguments hardly do more than revive an ancient idea. That propositions have a way of behaving like predictions and that predictions easily present themselves as if they were prescriptions has always been understood. K. R. Popper calls the second phase of this process the 'Oedipus effect' of predictions because in the Oedipus story the tragic outcome of Oedipus killing his father and marrying his mother are a consequence of its having been predicted.[22]

That this is the nature of prophecy was especially well explained by John Venn whose *Principles of Empirical or Deductive Logic*, published in 1889[23], strikingly anticipated the predicament of modern sociology. To give the reader the opportunity to relate Venn's own statement of the problem to my own account of it, I quote two relevant passages from his work in full: first, he affirms

. . . the impossibility of studying, or rather of publishing the results of our study, of the conduct of intelligent agents, without thereby producing a disturbance in their conduct. Any person can see that to draw inferences about a thing, and then to introduce a disturbance which was not contemplated when the inference was drawn, is to invalidate the conclusion we have obtained. But when the inference is about the conduct of human beings it is often forgotten that in the inference itself, if published we may have produced an unsuspected source of disturbance. In other words, if the results of our investigations be given in the form of statements as to what people are doing and what they will do, the moment these statements come before their notice the agents will be subject to a new motive, which will produce a disturbance in the conduct which has been inferred. We may make what statements and criticisms we please about the past conduct of men, but directly we commit ourselves to any statements about the future, or in other words, begin to make predictions, we lay ourselves open to the difficulty just mentioned . . . The publication of a Nautical Almanac is not supposed to have the slightest effect upon the path of the planets, whereas the publication of any prediction about the conduct of human beings (unless it were kept out of their sight, or expressed in unintelligible language) almost certainly would have some effect.[24]

In this passage Venn anticipated the predicament of the Gallup Poll which, at times, by virtue of having published its predictions, either invalidates them or amplifies the outcome predicted.[25] And finally he gives the following thought-provoking illustration:

> Giving the prophet (Jonah at Nineveh) the fullest recognition of his power of foreseeing things as they would actually happen, we must yet admit that he labours under an incapacity of publicly announcing them in that form. The city was going to be destroyed; Jonah announces this; in consequence the people repent and are spared, but had he foretold their repentance and escape, the repentance might never have taken place. He might, of course, make a hypothetical statement, so as to provide for their alternative, but a categorical statement is always in danger of causing its own falsification.[26]

There is one more consideration I must add here; we do not, on the whole, deny that our conduct exhibits a certain measure of predictability or uniformity. Indeed it is a frequently voiced complaint that 'you ought to know me better than to believe me capable of doing this or that.' At the same time we should probably react with irritation if mere acquaintances displayed so much knowledge of our nature as to be able to predict our behaviour in certain situations. It is at least probable that, should we be aware of these confident anticipations of almost mere strangers, we might with some angry determination do precisely the opposite of what we would normally prefer to do. It is conceivable that the counter-suggestibility which expresses itself in an individual in this way may also operate on a larger scale, swinging multitudes from one position to another. This self-stultifying power of some propositions and predictions may even be unconsciously wielded by communicators in certain circumstances. But whether deliberate or no, influence is, in fact, exerted in this way. 'To the extent that it enters into people's understanding,' wrote Barrington Moore, 'social science can nullify its own Cassandra-like predictions.'[27]

The seven arguments and the by now ancient insight notwithstanding it is still right and proper that the sociologist should, before going to work, do the 'sociologist's toilet', tuck in all the untidy elements of his thinking such as, for example, moral preferences and aversions. It has been and still is desirable to observe the rules of intellectual hygiene and to underwrite Max Weber's complaint that 'the identification of the psychologically existent with the ethically valid' is a bane both of the social sciences and of the moral philosophers for it 'obstructed the precise distinction of value-judgments from assertions of facts'.[28] This belief in the possibility of a total compartmentalisation of facts and values in social science statements is salutarily expressed time and again, and whilst it does inspire rigour and care it also misrepresents the situation. It is, by now, certainly clear that the sociologist is hardly as powerless as 'a seismologist watching a volcano'[29]; nor is he an architect of social reform. But those who assess, diagnose, interpret, and do these things publicly, are not uncommitted observers but active participants and initiators in the forging of man's fate.

I readily concede that it is not easy to produce conclusive evidence for a universal causal relationship between the so-called informative statements and behaviour. To prove that all communicated sociological propositions always ultimately exercise an influence on the situation about which they speak is not really possible, of course, partly on account of the adverb 'ultimately'. If we are not too exacting, and, for the time being, are willing to accept probability in lieu of certainty, I should say that the instances in which causal relationship between sociological communications and social change can be demonstrated are numerous.

> In the modern age – if not already before its beginning – side by side with the unfolding of scientific knowledge, man has behaved increasingly as if he had been committed to a naturalistic moral philosophy, or more precisely, as if he could not divorce his understanding from his moral judgment. The history of penal reform, our changing moral principles relating to responsibility, our consequent treatment of the poor, the criminal, the coward, the sexual pervert, and so on, on the one hand, and our appraisal of the great man, the hero, the patriot, the mystic, on the other, have become, to say the least, coloured by the discoveries of the social sciences.[30]

I fear that the generalities in this quotation may not satisfy many. But am I really committed to demonstrating in all perfect detail how an increase in our understanding of the workings of human behaviour inevitably affects our conduct? Is it not a commonplace that social awareness and social self-consciousness are factors in social change?

'The success of the social sciences,' writes E. A. Shils, 'in devising procedures of convincing reliability have led to their marriage with policy to an extent which could have been conceived only in principle in Weber's time.'[31] I think 'marriage' is too explicit and conclusive a term; for the time being, the social sciences 'live in sin' with social action, a relationship either condemned or blindly ignored by conventional sociological thinking. Yet it is a relationship no less capable of resulting in the conception of both new ideas and new social actions.

The lessons of this analysis in the context of the present study are manifold.

1. Those social scientists who participate in the training of professional workers and, especially, of the personal service professionals, are engaged in a task of indoctrination.

2. The professional workers, who have received instruction in one or other of the social sciences, tend to link their authoritative professional speciality with some of the general social science principles, which they have assimilated in the course of training. In their professional contacts with associates and clients they will extend the area of indoctrination, and thus maintain the process which was started in their own training.

3. Of course, the theoretical principles may be only superficially linked with their actual practice, yet here, from the point of view of the total cultural climate, mere lip-service, and occasional public reiteration of the principles have a cumulative, and therefore substantial effect.

4. Sociology, psychology, anthropology, and economics, taught without any reference to eventual professional tasks, reinforce a so-called 'pure-science-attitude' in human affairs. On their own these disciplines would encourage a manipulative stance, and not a counselling ideology. But when these pure sciences are incorporated in the professional training they somehow invariably acquire a professional justification: that they will be somehow *applicable* in practice, and, indeed, that they afford the scientific principles behind that practice as straightforwardly as physics, chemistry, and biology are claimed to provide the scientific principles of medicine.

The personal service professionals are taught some or several of the social sciences with oddly ambiguous or even paradoxical consequences. The illumination, the inspiration, the matter-of-fact understanding, to all of which social studies contribute, are accompanied by influences of a damping, disillusioning, and discouraging character. The blending of these two is easy to discern and I will single out for discussion one case of this divided influence which is central to my interests in this chapter.

The ethical rules which operate in the cultivation of all science are incorporated in the end-product, displayed in it, as it were, sometimes quite eloquently. These ethical rules of science are, and have been for some time, rationality and objectivity incorporated in a general code of scientific honesty. An insistence on scientific honesty is conveyed in the description of methods used to arrive at conclusions, both in the empirical investigation itself and in the logical appraisal of the findings. The moral commitment in the case of social science goes beyond the area of rules controlling the cultivation of science; all social scientists who expect that some betterment of the human condition will accrue from an increase in our understanding of social matters do also explicitly pledge that, in social action, the rationality and objectivity of science should be the arbiter, and not revelation or intuition, or a non-scientific way of knowing, or the arbitrariness and caprice of power. To create social science is to influence society in its very method of making fundamental choices, and it is to expect society to manage itself in a scientific way. So, on the one hand, we have the inspiration afforded to us by models of intellectual honesty, objectivity, and rationality, while on the other hand, it is impressed on us that a dispassionate and impartial standard is all that is being prescribed by the ethics of science and that the complement of service, of personal service, the application of personal concern, is not only extraneous to the scientific ethics but also that science is both irrelevant to personal service and, at its worst, inimical to it. Also, the discipline and rationality of the social sciences have understandably placed so much stress on calculability and determinism that they have contributed to the weakening of man's faith not only in the less extravagant eschatological and non-scientific categories but also in the phenomenological and experiential categories of thinking. In this way the influence of social science on society has been doctrinaire and ideological.

Especially in our time, the objectivity of science, and therefore also of social science, has been more and more a jealously guarded quality. This quality or standard of objectivity is often thought to be impaired by optimistic and often naively metaphysical doctrines about the nature and destiny of man. Hitherto, to the social scientist, being objective meant that he was able to ferret out the mean and mercenary motives and that he could be cheerfully sceptical and triumphantly pessimistic. In fact, one of the chief pursuits of social science thinking has been the pursuit of disclosure, or – as social science would have it – the analysis of ideological distortions of neurotic rationalisations, the analysis of ulterior motives and of hypocritically concealed intents. In our age there has been '. . . an intellectual preoccupation with covert forces that can explain the manifest content of the social world'.[32] Karl Mannheim noted this when he said that sociological exploration often took the form of 'unmasking'.[33] Methodological severity imperceptibly becomes moral scepticism and moral scepticism thrives on the respectability of intellectual rigour. Voices are still raised to say these things: for example, that the 'maximisation' of these attitudes is an ideological error of sociology has been powerfully argued by Nathan Glazer.[34]

There seems to be a masochistic hankering for being self-denyingly strict with ourselves, and for being thought virtuously free from complacency. 'The radicalism of our time', observed Woodrow Wilson, 'does not consist in the things that are proposed, but the things that are disclosed.'[35] And the high priests of this kind of radicalism are the social scientists. Social scientists have been tough-minded assessors of the motives that lie behind man's achievements.

The process is insidious and is to be demonstrated with the help of a reference to a school of thought which excels in its masterly combination of scrupulous objectivity with naive misrepresentation. This school of thought, behaviourism, occupies an important strategic position in the contemporary behavioural sciences and so a detailed reference to the mode of thought characteristic of this school is entirely apposite.

'In a demonstration experiment', writes B. F. Skinner,

a hungry pigeon was conditioned to turn round in a clockwise direction. A final, smoothly executed pattern of behaviour was shaped by reinforcing successive approximations with food. Students who had watched the demonstration were asked to write an account of what they had seen. Their responses included the following: (1) The organism was conditioned to *expect* reinforcement for the right kind of behaviour. (2) The pigeon walked around, *hoping* that something would bring the food back again. (3) The pigeon *observed* that certain behaviour seemed to produce a particular result. (4) The pigeon *felt* that food would be given it because of its action; and (5) the bird came to *associate* his action with the click of the food-dispenser.[36]

Professor Skinner soon corrected these 'mentalistic' aberrations of his students, for behaviouristic methodology does not credit statement about what pigeons or people *experience* with any scientific usefulness:

The observed facts could be stated respectively as follows: (1) The organism was reinforced *when* it emitted a given kind of behaviour. (2) The pigeon walked around *until* the food container appeared. (3) A certain behaviour produced a particular result. (4) Food was given to the pigeon *when* it acted in a given way; and (5) the click of the food dispenser was *temporally* related to the bird's action. These statements describe the contingencies of reinforcement. The expressions 'expect', 'hope', 'observe', 'feel', and 'associate' go beyond them to identify effects on the pigeon.[37]

Thus, for a rigorous behaviouristic social science, the global notions of 'hoping' and 'feeling' simply do not exist. They are at any rate not accessible to scientific examination and, therefore, they inevitably acquire an aura of spuriousness. Yet society indoctrinates us with terms and notions of this kind, and students use these mentalistic notions because they come to the experiment having been indoctrinated by the 'verbal community' (society). There is no doubt that the behaviouristic kind of methodological practice in social science entitles us to offer a hypothesis. And this is: that in a society where a strictly behaviouristic psychology advances, the stimuli of mentalistic imagery are weakened culturally and morally. These stimuli define man's self-image for him and this self-image becomes part of the real self.

This socio-cultural outcome is clearly perceived by Carl R. Rogers in the same symposium when he observed, 'objectivity can be concerned only with objects, whether these are animate or inanimate. Conversely, this way of knowing transforms everything it studies into an object, or perceives it only in its object aspect.'[38]

The personal service professional could not sustain the inevitable stresses of his career were he prepared for it exclusively through scrupulous behaviouristic training. The distinction between 'professional training' and 'academic instruction' has always implied this,

G

but what I am saying asserts a little more than this distinction. The objective perception and understanding of the external world notoriously overlooks the observing personality. It is part of the occupational burden of the professional to become proficient in the use of this observing personality, which, unfortunately, differs from the whole observed external world by virtue of being at the dead centre of everything else. In professional training, social science, which declares this area of experience as 'untouchable', suffers the inefficiencies and irrationalities of a conceptual caste system. Most professionals would say that the deliberate averting of the eyes from the quality and substance of subjectivity is no less a superstition than the ideological, rationalising or downright deceptive distortions of objective empirical reality. This is inescapable for those who function professionally in the context of human relationships. In their moral and inspirational declarations we have the testimony of all manner of paedagogues, instructors, and trainers that social science, far from being a 'sufficient' requirement for practice in personal service, is by its very nature incompatible with sustained service unless it is coupled with its antithesis, some uniting and global view, such as is haltingly provided by the counselling ideology of the twentieth century. It is becoming clear to anyone who studies the training principles and programme of professional schools that scientific training is undergoing modifications, and is collecting accretions from the recorded experience of personal practice, the lessons of which are not always convertible into verifiable propositions. The practitioners in medicine, from doctors to nurses, in social work and in psychotherapy have already been shown to rely on principles which they have not derived from their scientific education.[39] I shall now explore how the largest group of personal service professionals the teachers, and one of the most influential class of professionals, the managers of business, are using what I have called the counselling ideology of the twentieth century to supplement and modify the scientific training which they may have received.

And yet, the clinical and personal point of view in this ideology is still empirically based. Psychology and sociology still provide the base-lines of the practitioners' thinking. All accretion of knowledge in the positive social sciences is put at the disposal of the novice practitioners, and they have to assimilate social science intelligence in the mode and techniques of their day-to-day practice. Of course, social science will constantly bear on the style, method, and objectives of that practice. In this, social science will affect social change by affecting the work of the personal service professionals. *But, para-doxically also, the growth of the authority of this population of practitioners will constantly veto the claim of social science to eventually amounting to a system of total explanation for human relations.* The social scientific rigour has been the puritanism of the twentieth century. This protestant severity was followed by the counter-reformation of the confessional-counselling ideology. The personal service professional blends the influence of these two in a practice which aspires to be both an 'applied social science' and a personal commitment. This is not necessarily an antithesis, at every point a total clash of opposites: for example, the ethics of science speak the language of punctiliousness, and the virtues of personal commitment require the same language. The constant self-scrutiny of the counsellors, the systematic testing and review of one's insight is the same as the rigour of the empiricist. 'Know thyself' demands, if anything, greater objectivity of ourselves than 'Know the world'. This resolute and even religious quest for the hidden self, for the truth of it all, and, indeed, this belief in the possibility of succeeding with a quest of this nature, unify the influence of social science and of the counselling ideology.

The personal service professionals, as agents of social change, will for ever be receptive to the propositions of social science but they will for ever be reappraising these propositions in terms of what their subjective self-awareness does to them in the course of practice. Their subjective self-awareness as practitioners is not a bit less of an empirical fact than all the other facts upon which social science pronounces. Here lies a built-in limitation to the influence of social science on social change: the agents, the changers themselves, the personnel, the professionals, stem the tide of social science. And somehow they are not likely to desist from this in the future either. There are practices portrayed in the following section which will make this sound at least probable.

B. THE COUNSELLING IDEOLOGY IN TWO PROFESSIONS

The deep imprint of social science on social action is clearly legible though the meaning of what one is able to read is still somewhat indeterminate. Not a small part of the burden of the previous section is that the personal service professionals and others, trained in one of several of the social sciences, may receive tuition which is prejudicial to the practice of personal service. This is an anomalous conclusion when we are firmly resolved to believe in the usefulness of social science in social action of all kinds. Such a belief is a characteristic doctrine not only of training institutions – which are not entirely above the suspicion of having a vested interest in wanting to teach the social sciences – but also of most other contemporary intellectuals. I am not trying to suggest that the usefulness, indeed, the necessity of social science training for those who practise in some professional work of personal service is at all to be questioned. The point of the last section is to stress that social science training precipitates certain problems, which the practitioners have to resolve by evolving an orientation to practice from sources which are not only outside the area of scientific thinking but, at times, at variance with that thinking. The roles of 'applier of social science' and 'renderer of a professional personal service' are not coterminous and the latter is not even entirely inclusive of the former. Of course, the odious consequences of irrationalities and of plain ignorance shrivel in the glare of a scientific examination, and under the merciless analysis of the socio-scientific scrutiny the ulterior motives and false pretences of personal service are neutralised.

The situation brought about by the aseptic influence of science, is rather like that brought about by the indiscriminate use of antibiotics: they destroy not only the hostile bacteria which have invaded the organism, but they also eliminate all the benevolent, indeed essential, micro-organisms without which the organism cannot continue to exist. If there is such a thing as an 'antibiotic poisoning' of the organism, we may not be able to rule out the possibility that there is such a thing as a 'social science poisoning' of the personal service professional and, indeed, of society. Naturally, because of this 'overreaching' effect of antibiotics, and because of their part in the production of new strains, the antibiotics have had to be constantly modified and improved. Similarly – in our reliance on social science – numbing impartiality and sub-zero objectivity would have frozen practice altogether, but for a system and theory of pragmatic rules, which loosened up practice again. These rules have had to be evolved to cope, paradoxically and, as it were, thermostatically: practising with a heated resolve of scrupulously not doing any more than coolly applying science in personal service. This new body of rules has given scope to clinical practitioners, welfare functionaries, and staff management to operate in their respective fields without being morally frozen out by scientific methodology. And this new body of social-psychological tenets and pragmatic prescripts is what I call the psychotherapeutic or counselling ideology of the twentieth century. It is a product of circumstances and antecedents which I described in *The Faith of the Counsellors*. There, my brief was to show that this new body of tenets about facts and values was shared by those whom I grouped together in one sociological category: professional workers, mainly social caseworkers, psychotherapists, some psychiatrists, and doctors. Here, in this book, I am addressing myself to the whole area of professional work, the area of the personal service professions, in which the counselling ideology can be shown to have taken a foothold. The 'counsellors' constitute only a numerically small, though culturally and morally influential, section of the personal service professions and of the intellectual élite in our modern industrial societies. But because of their pervasively influential presence – the presence of a relatively small but especially alert and communicative group – other professionals who operate in the medium of close human relationships have by now been deeply affected and have assimilated much of what I call the counselling ideology.

The largest group of professional workers who have been so affected are the teachers. Of course, this is by no means a homogeneous group, and, if they are to include everyone from primary school to university, the range of ideological orientations in personal service is likely to be very wide. Yet I believe that, on the one hand, the core values of instructing, guiding, and helping will have been rephrased *for this whole range* in terms of the counselling ideology; on the other hand, a major dissent from the moral principles of this ideology will not be noticeable in more than a relatively small and dwindling minority. Writing about the culture of a society or of an age, one may misrepresent it by giving prominence to dissident minorities.

Another smaller though rapidly growing group is that of the personnel management professionals, the trained staff officers of our economic institutions. In this latter case I am thinking of all those who are either *trained* to manage, or who – though untrained – are influenced by the counsellors' beliefs about socio-psychological facts and associated values. My remarks will relate not only to the professional group explicitly labelled 'personnel managers' but to all those who are in fact engaged in the management of personnel.

As a lubricant, to make the ensuing documentation flow more smoothly for the reader, and also to impress on the reader that he is not being enticed into theoretical explorations outside the realm of social situations I propose to present two thumbnail sketches of personality development. One is of a professional career in education, another is of a professional career in management. These introductory illustrations are not offered even as anecdotal evidence, but merely as explanatory material. Yet, though the characters and events in these sketches are entirely fictitious they are representative of widespread trends in contemporary society. That this is so follows from the evidence and documentation offered throughout this book which warrant, at least, our entertaining an hypothesis on these trends. The description of the two careers will be followed up by documentation and testimonies from the two fields in which these two careers have run their course.

1. Sam is a teacher in a comprehensive school. He is himself a public school – Oxbridge product. Many years ago he ended up in school-teaching because, as a historian, he was not sufficiently a scholar to continue at a university, yet he was sufficiently a historian to wish to go on reading and talking about history. His attitude to children was one of bemused tolerance alternating with indifference. Even so, his choice of a paedagogical career was already then not entirely uninspired by an interest in his future pupils: he fancied himself as one who could persuade sixth formers that history was not only a subject but almost an attitude to living. Yet, if pressed, he might have confessed to more concern for his subject than for his future charges.

Sam began teaching in a public school, but unfortunately he was not given a share of any advanced work in the school. In addition to this he became oversensitive to the forlorn, dispossessed look on the faces of some of his youngest pupils who, from one end of term to another, saw little or nothing of their mothers and families. He came to the teaching role with no more than common human sympathies, and with an average capacity to feel for others. The residential situation, the sustained close contact between master and pupil, and his normal professional responsibilities for teaching them, slowly aroused in him a more

personal interest in the wider paedagogical role as distinct from
the role of a historian. Of course, even at the very beginning, he
had anticipations of what would be required of him but he met
these with vague resolves to do what was needed. Eventually, he
grew to be a purposeful enquirer into the why and the how of
public school education. Various normal developments in his
own personal life, such as marriage and children of his own,
further assisted this change. Finally he chose to move from this
walled, secluded, and in many ways exclusive teaching institution
to a day school in which the cultural and conventional principles
of staff-pupil relationships allowed him more scope, indeed more
plain freedom of expressing his slowly but firmly acquired
predilection to help children couple learning subjects with
learning to live. He was greatly helped and inspired in this transition by a lecturer at a University Institute of Education whose
classes in child development he attended, and whom he later
befriended. Through this contact, and as a result of much reading
about this newly acquired interest, he came in contact with a
collection of theoretical systems, principles, empirical studies,
characteristic of the so-called 'counselling ideology' of the
twentieth century. Thus he learnt to have his role as a teacher
redefined for him, and continued for many years to try to live up
to this redefined role.

Of course, there is a multitude of other avenues along which
teaching careers may run their course. There may be an early and more
determined as well as a more explicit preference for the global
paedagogical interests even at a definite expense to the academic ones.
Also, at the other extreme, the main consideration leading to a teaching
career might have been that the long holidays would compensate for
the drudgery of it all. Clearly, all these varied beginnings continue to
feature prominently in tales different from Sam's. Yet there is one
circumstance in all these tales which, in spite of all the great variations,
is common to all: the role of teacher is assumed, enacted, or played,
and even if the conception of the role itself has considerable latitude,
*it is not wide enough to stop certain powerful cultural pressures from
confining that role more narrowly*. Teacher training institutions, cultural
heroes and their public pronouncements, literary, artistic, and mass-
media-conveyed élite opinions have taken a strong stand on matters
such as corporal punishment, discipline, inflexible academic regimen,
sexual morality, parental responsibility, and the like, and it is hardly in

doubt that this strong stand has been made possible by a remarkable measure of unanimity on these matters prevailing in our teachers' training institutions. The informed public opinion on paedagogical matters is determined by the principles which have emerged in psychological and sociological thought in this century. Much of what is being advocated as a result of advances in these disciplines is supported by the prestige of the clinical practitioners in child care and guidance, a prestige which is derived as much from their personal service professional roles as from the inspirational and personal echoes of their tenets. The outcome is that 'the counselling ideology' has left its mark on the theory and practice of education and, consequently, on the role definition of the teacher.

2. Jim, just out of university, has taken up his first job. He is one of the assistants of the Manager (Personnel) of a large and well-known company. Jim is ambitious. He hopes to achieve both high income and high position. He wants to get ahead fast and is keenly interested in finding out what has been required of those who have got ahead already. He is also watchful to discover as early as possible what others like him are doing to forge their way ahead. There will be models of ruthless competitiveness to follow, and there will be the customary cases of scheming, or of single-minded currying of favours with the powerful. But there will also be the inevitable necessity of having to master skills, technical skills, social skills, and in Jim's job, specific professional skills of management. Indeed, early recognition of talent will very much depend on how efficiently tactful, and how plausibly reconciliating, Jim can contrive to be on those occasions when the management of personnel demands that he rapidly resolve delicate but potentially dangerous problems. The department in which Jim is employed is thoroughly permeated by the so-called 'Human Relations' type of thinking evolved in modern industrial sociology and social psychology. An outcome of this is that there is almost as much, if not more, talk about the foreman's problems of conflicting identification with the shopfloor on the one hand, and with management on the other, as about wage-differentials, and almost more concern with a particular key-worker's marital difficulties than with the disadvantages to the company accruing from keeping this worker off the night-shift.

The staff-functionaries in this sort of cultural climate learn to conform to certain intellectual and personal disciplines, which are necessary to assess cases such as these in the spirit of this climate or group-mores. The basic principles of the social psychological theory from which the group-mores have been evolved dictate that 'presenting' problems should be distinguished from 'real' problems and, consequently, that the manager of personnel be informed of the nature of these 'real' problems, and that he should also acquire some access to their personal handling.

In aspiring to assimilate these disciplines Jim discovers from the experience of practice that refining his tools of understanding will increasingly depend on a total personal curiosity which has never before appeared to him to be an obvious requisite of competitive striving, and indeed of a career in business or industry, and which in fact can be cultivated often enough at a moderate expense to that competitive striving. One might think that at this stage a role-conflict might well develop. Sometimes, no doubt, this will happen. But often the gratifications of the craftsmanship at first, and soon afterwards the personal understanding unintentionally acquired, tone down or even silence the considerations of pecking order, priority, and competition or recognition. First, Jim will seek understanding so that others may have their way. This, not because he has now self-denyingly abandoned getting his own way but rather because it is now his pleasure to get his way *by assisting others in realising their aspirations.* In the meantime he will stumble on the insight that imaginative rapport is not only more accurate when it is sympathetic but that it has also a kind of immediate reward built into it which may somewhat devalue the harsh goals of self-realisation which have monopolised his attention until now. He may be rendering personal services to employees merely to secure the industrial, commercial, and mercenary objectives of his company and to reinforce his own personal reputation in that company for competence, but he will also be enticed into rendering personal services in a total and sincerely interested manner – for otherwise these services would fail to achieve their intended goals – and he will imperceptibly become so engaged habitually.

Of course, Jim might have entered this particular job already so oriented in his personal interest and ambitions, that he actually expected to be employed in rendering personal services. If this was the case right from the beginning, the job was then a mere opportunity. One might even say that cultures vary according to the multiplicity and variety of other-regarding functions they have institutionalised. The bare existence of such positions, as those in the personal service professions will give people established chances to cultivate care and solicitousness; this is *in addition* to using the established avenues of self-advancement and self-assertion. What happens is that in some cultures more self-advancement and self-assertion are actually achieved through solicitousness and care than in others. If society multiplies these roles at the expense of others the cumulative consequences are likely to change the quality of the culture and of the society as a whole. When personal success and advancement are deeply associated with an achievement of beneficial change in others and when even personal ambition has to be blended with compassion for either or both to come to fulfilment, the synthesis offers an absorbing opportunity for a sociological reappraisal.

When writing about Jim, I took the more sceptical line deliberately and assumed that Jim had entered his job merely as an average candidate for the role of 'organisation man'. This, I thought, would highlight the discrepancy between an assumed and initially egocentric ambition and the need to fit it into role-functions in which he has to play caring and solicitous roles plausibly and even sincerely.

The significance of the initial discrepancy consists in the job's remarkable assimilating power which can neutralise the discrepancy: the values of those who are in a job gradually approximate to the values of the job itself. Nothing could be more tempting than to caricature my argument and say that – if what I am saying is true – service in a profit-making enterprise may sometimes have the power to elicit some sort of a moral renewal. Assuredly the way to negate the idea which occupies my mind is to make it sound more unequivocal and unqualified: then it will certainly look ridiculous. The example sketched here merely intends to illustrate the hypothesis that a professional role, lastingly assumed, may brand itself on the role-player in unexpected ways, especially if and when the aspirational characteristics of the role draw the self-seeker single-mindedly. It is in this case that the role can envelop the ulterior motives of the role-player and change their quality. But my hypothesis is not about Jim (of the sketch) or of the individual, but of society: through the establishment and multiplication of these aspirational role-types, in particular in positions of cultural leadership, the quality of culture changes too. The process is of two ways: the aspiring and restless role-players of established roles constantly renew and amplify the aspirational character of the roles, and through them culture; and culture proffers to the new entrant into the role a model of striving and aspiring.

The documentation in the two following sections serves the purpose of showing not only a widespread agreement among scholars and authoritative writers about the nature of some important features of the teacher's and of the business manager's role in relationships, but also that these professionals appoint themselves to be advocates of certain types of values which, by now, in *their* opinion, society would do ill to neglect.

1. *The Counselling Ideology in Education*

Teachers have always been enjoined to educate 'character' and not only 'intellect'. The moral teaching of the young, preparation for citizenship, for patriotism, for being a 'good, and god-fearing person', or a 'good personality-cultist communist', a comrade who 'loves Lenin warmly',[40] are some of the moulds into which moral education of the young has been cast from time to time. Today the mould is inevitably shaped by the socio-psychological sciences: a clinical, psychiatric, and counselling mode of thought determines the stance of the modern western teacher. He is no longer an instructor, but a 'model for identification', he no longer lays down the law, but elicits co-operation and compliance. Needless to say, changes like these are never complete and absolute, yet there are marked tendencies and trends in these directions. In some institutions – in some countries – the new directions in paedagogy may be explicitly and even emphatically specified. Elsewhere, they may exert influence only in an oblique manner. Yet again, elsewhere, the new paedagogy may be repudiated. The clinical point of view is an objectionable one to those who think that calling naughtiness 'insecurity', delinquency 'maladjustment', and serious crime 'psychotic break-down', is using, at least, mischievous euphemisms, and through misrepresentations of this nature, encouraging moral indifference, weakening moral stamina, and thus underwriting what is plainly wrong.

In spite of such a variety of responses, and especially since the second world war, the mental hygienist point of view in education and the counselling orientation of paedagogical personnel have steadily gained ground. The whole paedagogical literature is permeated with strong advocacies of 'educating for motivational and affective sanity', however this desirable condition is defined. The whole attack on large schools, comprehensive or otherwise, to mention only one example, is based, at least partly, on the complaint that they lead to impersonality, to a lack of warm personal contact between teacher and taught.[41] In fact, the academic, skill-forming, and instructional 'pay-offs' of education are often regarded as by-products of a mutually warm and creatively cooperative teacher-pupil relationship. The doctrine – sometimes openly conceded – is that you learn in the context of 'relationships' which pass the counsellors' scrutiny, or you don't learn at all!

The process of recent changes in paedagogical thinking is usually well outlined and extensively documented in the authoritative *The Yearbooks of Education*. In the 1955 volume much is written on the so-called 'guidance-movement' in education. According to Sir Cyril Burt, 'guidance is not something to be undertaken for exceptional pupils at exceptional crises of their school career; it should be a continuous process available for all'.[42] And Burt concludes that, 'the principle of universal "child guidance" has at length gained unquestioned support and official recognition'.[43] This declares that the counselling ideology has irremovably established itself in educational thought and that this has received official recognition. If in terms of appropriations voted, institutions set up, and posts created, as well as suitably filled, this diagnosis goes far beyond the actual state of affairs in Britain, Cyril Burt's testimony – to my contention that the counselling mode of thought characterises our paedagogical ideas – is in no way weakened. It is also interesting to note that, in the same *Yearbook*, Ben Morris (Professor of Education and a trainer of teachers) himself a cordial supporter of psychoanalytic thinking, translates his metapsychology into the language of the creeds of which I wrote at length in my *Faith of the Counsellors*. Morris thinks that we are in danger of looking upon 'guidance' as 'purely technique' or 'means'. He suggests that a separation of the so-called revealed and inspirational from the technical and positive in paedagogy is a forlorn try. If I understand him right he appears to subordinate paedagogy altogether to the concept of 'guidance' of which he writes,

'guidance' is identical neither with education nor with teaching, nor with the treatment of behaviour disorders, although the greater part of all those spheres of action may be approached from the standpoint of guidance. It is both an approach to the problems with which they deal and a particular kind of activity which may inform all that is done in their names.[44]

He requires a balance of concern and detachment from the 'guide' in the paradoxical manner in which the counsellors are expected to be functioning.[45] In the 1958 volume of *The Yearbook of Education* we find an especially carefully documented account of these changes in educational ideas by W. D. Wall.[46] It is not so much that the new educational thought of the mental hygienists, the counsellors, the 'guidance people', or call them what you will, is destructively anti-thetical to some of the principles and precepts of Comenius, Rousseau, Pestalozzi, Herbart, Montessori, Froebel, William James, Dewey, and Makarenko, as that this new educational thought is distinctively Freudian in origin, in psychological and philosophical conception, and does constitute a fundamental departure from established ideas. Above all, this twentieth-century account of personality development discredits traditional and conventional claims for the efficacy of certain authoritarian and disciplinarian methods. Instead of moral or religious qualifications the teacher's psychological 'toilet' has now seriously come under inspection, and his training in educational psychology absorbs an increasingly larger part of his time in training.

In R. F. Butts' *A Cultural History of Western Education* we read that 'despite much opposition to the specific interpretations of the psychoanalysts, they have had enormous influence in turning the attention of the educators to the importance of the early childhood years in shaping human behaviour'.[47] 'Enormous' is certainly not an excessive attributive to use. The teacher's professional role has been thoroughly redefined under the influence of this kind of thinking and he is now systematically trained, if not indoctrinated, to absorb certain principles about the nature of man and about the teaching procedures which are appropriate to that nature.

First, the new account of personality development requires the would-be teacher to accept the importance of the unconscious motivation of acts, whether destructive or creative. *Secondly*, it requires the teacher to abandon punitive or even judgmental attitudes towards manifestations of sexuality and sensuality in the child. *Thirdly*, it requires the teacher not only to try to resist the temptation of retaliating the aggressions of those who are in his charge, but also to respond to aggressive behaviour by reassuring the aggressor so that the aggressor will not be blinded by guilt or by self-righteousness, but can be guided towards self-understanding, and, eventually, self-control. *Fourthly*, it requires the teacher to search out and control or reappraise his own defensive and distortive responses to the behaviour of the child, and to be for ever on guard not to succumb to temptations of using his charges for the abreaction ('acting out') of his own personality problems. *Fifthly*, he should always temper his judgmental-ness by recalling the profoundly deterministic quality of the human developmental process, and especially, of the infantile history of the person, over which the individual's own responsible control is evidently very limited. Yet, contrapuntally to this fifth point, and *sixthly*, the modern counsellor, and following him the modern teacher, appears to bring out the latent idealism of the Freudian *credo* by inconsistently granting autonomy to the 'will-to-be-sane' irrespective of a wretched past. It is important to say again and again that the first moral appeal of this kind came from the arch-counsellor, Freud himself: 'Where there is *Id* there shall *Ego* be!' Already for Freud, this appeal meant backsliding into moral language. But later, psychiatrists, emancipating themselves from the total deterministic régime of science, became existentialist fellow-travellers at least, who postulated a core-will to sanity in the patients they have undertaken to treat, a will to self-regeneration, a will to pull themselves up by their own boot-straps. The teacher, an inheritor of centuries of moralistic paedagogical preachings, secretly welcomed this *tour de force* of the counselling ideology: and the concession to the mythology of free will in the faith of the counsellors made the adaptation of the counselling ideology to paedagogical purposes so much easier. In case Marxists might feel drawn to dismiss this latest of the bourgeois contrivances to remain free amidst total unfreedom, they should remember that they have been following the same path when insisting that all morals, art, and ideas are the products of merciless material exigencies and, at the same time, enjoining others – and their morals, their art, and their ideas – to rise against their merciless material necessities! Proletarians of the world are supposed to unite even before production relations have changed sufficiently to bring this about *without* the moral challenge that 'Proletarians of the world shall unite!'

In this book, my function is to be a student of a complex of ideological notions and values. I am not here to act as a critic of this complex. It does not concern me, here and now, whether holding these six positions is consistent and logically defensible. As a sociologist, I am putting forward the proposition that these six positions are being conjointly held by counsellors and, *following their example*, by teachers. Teachers increasingly hold the views characteristic of these positions. This is so, mainly because the institutions in which they are trained, and the culture in which they function, persuade them to assimilate and advance views such as these. It is not only that eventually the pupils they teach will be affected by this. Long before this has a chance of making its mark upon a new generation, the army of well educated adults, the teachers themselves, become the members of the élite, the new carriers of culture and the definers of its modes and content. The counselling ideology changes the teacher before it changes the pupil. 'The true contribution of psychology', writes W. D. Wall, 'to the modification of secondary curricula therefore lies as much in the application of psychological methods to the further training, and advanced training of teachers and administrators as it does in direct exploration of child and adolescent growth; neither can usefully exist without the other'.[48] Thus the counselling orientation of paedagogical training institutions encourages research effort to be expended on the so-called 'emotional-developmental-aspects' of personality and individual growth. Above all, there can be no doubt that in addition to this preoccupation with the emotional development of children and adolescents, a logically indefensible conversion of psychological propositions into moral imperatives has also been going on under the tutelage of the counsellors. Indeed we have already reached a stage in the United States, where 'mental health . . . by its coincidence in definition with the healthy personality – the normal personality – and by its concern for the development of effective, satisfying behaviour, relationships, and action in society, is looked upon by many educators as a primary function of the schools'.[49] When teachers are being trained to regard 'the personal well-being of those with whom they work as their paramount goal',[50] we are confronted not only with a redefinition of paedagogical objectives, but also with a radical ideological re-education of a large complement of society's intelligentsia, the teaching profession. Here we must remember what was said in the first chapter about the importance of social positions occupied by teachers and ex-teachers in contemporary society so that we may be adequately prepared to follow the consequences of this ideological re-education.

In our training colleges, university departments of education, institutes of education, and in some other institutions of teachers' training, the influence of the counselling ideology is ubiquitous, prominent, and deeply embedded. This influence is usually exerted through the Psychology of Education curriculum, though it may be identified in programmes which run under the names of 'Principles of Education' or 'Methods' courses. The Sociology of Education courses do not as a rule accommodate instruction along these lines, but some of the Social Studies courses do. On the whole, the basic characteristics of the professional counsellor's stance are constantly being incorporated in what is regarded as the notion of the 'good teacher' in more than one stream of the training programme. Several, though not always all, of the six specifications listed earlier appear in the new cookbooks of paedagogy. Of course, the seasoning prescribed can be deceptively conventional. If the counsellor is enjoined to be 'non-directive', the teacher is invited to respect the spontaneities of the child's thoughts, sentiments, and behaviour. If the counsellor is told that he must use his personal concern and warmth in a professionally controlled yet recognisable manner, the paedagogue is not discouraged from believing that liking his job *a fortiori* means that he likes his charges. If the counsellor is warned against his 'negative countertransference' – plainly, his dislike of his client – the teacher is also prepared against the eventuality, and is shown the ways of handling his own anxiety, if and when the eventuality arises. Moral failure or alienation will become a technical impasse to be treated technically. Yet, both counsellor and teacher will also be told that no amount of technical competence, however brilliantly conceived and assiduously drilled, can succeed in application unless sustained by an unqualified total application of the personality to the client which is made possible by genuine personal concern alone. Of course this notion of a 'genuine personal concern' is almost wholly mystical and, therefore, unscientific. Whatever my own views about its reality or significance may be, it is not my present task to advocate these views. I am anxious to disclose the heart of the ideological complex, which is actually pulsating in the belief-systems of the professional practitioners, whether they are aware of it or no, and whether they are willing to confess to it or no. The point is always there but we refuse to recognise it. Whether one reads the Soviet Makarenko or the Western counsellors in education, the commitment to personal service is, at least, taken to have been stipulated, but mostly in fact, it is expressly demanded.

It might be argued that two thousand Christian years, as well as the enlightenment and humanism of more recent times, have between them been responsible for the contemporary professional humanism. The meekness and the businesslike kindheartedness require no elaborate historico-sociological rationale: intelligent man is just being himself, might be an answer. But surely, in this age of all ages, in which positivistic philosophies, behaviouristic psychologies, and conflagrationist (mainly Marxist-Leninist) sociologies have dominated our thoughts about ourselves, neither the age-old Christian assets nor the more modern humanistic increments could have alone sustained the contemporary personal service professional's moral aspirations, self-discipline, tolerance, and acceptance. Much of these resources has come to hand from the sheer diligence of application to the job, the resolute concentration on the task, which – in the case of the personal service professional – is a human and personal task.

The practising professional still covets the respectability of an applier of science and would feel ill-at-ease if his sole credential was some mere revelation. In fact, the systematic scrutiny of our manuals in psychology and in social studies used in our institutions of teacher's training will show to anyone who cares to look that it is under the banners of scientific instruction that we powerfully strain ourselves to exert a lasting moral influence on our future teachers. Of course, we need empirical evidence that this indoctrination 'gets home' and that the theory as well as the practical training does not go down the drain soon after graduation or qualification. The fact is – and this is surely not being questioned – that we are devoting substantial sums from our national resources to teachers' training and that some of these resources are used for the purposes of the kind of indoctrination I am here describing. Thus the reader is not allowed a moment of suspicion: it is not at issue here whether we deplore or salute this indoctrination but whether it goes on at all! In the understanding of my thesis this indoctrination means that we train our teachers to adopt role-elements of the counsellor. The teacher's role – the role of the instructor and of the trainer – is to be blended with adapted elements from the roles of clinician, of the social caseworker, of the child guidance psycho-

H

therapist. One might say that these elements have been called in to fill the places vacated by the missionary, the gospeller, and the priest. In the meantime suggestive intermediate models are also being invented; for example charismatic models of the Lyward-type[51] operate half-way between class-room and consulting-room, though in certain cases the consulting room vaguely resembles the confessional box. Monographs are published on avant-garde educational experiments by inspired and exceptional teachers presenting new models of the teacher's role and the average teacher in a secondary modern school, say, a form-master of the C-stream school-leaving group, is invited to read, reflect, and respond.

In the meantime, the appeal, which is being made to student-teacher and teacher alike, is made in the dispassionate clinical or scientific psychological terminology of our times. For example, in our textbooks on educational psychology, 'the establishment of male identification' is described as dependent on a 'rewarding relationship' with the father, or father-substitutes, and the teacher is enjoined to use his own personality as a model for such an identification as this. The circumlocution and the inverted euphemism are probably entirely warranted in terms of the psychological theory to which they relate and which gave them rise but they are, at core, only refinements of the proposition that liking the child will help in educating him.[52] Trainers of teachers no longer pretend that there is a clear dividing line between the clinical and the paedagogical. Already a good few years ago Dame Olive Wheeler told us that a '. . . deeper insight into the problems of adjustment' will improve the professional training, and indeed the literature of training is not lacking in passages which are written with the purpose of deepening this kind of clinical sensitivity in the future teacher.'[53] But if mental health and mental hygiene are to become paedagogical objectives they have not been advancing into the forefront shyly or reluctantly. Professor Peters very rightly observed that 'We no longer talk of turning out Christian gentlemen; we talk of letting people develop mental health or mature personalities.'[54] And even though he wonders how the counsels of mental health could ever provide positive ideals he, too, dutifully concludes that mental health is 'something that educators should never neglect while they educate people'. Surely, it is not probable that either Christianity or modern humanism could have elicited such a firm avowal of a paedagogical precept without the support of the counselling

ideology of the twentieth century! This is not to say that the counsellor's mentality is not in the European tradition of educational
thought. This mentality did not have to be grafted on an alien plant.
Professor G. H. Bantock properly pointed out that some of the
counselling ideology could be traced to Rousseau.[55] No doubt there
were other related, and still ongoing streams. But even if the distance
between Rousseau and A. S. Neill is shorter than we thought, the
distance would never have been travelled without Freud and the
post-Freudians, and without all those whom I call counsellors. The
moral insights of earlier times have had to acquire a clinical and
scientific authoritativeness to survive, for in this age it is deemed to
be in a far better taste to aspire to mental health than to goodness, and
this has been entirely the work of the counsellors.

J. S. Brubacher, in his widely used textbook on *Modern Philosophy
of Education*, remarks that ' . . . an educator today frequently invokes
Freud rather than Rousseau . . .'[56] Of course, more often than not
the invocation is unconscious, and Freud's name is not mentioned at
all. The counselling principles which originated from the psychoanalytic consulting-room have become so widely and thinly dissem-
inated that they are not recognisable by the naked eye. But they are
very much there and they penetrate every nook and cranny. One of
my favourite passages to illustrate this point, and a passage with which
I am incidentally in sympathy, was written by another distinguished
paedagogue, Professor W. R. Niblett. It goes like this,

> We pay a great deal of attention to securing that children shall
> memorise facts and passages of verse and even prose. But at least
> equally important is a training of ability to recollect moods and
> past experiences. This capacity is difficult to train because it is so
> much less within the teacher's knowledge and because classes
> in any case are so big. But to be able to recollect at will one's
> own childhood and growth can be a great bulwark of indivi-
> duality. . . .[57]

Indeed, it can be so, and the first man who argued systematically
that this was so was Sigmund Freud, the arch-counsellor. This aesthetic
and cultural overspill of the counselling mode of thought into the
general area of intellectual consciousness, or the somewhat narrower
area of aesthetics, coincides with the use of the Freudian anamnesia
in such contexts as, say, in Marcel Proust. Literature and the arts in

general don't appear to be able to escape the influence of twentieth-century psychology and sociology. Consequently the paedagogy in the arts is also invited to act on some of the pointers which the counsellors have been offering all around. Indeed, it is the prevalence of the counselling ideology that alone can explain why the seven recommendations of the British Council of Churches on *Sex and Morality*,[58] are almost entirely taken up with demands for more instruction in psychology, social science, and human relations. They take it upon themselves to advise University Institutes of Education that 'these institutes should provide courses on human relations which seconded teachers could pursue perhaps for a recognised qualification'. Here is a plea coming from outside the paedagogical battalions, from 'the competition' as it were, which setting itself up as a kind of public conscience, tells the community that the teachers must be trained in human relations. It goes without saying that the clergy too shall be trained in the counselling techniques, and the recommendations include this as well.

The collective term, 'the Social Sciences', this nebulous plural, this assortment of sundry theories, this collection of rare and lean propositions, is now being credited by church people with the power of 'giving man better insight into the practical ways of expressing his affection and using it for constructive ends'. The contemporary moralists can be heard in increasing numbers to advise, 'go and study the social sciences and you will be a better man, a better counsellor a better teacher, or a better what you will'. It is hardly surprising if the redefinition of the teacher's role has gone on along these lines. Claude Russell noted not long ago that 'to an even greater extent the teacher is now becoming a social worker';[59] and Mrs Jean Floud could recently be caught toying with the idea that 'the teacher-social worker' might well be substituted for the 'teacher-missionary';[60] and that sums up a good part of the socio-cultural and role changes about which I have been writing.

I am not unaware of the fact that a multitude of schools, schisms, and varieties of psychological as well as sociological theory is being offered to student-teachers in our institutions of training. Yet, in the face of this, I maintain that there is a sufficiently large body of shared information and precept to justify my hypothesis that the counselling ideology permeates the principles of teachers' training everywhere. I say this, in spite of the obvious and energetic initiative of a so-called behaviouristic mode of thinking, at any rate, in some schools of training, where a connection with any kind of counselling ideology would be strenuously disclaimed. I have already explained elsewhere why these disclaimers could not be really accepted.[61] Here, I will merely repeat that so long as the behaviour therapists continue to solve all their insoluble problems by referring to an unanalysed and global 'social reinforcer' or 'clinician contact' – the personal presence of a persevering, and interested professional worker, their account will remain suspect. This is a theoretical objection of the first order. But there seems to be a pragmatic anomaly as well: in a very important sense it is, I think, true that a behaviouristic psychology is no more serviceable to the teacher than a physiological account of passionate sexual love is a cure for impotence. Perhaps it is for this reason that a rigorously behaviouristic account of personality growth and of professional roles has not yet disposed of the counselling influence in paedagogical training. Of all times, today, when mechanical aids to teaching have spread beyond our expectations, the very staying power of a counselling mentality must somehow be explained. The personality of the teacher, and the 'human relations' context of teaching, are still the dominant notes of paedagogical moralisation and indoctrination today. I have no doubt that the dominant view indoctrinated in the student-teacher at the present time is that the behaviouristic fragmentation of the total personalistic account may be intellectually satisfying some of the time, but in professional practice it is too often either inapplicable or irrelevant or, indeed, incapacitating. This is what our leading educators still teach, and this is what Professor Ben Morris must have meant when he concluded that the teacher '. . . through his attitudes to his pupils holds the fundamental key to learning'.[62] There has been no change in our views on this matter and, in fact, our never slackening demand for the personal attention of the teacher to the pupil testifies to our faith in a personalistic psychology, in a human relations concept of the teaching role, and also, of course, in a counselling bias. And it is not a bit acceptable to argue that we plead for the *personal* attention mainly because of its superior 'instructional efficiency', because it is expedient, for the plea is moved by aspirations which are inextricably bound up with our faith in the intrinsic value in global personal relationships. One might even detect a spiritual utopianism in the 'small class movement' for it is never clearly stated that there is an optimum smallness for an educational group, other than the communion of a twosome. Perhaps the educational utopianists unconsciously envisage that the 'second coming' of the 1944 British Education Act will dispose of classrooms altogether! I must give this some emphasis because I feel that the demand for smaller classes, for personal attention, for individual treatment, is very often symptomatic of a desire for a counselling type relationship in education. The student-teacher may not be importuned and harassed with psychoanalytical concepts such as transference, countertransference, ego-supportiveness, and the like, and yet the concepts which these terms connote are indelibly in the minds of most psychologists of education when they speak of the teacher's personal influence. After all, this is vividly borne out by the widespread practice of describing educational difficulties of the children, and class-room control problems of teachers, in clinical terms.

For years I was associated with a paedagogical reform movement, called 'Interprofessional', which advocated the linking, merging, or combining of teachers' training with social casework training in special interprofessional courses. I also repeatedly argued for the inclusion of some interprofessional educational element in the training of all personal service professionals. Today there are several institutions of teachers' training in which the advocacies of the first five Interprofessional Conferences[63] have been translated into the practice of concrete training programmes. Not having been an inconspicuous advocate I might be forgiven for hoping that the outcome of my efforts was not entirely negligible. Of course, on reflection, the counselling ideology was encompassing the training courses already, and I merely voiced what must have been in the minds of many people at the time. At any rate, the response to my initiative certainly encourages me to think so. That, in my time, I too spread the counselling ideology in the training of teachers, is offered merely as a testimony to the effect that I have had direct experience of how this sort of thing is done, and a special sensitivity to perceiving when it is being done.

It was after the first Interprofessional Conference at the University of Keele in 1958 that I organised an Interprofessional Committee to work out concrete paedagogical programmes of an interprofessional kind. Professor J. W. Tibble very readily took up my initiative and agreed to act as Chairman. He has faithfully carried on as Chairman of that Committee ever since. A professor of education, and a former head of the School of Education in the University of Leicester, he is

yet another educationist who explicitly identifies the paedagogical
with the therapeutic, the educational role with the counselling role.
'Both education and therapy', he writes, 'involve bringing about
changes in pupil or client which will enable him or her to fulfil needs
and cope with problems adequately. In both cases something has to
be learnt – skill, attitudes – which are relevant to the need. The
difference can be most profitably thought of in terms of education and
re-education, since the social worker is more likely to be specifically
involved in repairing defects of knowledge, changing unsatisfactory
attitudes, relearning social skills and so on. But clearly, also, many
teachers need skills in remedial work and have to cope with effects of
unsatisfactory home backgrounds and defective relationships between
child and parent'.[64] According to those of us who have been advo-
cating a new 'interprofessional' formula for professional education,
almost all those who are engaged in the helping professions are
engaged in essentially the same task, the liberation of another person's
potentials. This liberation is both a process of education and one of
therapy. The pursuit of this line of thinking meant that the difference
between the role of the teacher and of the counsellor, the difference
between 'teaching' and 'counselling', has become blurred. I digressed
to mention the activities of this Interprofessional Committee because
it received widespread support from educationists of many kinds, and
its existence corroborates my present thesis that the counselling
ideology has permeated educational thinking in our time.

But it is not only the passing generation of Tibble's and mine that
has gone in these directions. The younger educational theorists are
also interested. Maurice Craft, for example, redesigns the role of the
teacher, and asks us not to leave it to chance whether the teacher
knows about the social and family background of the pupil: the
teacher must be thoroughly familiar with the social context of child-
life and this familiarity, this knowledge, is supposed to be 'the central
tool of his trade'![65] Eggleston and Caspari, using social casework
supervisory techniques in the training of teachers went in this direction because of the need for a redefinition of the teacher's role: the
teacher needed a new kind of 'sensitivity-training' which he would
not normally get in routine class-room supervision.[66]

Perhaps the most conclusive evidence for the 'ecumenical' spread
of a uniform counselling point of view is the organisational and
statutory realigment which it seems to encourage. First, it was only

the professional social caseworkers who started talking and even organising along *generic* lines, having identified a largish body of generic skills and information which all must share. At first this was no more than the highest common factor in the requisites of being a probation officer, or a psychiatric social worker, or a medical social worker, or a child care worker. But now it is rapidly coming into view – and this book explains why – that there is also a generic factor in all the personal service professions of teaching, social work, nursing, doctoring, and so on. This factor may not be very large but it is substantial enough to make an enormous difference to a student of culture and to a student of the great societies of our time. The moral consensus of the personal service professions need not affect every move or function of the several professions to have a far-reaching social and cultural significance. Though this consensus is implicit, and even unconscious, most of the time it determines the moral quality of the contemporary intellectual élite, and, through them, the moral quality of the society at large. It is this that we must keep before ourselves when we are tempted to dismiss the conclusions towards which my arguments point. It will be said that the tasks of the several kinds of 'personal service professionals' are so different, their training, their thinking, their values so much at variance, that no unitary cultural phenomenon could be explained with reference to them as a discrete social entity. It is fundamental to my diagnosis of the current cultural changes that this kind of objection is mistaken.

The reports submitted to the British Government, such as for example, Robbins, Newsom, Plowden, and now Seebohm, all identify the need for integrating major personal services under the control of some coordinated system of principles. It is taken as read that we have already agreed on a coordinated set of principles of betterment and that the values of social life are not eternally under dispute. When one tries to identify the area of assumed consensus in the grey paragraphs of government reports it is not difficult to see the influence of the counselling ideology on the principles of betterment embodied in these reports.

Take Seebohm, for example. Paragraph 141 has no doubts at all about this: 'the need for a more unified provision of personal social services has been made plain by growing knowledge and experience. There is a realisation that it is essential to look beyond the immediate symptoms of social distress to the underlying problems.' It is interesting to observe the connection between these two sentences. The first commends that we use generic concepts, the second that we look out for the unconscious motivation, the concealed and ulterior motive. The linking of the two sentences means that we can't expect to be able to do what the second says unless we comply with the first! The 'generic' equals that which is fundamentally and universally human, and the propositions of a counselling psychology – including the one about 'presenting problems' and 'unconscious motives' – are readily incorporated in the government report, taking it for granted that the propositions are beyond dispute. 'Of course, important administrative boundaries will remain', continues the same paragraph. 'Responsibilities for medical care, education, and housing will continue to be separate, although the problems they deal with also have an obvious social component.' And so the 'generic' *social* embraces *all* the personal social services and not only those of social work to which this report is mainly devoted.

In sheer numbers, the teachers are the most prominent among the personal service professionals. If and when they become carriers of the counselling ideology they inevitably spread the precepts of that ideology far and wide. This is not at all a naive generalisation about *all* those who teach: there are large numbers of teachers who are not at all susceptible to this ideological influence. There are also large numbers for whom the teaching vocation is predominantly academic and almost impersonal. Just the same, the main stream of the profession, with conviction or convictionless, reiterates the counselling principles and redefines the professional role accordingly; it matters little that there may be extensive peripheral elements who pay little or no attention. The moral reappraisal comes about without them or in spite of them.

Of course, the notion that the teacher is to exercise a kind of pastoral care over his pupils is very old. But without the injection into this notion of a large shot of clinical and socio-psychological ideas, our agnostic world today would have rejected pastoral and personal care as a sentimental and old-fashioned indulgence. In the world of teaching machines, in which pupils are 'processed' and 'programmed', the traditional 'moral tutor' or 'guide' is almost a figure of superstition, and even of ominous reaction. It was through the counselling ideology that hypotheses have been presented in the manner, and, approximately enough, in the method of a social science. Though, alas, the verifications of these hypotheses have often been put off *ad graecas calendas*, happily, the stance of personal care has as often been rehabilitated in the educational setting. Without this service rendered by the counselling ideology of the twentieth century, the old, entirely mystical concept of pastoral care would have had a very hard time of it during the recent decades of progressive disillusionment.

But, as I explained at the beginning, my objectives go far beyond merely suggesting that the counsellors have had some sort of an influence in education. Through our education systems in the West, the counsellors, in league with legions of indoctrinated paedagogues, spread their sway, and exercise an unprecedented moral control over society today. Of course, the teachers, who constitute the most populous branch of the personal service professions in all the advanced industrial societies, may be evolving a body of tenets, a paedagogical ideology, a contemporary version of the ideology of education and in doing so they may be incorporating in this some of the major features of what I call the counselling ideology. It seems to me, that the personal service professions – all of them – are engaged in doing this, and it so happens that much of the ideology of the personal service professions is, in fact, nothing else but the counselling ideology itself.

That this is so, can be vividly shown if we leave the class-room and the clinical consulting-room – places of much other-regarding effort – and go over to an area of life in which we would not expect to be treated with so much consideration for our own welfare alone: namely, the world of business and of determined profit-making. To our surprise we shall find the same familiar slogans and precepts laid down for the management of human relations even there.

The second section of my documentation is devoted to this area of activities.

11. *The Counselling Ideology in Business Management*

The dissemination of the counselling ideology in educational thought and practice is paralleled by a similar process in industrial and business management. This is an unexpected development because whilst counsellors and teachers are committed to a career in personal service, business managers are not. Though the advancement of an enterprise of profit-making is of obvious service to the few and possibly even to the several, it is certainly not primarily an enterprise of rendering personal services to the many, let alone to everybody. Business managers in industry and commerce have nevertheless been making much effort to change the roles which they have been hired to play, with the result that these roles are in the process of acquiring outlandish elements of personal service, as newly discovered requisites to the role of being an effective business manager. The accretion in the business manager role has continued in this direction so that certain personal service criteria of suitability are beginning to be raised already at the moment of hiring instead of waiting for them to emerge spontaneously later. Naturally, we may be tempted to doubt that what is being grafted on the manager's role is altogether the same complex of norms which operates in the personal service professions.

Of course, we may heartily doubt that professional ethics will survive a translation from professional life into the business world. We will certainly require evidence to the effect that it does happen at all sometimes, or that it happens often enough to count. My hypothesis is that mainly as a result of the sheer multiplication of instances in which business is influenced by professional expertise, a certain discolouring of the banners of 'Profit First' is noticeable. *On the one hand*, patriotic slogans such as 'Efficiency First' or 'Productivity First', especially at a time when these are national objectives, exert some influence. *On the other hand*, the businessman is learning to look up to the professional expert whom he employs in ever-growing numbers, and whilst trying to perserve his tough-minded entrepreneurial approach to the things of this world he is slanting this approach so that some, by no means unimportant, accommodation takes place between his tough-mindedness and the relative tender-mindedness of the professional man. Of course, what is professed and what is practised are not necessarily the same. My view is not that an overnight revolutionary moral change has taken place but that the moral precepts of leadership have been undergoing a slow but sure amendment, and that this amendment is affecting even the long established responses of the businessman's utilitarian calculus. I also believe that this conditioning by professionals affects not only the manner of the businessman's dealings with people but, through him, the moral climate of the society as a whole. Even when, in the business setting itself, the publicly avowed philanthropic considerations, the lip-service, have as yet little or no substance in them, the sheer fact of their anxious repetition is almost certainly to exact some sort of delayed response from future managements and leaders.

The point is that, though business is strategically important in the scheme of labour in society, it is rapidly being rationalised, concentrated, and deprived of the freebooting, unshackled, and unscrupulously licensed initiative which used to be its *sine qua non*. More and more professionals will be needed to furnish the technological know-how, the administrative expertise, and the scientific overview necessary for the planning of business activities. Of course, for business management the shareholders come first, but strangely, sometimes they have to come second, so that considerations for good 'human relations' can be given first place. On such occasions the hard businessman will apologetically explain to his board of directors that to be 'good' is good for business, and it rarely happens that anybody demands evidence that it is really good for business. Lately, however, there have been some research results sadly showing that it is not always good for business to be 'good' – but the lessons of these results have not yet been assimilated.

A standard method to dress up a businessman's philanthropic conscience is for him to call for a professional, the human relations expert. Indeed the managers nowadays not only call for him but also elect him to the board of directors. It is thus that the professionalisation of business brings into the world of profit and loss a curiously outlandish and possibly disturbing set of moral precepts, for, as H. D. Lasswell observed, 'running a business often involves a calculating posture toward other people'.[67] But the newly recruited professionals to business, are 'tainted' by other proclivities as well. For example H. R. Bowen writes, 'in keeping with the businessman's production-oriented economics, he regards his primary responsibility to be the achievement of ever-expanding production. . . . In achieving the goal of increasing production, the businessman regards the making of a profit as his first and foremost duty. To him, a business that fails to make an adequate profit is a house of cards. . . . In the long run it cannot survive. . . .' But he concludes, '. . . once the *sine qua non* of a reasonable profit has been attained, then according to these views, it becomes the duty of corporate directors and managers to conduct their enterprises with concern for all the interests affected. . . . An increasing number of businessmen are beginning to regard management as a profession having underlying ethical principles and social responsibilities similar to the learned professions of medicine or law.'[68] In the days of unashamed plunder and chicanery, 'social responsibility' was what the lazy, good-for-nothing workers did not have and what the hardworking and resourceful owners of business were proved to possess by virtue of their hardwon success.[69] Even if today the whole social change is merely a transformation of styles in greed we must seriously consider the possibility that the change in styles may well affect the substance of human intentions and actions as well as the moral climate of the whole society. This development was anticipated by Emil Durkheim, in his *Professional Ethics and Civic Morals*,[70] and its initial signs were noted by R. H. Tawney in his *Acquisitive Society*.[71] In a study of *The Professions*, by A. M. Carr Saunders and P. A. Wilson we read,

> We may . . . suppose that, under a system of large-scale commercial and industrial organisation, all those who occupy the important positions will gradually come within professional associations, or at least under professional influence . . . the incompatibility of profit-making with professionalism is ceasing to be an obstacle in the way of the spreading of professionalism throughout the world of business.[72]

Another American writer, A. H. Cole, exclaims, ' . . . it is important to notice, especially over the past two or three decades, how considerably American corporations have modified any rule of financial maximization that may have existed, so that corporate longevity, community relations, or public responsibilities might be taken into account'.[73] Guy Hunter reporting on a study group's conclusions about the role of the personnel officer lists the main components of this role in the following three points:

> 1. . . . the personnel officer, like any good citizen, must feel it his duty to improve the ways in which industry fulfils its task;
> 2. . . . in doing so, he does not act by higher standards than those of good management; but, because he will more often be faced by problems of social morality and will become in some sense experienced in their nature it will be his responsibility to remind management both of their duties to their employees and of their wider impact of their policies on the life of society outside;
> 3. . . . as a member of the management team, he must bear in mind

equally with them the limitations of social idealism which may from time to time be imposed by the current conditions for economic success.[74]

Though the third point certainly moderates the personal service bias of this professional worker there is no doubt about his commitment to certain 'limitations of social idealism' on the one hand, and about his moral influence on the rest of the management team on the other. Yet another American writer, T. C. Cochran, clearly outlines the abandonment of an obsessionally economic and technical logistic in business, 'the managerial ideology [of the earlier 1950's]', he explains, 'so emphasised education, cooperation, and success through personal relations, and disapproved so strongly of egoistic individualism, ruthless dealings with competitors and of any quest for high profits dangerous to long-run security that the managerial creed [of the period] seemed to be in a transitional stage towards a doctrine in which the goal was to achieve a position that conferred power and prestige, rather than personal wealth'.[75] And Cochran rightly observes, 'once the *major* aim is transferred from extra profits for stockholders to the welfare of the organisation, the critical step has been taken in the direction of a new social adjustment. . . .'

Side by side with these developments which have increased preoccupations with the non-pecuniary incentives, we have also a growth in the influence of the *ethos* of higher education. B. M. Selekman, the author of *Moral Philosophy for Management* notes,

> Recent decades witnessed a veritable explosion in business education, with large enrolments in business schools affiliated with universities. Association with a university immediately projects any calling on an impartial and moral plane, with the challenge to meet standards already established in the older professions of law, medicine, engineering, architecture, the ministry, and teaching. With the concept of a profession comes also self-consciousness, a desire to develop standards of technical performance as well as an ethical code, both of which give stature to those who enter the calling . . .[76]

and Selekman adds: '*I am impressed with the greater concern with religious and moral values in business schools than among scholars in the humanities*'.[77] (my italics). Those who seek the professionalisation of management will, of necessity, divert much of their attention to getting the more obvious obstacles out of the way: how can they get the same mix of honoraria and honours, as, for example, doctors are getting? How can they elevate the non-pecuniary rewards to a level which would not be too far below the levels of this kind of reward in nursing, social work, or teaching? Clearly, the operators of businesses in washing machines, groceries, bedroom suites, and what you will, are severely, and one might say, irreparably handicapped in this progress towards realising an aspiration. Yet the sheer technological and administrative complexity of the procedures, which increasingly characterise the larger organisations at least, involve management in an exceedingly prolonged and all-absorbing concern with staff-relationships and staff-management. It matters little whether the corporate enterprise is about cigarettes or surgical instruments, its corporate nature will make the same demands on its leadership of personnel, though, of course, the moral implications of the product may have some differential effects. I assume no more from this than that we have radically altered our conception of what it means to be qualified to manage. Today, to be qualified no longer means the possession of a mixture of economic, technological, and administrative efficiencies only. Managerial dexterity is increasingly defined in terms of the so-called human relations ideology. Naturally, this is more in evidence for some positions and less for others.

The candidates who groom themselves for managerial positions are nowadays increasingly 'intellectuals' who are eager to embrace the new standards: they are often marked by a moral squeamishness alongside intellectual discernment, logical pernicketiness, and an intolerance of cant. *For the intellectual, consistency of principle tends to spell a universalistic moral philosophy, and this kind of philosophy disturbingly retains all interested parties in the picture: not only those who gain, but also those who lose.*

And mainly for this reason intellectuals who find themselves in business are restive about their job. According to R. K. Merton intellectuals in business are introspectively self-critical about their place in the scheme of things and either give an altruistic reappraisal of the role they have assumed or indeed become 'alienated from the assumptions, objectives, and rewards of private enterprise' altogether.[78] J. K. Galbraith concludes similarly when he says that 'pecuniary compensation, as an explanation of effort, has now a relatively much diminished role',[79] and talks refreshingly about 'the marginal utility of income'.[80] Galbraith thinks that 'identification and adaptation may be driving forces'[81] and that 'pecuniary compensation need not be the main motivation of members of the technostructure'.[82] But the fascinating difficulty lies just in the inextricably mixed motives of power and identification: if the first is clearly ego-centred this cannot be said about the second. One's sense of power is enhanced by identification with a larger community, but identification with a larger community spells the mortification of the self. Either way strange, unbusinesslike, non-mercenary considerations get mixed up with double-entry book-keeping. When Galbraith says that, 'I may even pay something for what is called a good employer image',[83] it becomes urgent to decide what we mean by 'pay'? Does it mean that the image will demonstrably register in the balance sheets? Or, at least, that it does so register though we are unable to prove it? Or, perhaps, that it does not have any substantial material effects on anybody's pockets but much rather on their composure and sense of integrity? If a transaction enhances these unquestionably valuable things in our lives we should have little hesitation in saying that the transaction has *paid off*. No doubt, having a 'good employer's reputation' can have fiscal consequences, both positive and negative. But even if all the consequences were financially profitable it is not at all to be taken for granted that this is what makes them solely or even mainly desirable.

Because it is imperative that we keep this thought well in the focus of our attention, and because this thought is close to the heart of my argument I should like to quote, in full, three passages from the *Psychological Analysis of Economic Behaviour*[84] both to elaborate this thought, and even more so, to show that I am not introducing a novel interpretation or an utterly unshared impression.

... [If] the term 'maximisation' must include such considerations as maintenance of the firm's good will or the reputation of its brand name . . . [then it] is not the only qualification we have to consider . . . If businessmen strive for profits but not for maximum profits, what is their aim? It may be that they attain 'satisfactory' profits. Satisfactory profit is a psychological concept. . . .[85]

If all motives were ego-centred, one might argue that the managers strive to maximise their own salaries or remuneration.

The objective of getting the highest profit for oneself from the corporation's activities, that is, the objective of 'milking' the company one directs, may prevail in one or the other exceptional instance, but it is contrary to the institutional patterns prevailing in our economy. . . .[86]

. . . in all probability, the point of view, repeated over and over again, changes the psychological field both for those who pronounce it and those who hear it. The motives and actions of businessmen who proclaim publicly and proudly their objective of making large profits may differ greatly from those businessmen who are apologetic about their profits.[87]

Two important ideas must be highlighted in these passages. *First*, that the 'institutional patterns prevailing' in our contemporary culture – in Western societies at least – are already *imposing* some gestures, rituals, observances, and a general conformity with the norms of a personal service ideology on those who deal with personnel in our economic institutions. Both those in the key-positions of leadership and the rank and file are both becoming acclimatised to manners, conventions, and ethics of colleagueship, of superiority and inferiority, of sharing and participation, an abandonment of vindictive secretiveness, and an adoption of the habit of exacting service through positive incentives instead of through threats, or sanctions, and so on. The changes in the climate of work have been called into being in our time because the counselling ideology afforded a suitable rationale for re-arranging human relationships in the work-place. Naturally these changes could not have succeeded but for the retreat of authoritarian and classical-capitalist employment systems. But this retreat, born of major political changes, could not have achieved the restructuring of the microsociological thinking about simple human relationships in the work-place or in staff-settings; in fact, there is ample evidence to show that exploitive, authoritarian methods continued in those industrial systems which have totally abandoned capitalist economies. The nationalised industries of the semi-capitalist welfare states, and far more so, those of the communist peoples' democracies, ruthlessly enforced a code of employment and, if anything, justified it by noisily advertising that the code served the common good and not the capitalist.

Secondly, it is to be remembered that the sheer reiteration, and

I

acting-out of these personal service observances, profoundly change 'the psychological field', that is to say, the cultural context and, in the event, call into being a new institutional pattern in which the very conceptions of 'profit' or 'advantage' may undergo some striking changes. It is customary to smile at the psychotherapeutic effectiveness of 'everyday in every way I am getting better and better', but there is little doubt of the power which autosuggestive definition of one's own condition has over that condition. The role-definition, the re-iterated description of one's function and purpose in the productive system exacts an effort to conform in fact with the definition in thought and word.

Certainly, the presence of the effort to be less mercenary, more public-spirited, is itself a proof of discrepancy: the definition of the management's role is ambitious, and goes far beyond the facts of the case. It is, in fact, an aspiration. I agree with Bernard Barber that professionalism in business remains more an ideological aspiration than a social fact,[88] but I must stress that the widespread hankering after the dignity and honour of a professional status among Western management leaders and businessmen is itself also a socio-cultural fact, which clearly signifies a profound discontent with an exclusively mercenary role-definition in the world of business, and a nostalgic longing to amend that role definition. I do not assume that business has become professionalised already, but rather that the fact of its growing aspiration to become professionalised has a powerful contribution to make to a general moral change which is accelerated by a more realistic professionalisation in other sectors of life.

Certainly, we need not be excessively impressed by measures such as, for example, the announcement of workers' birthdays over the public address system in the cafeteria.[89] But this conclusion is inescapable: managerial personnel, which concerns itself more and more with the policies of kindness and generosity, with the susceptibilities of others to courtesy, friendliness and sympathy, will certainly be 'contaminated' by the practice and cultivation of these concerns. No matter how hypocritical and mercenary we judge the motives behind these measures and tactics, the new habits of tact and consideration substantially reform the standards of our human relationships.

The social situation in which the leaders operate is constantly though almost imperceptibly being redefined. It is being redefined by their own hesitating, half-meant, and groping initiative to change some of the norms of their own functioning. 'The assumption,' writes Sir Geoffrey Vickers,

> that business success should be measured solely by the criteria applicable to managing an investment, derived its validity – and still derives such validity as it has – from the fact that it was and to some extent still is incorporated in the mores of society. In so far as it is no longer so accepted, the reason is that society has developed wider and different expectations of business; and, in consequence, business management, itself an integral part of that society, has responded by accepting these expectations and partly incorporating them in its own standards of success.[90]

The process of change is a circular one, until a new factor breaks the circle, the somewhat spruced-up self-images are forced upon us by society, which in turn will so much the more insist on these as we perhaps reluctantly submit and conform. And again our submission to and conformity with a qualitatively new standard and a new role will become more and more automatic as society's resolve to expect us to conform is consolidated and reinforced by our own conformity.

A prominent feature which comes into view upon the closer analysis of the professional stance in the personal services imported into the world of business is the worker's aspiration to be 'scientific' in general principles and in their technical application. The professional – in the majority of instances – assumes that he is an applier of science or at least of a set of empirically verifiable principles about some aspects of the world. Invariably there is a bid to ascertain and verify the validity of certain procedures and techniques. The entrepreneur of earlier times might have evolved these techniques by trial and error, without reference to tested basic principles in psychology or sociology or economics, and it did not occur to him to hanker after a scientific validation of his spontaneously acquired business acumen, and of his intuitive cleverness in 'handling men'. But nowadays, a growing number of high-level decisions in business, reached in the headquarters of the enterprise, follow haruspication by human relations consultants, and socio-psychological experts of various kinds. Hunches are receiving less and less mention, and have certainly lost much of their erstwhile mysterious authority, whilst the resourcefulness of the experts tends to be boosted beyond the heights which they are able to live up to. It is almost as if it were said, that if we must rely on their judgement, because the scientific age demands it, we may as well build up confidence by convincing others, and incidentally ourselves too, that what we are relying on is near enough infallible. The result, as Wright Mills put it, is that 'the organisation expert becomes a key person in the managerial cadre . . . a sort of manager of managers',[91] with a scientific staff of his own. The demands made on this professionally qualified manager are not inconsiderable. He is not only expected to secure the solvency, and indeed the profitability, of the enterprise but he must also have 'interpersonal competence and extensive skills in a wide variety of management sciences, such as statistics, economics, and linear programming'.[92] Because of society's status system in which the professional expert tends to rank higher in impartiality, in educational achievement, in non-materialistic interest in his expertise, inevitably these managers of managers come to cultivate the scientific components of their roles at the expense of the profit-pursuing business elements of those roles. Of course, the 'applied behavioural scientist' employed in business may well be classified together with all the other kinds of scientists and technologists similarly employed. But the behavioural scientist's professional ethic does not seem to be the same as the professional ethic of scientists in general. 'The responsibility to safeguard the proper interests of those studied or affected' is explicitly stipulated in a 'Statement of Ethical Principles and their Application to Sociological Practice' presented to the Annual General Meeting of the British Sociological Association (April 1968). This sort of stipulation creates a signal difference between (human) behavioural scientists and other scientists. No subject matter of science, other than man, can be said to be afforded comparable safeguards! The non-human subjects of other sciences do not possess moral integrity. The code regulating the use of laboratory animals does not protect their life or integrity. The social-scientific stance of the management expert implies that he will have been indoctrinated against treating his subject as means, as 'things', and against taking up an 'I and It'[93] attitude towards them.

Unlike Professor Tom Lupton,[94] I do not feel that being a behavioural scientist sterilises against the bugs of a 'philanthropic ideology'. In fact, I am persuaded that intellectual and moral interest in the cultivation of a social science of social problems and in the digestion of social problems, is teeming with purposeful micro-organisms – a life-giving flora – which make the peristalsis of social action effective.

Apparently, this is yet another case in which bugs are good for us.

But while the professional duty 'to apply science' is not a new feature of professional life, the popularisation of the counselling 'idiom' of applying it in human relationships is unprecedented. The 'Human Relations' doctrine is shot through and through with this idiom. It is under the banner of 'Human Relations' that the clinical and socio-psychological principles of counselling have been brought into the tough-minded world of business leadership and organisation. 'Human Relations' is, in fact, largely a collection of propositions which adapts counselling principles to the handling of staff-relations in formal organisations of all kinds. The principal contribution of this school has been an illumination of the part played by the non-economic rewards in the motivation and contentment of the workers. Nowadays – in spite of a reawakened scepticism – the basic notions of the human relations account have not been repudiated. According to this account the worker does work for a wage but could not work for a wage only. Among other things, workers rediscover companionship in the enforced togetherness of the work situation; they acquire a more clearly defined identity through the way the work-group casts them in a role; and through their skill and performance they enhance their sense of worth which the group's estimate and esteem will confirm. They work not only for a wage but also for companionship, for the strengthening of a feeling of identity, for being recognised as skilled, responsible, and valuable in productive or social ways.

Summarising the so-called 'employee-centred' leadership ideology of the Human Relations type of business management, James H. Mullen presents the main points of agreement in the following requirements,

The successful leader in the modern business organisation:
1. generally puts the welfare of his subordinates before his own personal advantage;
2. maintains contact with his employees on as informal a basis as he can;
3. attempts to utilise employee knowledge and initiative through as much delegation of authority and participation in decision-making as he possibly can achieve;
4. communicates frankly and openly with employees on all matters affecting their welfare and lets them know where they stand at all times;

5. uses praise rather than criticism wherever possible in counselling and guiding his employees; and

6. tries at all times to maintain with subordinates the 'I-Thou' (Buber) relationship, the person-to-person approach, and eschews the 'I-It' relationship, the person-to-thing approach, with all its implications of manipulation and deception.[95]

On the face of it, the altruistic and service orientation of this list of directives for successful business leadership must *per force* appear to us as hypocritical. But the whole case of the present volume rests with the thesis that we would be grossly mistaken to believe this impression. A later chapter devoted entirely to the problems of insincerity and of hypocrisy in professional practice is an important part of the argument in support of my thesis. For the time being I will note that in addition to the altruism of these precepts, and in addition to the mysticism in the references to Buberian teaching, they comply with the principles of permissiveness and acceptance which are integral parts of the counselling ideology.

These prescriptions faithfully reproduce the philosophical orientation of contemporary management literature and of at least some well publicised contemporary aspirations in practice. They do not represent a minority point of view. 'The contributions in the area of social responsibilities in particular,' writes one theorist of management, 'have paved the way for a philosophy for professional management. These contributions have changed management theory from an often exclusive orientation toward economic goals to a wider view of interrelationships between business and other social values and responsibilities.'[96]

During the recent three or four decades, more specifically since the classical Hawthorne studies in the 1920's, the intellectual genealogy of the human relations school of industrial psychology and sociology has been intimately linked with that of the counselling ideology. In a recently published textbook, *Leadership and Organisation*, a competent and thorough work of its kind, we have an excellent and concise statement of this ideology which I will cite in full:

We have been fortunate to be working in times that academically have been ripe with ferment and stimulation. Clearly, it is impossible to trace or detail all the major influences under whose impact our ideas have taken shape. The towering notions of dynamic psychology, as originally developed by Freud and his disciples, undoubtedly made their mark. So did the brilliant writings of Kurt Lewin and of his students, whose formulations concerning relations between individual and group no doubt can be traced in our work. We have been strongly influenced by the thinking of Carl Rogers particularly with respect to the concepts of client-centeredness, acceptance, and listening; by J. L. Moreno, in areas of sociometry and psychodrama; by the pioneering contributions of Elton Mayo and of his associates, enriching our understanding of the industrial civilization that provides the broad context of our research. The approaches of the National and Western Training Laboratories in group development have interacted with many other approaches to human relations training in the evolution of sensitivity training. Vast areas of practice and experimentation, such as group psychotherapy, classic and 'modern' organisation theory, group dynamics – these and many more have been significant sources of ideas.[97]

The authors of this work, one of the better ones of its class, already numbering scores, are the inheritors of ideas of counselling theorists of many kinds, though it would not at all be difficult to show that the common ancestry of the 'greats' listed in the above excerpt is psycho-therapeutic, if not psycho-analytical, and that the single-minded interest and orientation of many of them is a psycho-therapeutic and counselling orientation. The gallery of portraits is gathered up almost exclusively from the clinical world: most of the original thinkers are authoritative innovators in some field of counselling. Here is a statement which does my work for me thoroughly: it testifies that modern thinking in industrial and management theory is inspired by the concepts and propositions of counselling practice. However, the book from which I have quoted is not offered as a clinical manual: it is supposed as a textbook of applied industrial sociology! It is intended to be a manual for the students of management, and of industrial organisation. The analysis of the basic principles discloses the presence of the same principles of operation which characterise the principles set out in textbooks of social casework, and indeed in the textbooks of the various schools of psychotherapy. The authors of this book make no secret about this, and not only give Freud pride of place in the 'credit titles' in the Preface of their book, but follow this up by listing all the other principal innovators in the field of the clinical repair of the personality, everyone of whom, on their own showing, and in their own published work, have admitted, or at least implied, some large debt to the originator of the counselling ideology, Sigmund Freud.

The emphases, the names, the schools of thought singled out for mention cannot be expected to be identical, but the similarities are unquestionable. Another much respected authority on this subject, Chris Argyris, writes,

> From the literature on scientific management, industrial economics, and public administration we learned about the properties of formal organisations. From the literature in clinical, social, child, and adolescent psychology, we learned much about the human personality. Putting together our two pictures of personality [in our culture] and formal organisations, we developed some propositions which became our first attempt at a theoretical framework.[98]

Even if we do not dispute that these propositions take an equitable fifty-fifty per cent of knowledge from the two areas, it would still be an impressive share conceded to psychology in the development of the theoretical framework. And it is of the greatest importance to say again that for much of what is called 'psychology' we must read 'counselling psychology', for even if there is often a determined attempt at emancipating ourselves from the doctrinal, speculative, and unverified propositions of counselling psychology and translating its propositions into the language of, say, learning theory, the practical prescripts are still based on assumptions about facts in human relationships which are not distinguishable from the assumptions about facts in the thinking of the counsellors.

But often enough the parentage of the ideas is blatantly stated: 'The psychoanalytic study of personality and character (as developed by Sigmund Freud) provides potentially the fullest and most challenging statement of conditions in human development that determine the way executives pattern their role.'[99] And if this is not definite enough to document my thesis about the prevalence of the counselling ideology in much of our industrial, social-psychological thinking, Zaleznik, who is Professor of Organizational Behaviour, at Harvard University's Graduate School of Business Administration, has also this to say:

In reviewing the evolution of organization theory I have suggested that the unsolved problem in understanding man in organization, centres around the inability of existing theory to grasp the essential dynamics of the individual, and from this understanding to formulate a truly psychosocial theory of organization and leadership. Psychoanalytic psychology as a psychology of the individual has provided and continues to provide the lead in this direction, whether the lead is pursued remains to be seen.[100]

Of course, not all professors of business administration are also 'Associate Members and Research Fellows of a Psychoanalytic Society and Institute' (Professor Zaleznik has both these qualifications in respect of the Boston Society and Institute). But it is, to say the least, significant that a prominent academic institution such as Harvard's Graduate School of Business Administration should deem the qualification of 'psychoanalyst' highly relevant to teaching and scholarship in the field of human relations in business organisations.

Of course, it is repeatedly stressed that 'Mental Health is not a matter of managerial concern because it is humanitarian to have such an interest or because it is believed to be "good for" employee or public relations'.[101] No, the executive is a 'Remedial Agent'[102] because this will get the job done.

It is important to realise that the spate of books and the multitude of papers which have been written by the ever increasing numbers of dons of the ever increasing numbers of business schools serve as the teaching vehicle, indeed as the major substance of a new discipline, business studies, and that what is taught and advocated in them is in the process of becoming the ideological mainstay of industrial and commercial management, and of the management of profit-making formal organisations everywhere. In his *A Moral Philosophy for Management*, B. M. Selekman writes,

Recent decades have witnessed a veritable explosion in business education, with large enrolments in business schools affiliated with universities. Associations with a university immediately projects any calling on a technical and moral plane, with the challenge to meet standards already established in the older professions of law, medicine, engineering, architecture, the ministry, and teaching. With the concept of a profession comes also a self-consciousness, a desire to develop standards of technical performance as well as an ethical code, both of which give stature to those who enter the calling. . . .[103]

Britain is hardly being left behind in this development although she has been very much a late comer to the idea that 'business schools' are an integral element of modern higher education. In 1965 there were in Britain no fewer than 12 universities and some 40 technical colleges and colleges of advanced technology offering courses of one kind or another in management studies, and during the last four years there has been a further growth in the number of these courses.

There is a good deal in contemporary management training literature which proves that strong pressures are exerted in the direction of more elaborate and more sophisticated social science training of all candidates for business leadership including technologists and scientists. However, many writers complain that 'merely adding to the main technical courses a few hours weekly of general or social studies and taking it on faith that this will broaden the powers of judgment of the technologist when he qualifies',[104] is not going to make a mark on the student. But even writers like these observe that there are courses of training for technologists which '. . . are more imaginative and incorporate into the main body of syllabuses a study of the history of technology and of its social and cultural effects, as well as a study of management and the sociology of science'.[105]

Before this book went to press I had asked four technological universities (two in England, one in Wales, and one in Scotland) to answer the following two questions:

1. What is the total number of full-time students in your institution reading any of the pure or applied natural sciences or technological courses (*not* including the social science and domestic science courses!) during the session, 1968–69? In all:

2. How many of these students attend a set course of more than one term duration in any one of the following subjects or cognate subjects during the session 1968/69? In all:

('Psychology', 'Social Psychology', 'Personality Development', 'Human Growth and Development', 'Human Relations' ['in Industry'], 'Industrial Relations', 'Sociology of Industry', 'Industrial Management', 'Personnel Management', 'Sociology', or any other course, which one or two of the foregoing might equally well describe.)

The replies which I have received have been as follows:

TABLE XXI

Institution	(1)	(2)	(2) as % of (1)
Bath	1,408	329	23
Loughborough	2,024	392	19
Cardiff (UWIST)	1,235	183	15
Glasgow (Strathclyde)	2,758	255	9
Total	7,425	1,159	15

Roughly one in seven science or technology students is exposed to some form of instruction in the social sciences described in (2) above. It is understood that this instruction varies very considerably from the type of exercise in 'civics' which registers little intellectually and not at all in terms of the personalities of the student to the type of instruction described by Sofer and Hutton.[106]

It is remarkable that the Council of Engineering Institutions examination has chosen to make only one final paper compulsory – The Engineer in Society. F. E. Warner writes about this: 'This is not an attempt to sprinkle engineering with Liberal Studies, but to relate the work of an engineer to his social environment. It deals in the main with the duties of an engineer to his employer, to his co-workers and society. If there is a dominant theme, it is the correct use of resources in the widest sense. Any engineer who takes the paper should be the better for it.'[107] We have here 'duties' consorting with the 'correct use of resources' and no wonder that – in these circumstances – the social science indoctrination of engineers continues to be concealed by ambiguity. But concealed or no, it goes on.

On the whole there is a tendency to expect more of the social sciences than they can as yet supply: the on-going processes of educational and training reform have added new demands for social science information and know-how. The young scientist or technologist, as well as all other respecters of modern science, will confidently await to be instructed in social *science* so that the managerial roles, which they look forward to playing, can be filled by them competently, and in full possession of the latest scientific information which is relevant to these roles. There are reasons to believe that those who eagerly seek and learn *to apply* social science tend to overestimate the value of what they can usefully wring from their social science expertise so that they do not lose heart over what effort and confidence they have already expended. This constitutes a built-in mechanism, perpetuating and reinforcing the compact between practice and social science. On the other hand, this overestimation of social science may encourage the scepticism about the brevity or superficiality of social science training. Nevertheless, the growing respect in which the social sciences are held tends to increase the prestige of those who learn their mode of formulating and resolving problems in the area of human relations. Even if only the conceptualisation is mastered, worse still, even if only the vocabulary is learnt, there is something to be gained in the long run. The seeming emptiness of this kind of learning may be reprehensible, but the cumulative effects are not: the new recruits still apply a more enlightened régime, even if at first without much conviction.

Of course, in the vanguard of the arguments offered in support of these developments we find invariably the utilitarian and even ostentatiously mercenary considerations that these courses of training and these technological schools will turn out appropriately qualified leadership and staff for our economic institutions, and that, therefore, they would primarily benefit the material efficiency of the formal organisations of business. The schools were assumed to be offering their services to the present and future leaders of business and of industry, who were primarily interested in efficiency. They suggested procedures which seemed able to put an end to loss, deficit, waste, and half-hearted enterprise. At the same time the leaders of business were also attracted by the idea of developing a new interest in, and a sensitivity for, issues more uplifting than their concerns for profit and loss have hitherto been. Also these leaders have frankly and eagerly begun to seek justice and fairness for those who work for them, simply because their newly educated consciences demanded of them that they should enjoy profitability, and material advantage without the pangs of conscience which indolence about the welfare of others would have brought upon them. The remarkable and initially unintended outcome has been that, no sooner have they established the solid solvency and profitability of their enterprises, than these leaders have become increasingly absorbed in studying or advancing the so-called human relations objectives of their formal organisations. Now their consciences can sometimes be observed to function in an inverted manner; they can be seen and heard protesting that these new preoccupations of theirs are no more than 'sound' business sense and intelligent as well as profitable management. Also, it is becoming very much a matter of pride for industrial leadership to be able to say that this or that plant has been able to avoid industrial conflicts, unofficial strikes, and other disputes. If human relations consultants can provide early diagnosis of impending troubles and proceed to recommend workable and effective preventive measures, then leadership, anxious to protect its reputation for wise management, will refer to them more and more and, follow their guidance, as well as assimilate their ideology. But whatever the motives, the preoccupations with a human relations type of thinking, and the fascinated, if not mesmerised, reverence for a leadership which observes the human relations principles of management continues. 'In 1956', wrote M. P. MacNair,

> the Inland Steel Company appointed a vice president of human relations. The Inland Steel Company, of course, is big business; but little business is not being neglected, for I note that the McGraw Hill Book Company Inc., is publishing a book on Human Relations in Small Industry. The Harvard University Business School has had a chair of Human Relations since 1950; by now the number of courses in Human Relations in Schools and colleges has multiplied substantially.[108]

And the process is not by any means restricted to the United States. Ever since Eliot Jaques' *Changing Culture of a Factory*[109] the thinly disguised psychotherapeutic and sociotherapeutic consultancy of industrial personnel has grown considerably in Britain as well. In a personal service society the consultancy afforded to management and staff is a personal service, never mind the strenuous self-reminders of both consultants and management that, after all, this is all done for the utterly unsentimental and businesslike rationality of efficient functioning. If at the same time they confess to aiming at harmonious cooperation, at the generating of growth, at the dispassionate examination of friction, and at contentment with human relations in the work setting, these aims are not to be proclaimed too loudly for they might make people think that the consultants are too starry-eyed to realise that the formal organisation is in existence to provide goods or services or both at a profit, and if it is to continue being an occasion for those counselling services it must also continue being a lucrative enterprise as well.

The area in which the conquest of the counselling ideology is most unexpected is in the area of technological and applied science training and education. An excellent document to draw on to show the nature and scope of the ongoing ideological process is *New Ways in Management Training* by Cyril Sofer and Geoffrey Hutton.[110] This work is one of the better studies of combined technological-managerial training. The theoretical premises of this study, the techniques and procedures adopted in its execution, the obvious technological preoccupations of the students undergoing training, and so on, are typical of what was to arise in numerous later courses of training of a similar kind. For this reason it is appropriate to refer to this study in some detail to bring out in high relief the principal elements of the 'human relations mentality' controlling the educational policy and programme designed to meet the needs of industrial, business, or formal organisation management. There is evidence everywhere for the overspill of a personal service mode of thought into the areas of impersonal skills, techniques, and into the area of technological know-how.

In this case production engineers were being trained. What was unusual was this: management training was an explicit and integral part of the general programme and not just a kind of 'liberal studies' ornamental addition, a lipservice to so-called cultural needs in technological education.[111] The students themselves were well enough motivated to pursue the study of production engineering but they seemed to be interested in the human relations issues only when these were presented as intrinsically relevant to the technological-production procedures. In fact their reactions to the searching examination of personality problems and their reactions to the claims that the problems were very relevant to human relations in industry were often defensive and anxious.[112] We are told by the authors that the student was invited to review 'in an unfamiliar way . . . apparently familiar events'.[113] Clearly, the students were led to scrutinise their own responses to human relations issues arising from their own training-employment in a technological setting, and their attention was drawn to analogies between these situations and reactions to those that they might have already recognised or might in the future recognise in the private sector of their lives. Naturally, the student wasn't 'taught' or 'instructed' in the conventional sense: he was guided more or less the same way as the client of a caseworker or even as the patient in psychotherapy. 'The distinction between education for management', write Sofer and Hutton, 'and attempted psychological therapy was difficult to draw',[114] and it would be unreasonable to expect that such a distinction would be drawn for, in fact, a separation of the two procedures – were this at all possible – would entirely liquidate the claims for effective training in human relations management. To put it in another way: if the education in human relations is not psychotherapeutic it falls short of being an education in human relations. As always, these must have been a mixed batch of candidates for this training, whose susceptibilities, in the face of searching enquiries, varied. There must have been some cases in which paedagogical brinkmanship was practised, though there is no doubt that those who were in charge played their paedagogical roles with care, competence and conscientiousness. And yet, the conclusion is entirely inescapable that these management tutors functioned as 'counsellors' to their students and, in some cases, probably those which the tutors regarded as successful, students themselves in turn were prepared to function in their future industrial employment as counsellors to those who were to be associated with them. Sofer and Hutton do not conceal that the 'training' procedures activated personality problems in the students who subsequently found it necessary to seek personal help.[115] Even in their so-called Group Discussion procedures they attempted to 'clarify' group-processes 'at both the overt and covert levels' which means that they must have interpreted manifest responses with reference to their unconscious background. No doubt the tutors worked gingerly, but who can be in any doubt about the powerful and central *clinical* orientation of this training approach and, therefore, about the counselling character of these methods of training?

In addition to these decisive indications the reader of this report is told explicitly that the theoretical basis of teaching was psychoanalytical. For tutors and industrial consultants, technological or some general social science knowledge was not enough. 'Efforts were made by the College [Brunel College, Acton – now Brunel University] to secure financial help for those who wished to undertake a course of personal psychoanalysis'.[116]

We learn from Marie Jahoda's book on *The Education of Technologists* that what has become known as 'socio-technical system analysis'[117] which makes use of all the behavioural sciences, and not only psychology and sociology but also anthropology and biology, 'have guided much recent research at the Tavistock Institutè of Human Relations'.[118] It would seem that the orientation of this Institute having determined the character of the 'social studies' taught to students of engineering at Brunel College[119] got through to these technological students: Marie Jahoda defines 'the essential impact of a human relations approach'[120] and testifies that the students, even in their first year, claim to have acquired 'ability to supervise staff and to coordinate the activities of different people or groups of people.[121] In this book we have one of the earlier testimonies to the effect that the personal service ideology of the counsellors is being transmitted to members of the impersonal service professions, in this case engineers, and that industrial personnel trained in the experimental sciences or in the technologies are also being indoctrinated in this manner.

It would be inaccurate to conclude that the counselling content of the human relations ideology in industry is exclusively or even mostly psychoanalytical: it is generically and eclectically psychotherapeutic, psychiatric, and of a 'mental health' or 'mental hygiene' interest. It is, after all, not without overwhelming significance that, in the United States, a large number of human relations studies in industry have been sponsored by the National Institute of Mental Health,[122] and that in Britain The Tavistock Institute of Human Relations, a social-psychiatric research institute, has been in the forefront of these studies with their staff having been responsible for most of the original and distinguished pioneering work done in this field. Of course, some of the 'counselling' would be performed for the organisation as a whole, and would aim at 'restructuring' it. This would appear at first an impersonal process, in which the 'client' is an organisation. But the principles, which guide any attempt at 'restructuring', are those of the counselling ideology. There is a kind of functionalism implied in all this in which the decision, on what is or is not a disfunctional factor in the organisation, is determined by the 'human relations' psychology and sociology of the consultants. Of course, productivity must respond to the changes initiated by consultants. But what if productivity, profitability, or even solvency would respond negatively? How much leeway is allowed to the consultants?

In his recent survey of the contribution of the Tavistock Institute of Human Relations to the development of Industrial Sociology in Britain, R. K. Brown observes that 'most of the empirical studies [of the Institute] have included an element of consultancy . . .'[123] No matter that this was most of the time a 'research convenience', for, of course, it was easier to gain access to the field of research and to secure the cooperation of industrial staff if the approach was made in response to request for help. 'Action-research' is research in the course of therapeutic or consultative action: it is both research and counselling. According to Brown the 'theoretical sources' of this work were rather 'limited'. By this he means that, at any rate, in the beginning, in the work of Jaques and his immediate successors, psychoanalysis loomed large indeed. Gestalt psychology and some Lewinian concepts were added at an early stage but as late as 1963 Higgin records that though 'the particular concepts of psychoanalysis as such play little direct part in the work of the Institute . . . *the form of thought of psycho-analysis is central to the tradition it draws on*'.[124] Brown comments on this, 'The situation however is not quite as simple as this statement suggests. In the first place, psychoanalysis and especially Kleinian object relations theory, affects their conception of man; secondly, there is a tendency to explain social phenomena in psychological terms; and thirdly, group psychoanalytic concepts have been stressed in a number of studies.'[125] There is no remaining doubt at all that the guidance, inspiration, counselling bond, direct teaching, and even indoctrination of future, and already present, management leadership in business, industry, and in formal organisations in general are characterised by a mode of thought, a system of values and of assumptions about facts, which, in their totality, I call the counselling ideology.

The social science indoctrination of the technologist-managers is by no means a mere Anglo-Saxon curiosity. In the École Nationale d'Administration the *ingénieur-élève* is not only expected to study several of the social sciences but this part of his course is ' . . . designed to show the primacy of social studies over technological studies, and to humanise the extreme scientific outlook which is the normal result of intensive theoretical and practical training'.[126] It is not only here, in a school of administration, that engineers are trained in this way; similar 'digressions' can be observed in the École des Mines or in the École des Ponts et Chaussées. In Holland, those in the civil service who receive advanced training in 'organisation and methods' must receive instruction in economics, psychology, sociology, and statistics.[127] This is a broad spectrum and the direction of the socio-psychological teaching may well be varying or non-specific. Yet there is no doubt that the very presence of a social science orientation sustained by the available social science literature of modern industrial societies stamps its mark on those who receive this training. Social concern is not only boosted, but also subjected to an intellectual discipline which, in turn, lends this concern an intellectual propriety. The tough-minded scientist-technologist need not trouble himself about the dangers of becoming sentimental: he is being persuaded that he can present his concern in the garb of technological manipulativeness.

Leaders of the communist states are, if anything, even more anxious to increase the productivity of labour than our capitalist 'exploiters'. The communist leaders' concern with productivity had to land them, sooner or later, in management research, and in industrial human relations studies. It is hardly surprising that the lessons laboriously accumulated in the west will be consulted and considered by communist management, if only to save them time and effort. The communist leadership, of course, will assume that they have an obvious initial advantage: theirs is a just and equitable industrial system, and the Western lessons either do not apply to them, or if they do, the lessons are on strictly technical, organisational, and somewhat peripheral gambits of management, useful hints, simple stratagems, which, in some cases, can be adapted to a morally superior situation, the communistic industrial order.

In the area of science and technology the very efficiency of their enterprise dictates that they strictly adhere to the principles of scientific objectivity and rationality. If they allowed Lisenkoist type of pseudo-science to interfere with their productivity or their space-research they would soon come a cropper. The principles of a scrupulous care for evidence, for suspending judgment until verification can be secured, for refusing to reject out of hand – on grounds of some metaphysical-dialectical doctrine – hypotheses, which the evidence may subsequently justify, are slowly becoming complements of the communist professional man's self-concept and role-organisation. Needless to say, there are difficulties and some delays: the ubiquity and weight of the doctrinal control is still there, though it reluctantly has to yield to the priorities dictated by the industrial programme, by the needs of production, and by the desire for prestige. And so, the communist technologist-manager-professional must increasingly seek to do what, according to him, and not so much according to the doctrine, is the right thing to do. The intelligent and insightful handling of human relations and the socio-psychological analysis of the problems of human relations throw up conclusions, or at least tentative observations, or provocative questions, which seem to go beyond the current version of Marxist-Leninist principles.

Generally, if one is to judge from the books and papers written by these professionals, the cracks in the ideological edifice are papered over by slogans almost as mechanically repetitive as the pattern of some wallpapers. Nevertheless, even this solution cannot persist when the obvious intelligence and integrity of the professional worker, the communist writer, demands that the new insight be described and discussed. In spite of some recent signs of a relaxation in the former rigidity of doctrinal discipline, no writer would omit 'saying grace', that is to say, declaring his allegiance to Marxist-Leninist principles, and even insisting that what he is going to say *follows* from, or at least is *in harmony with*, Marxist-Leninist principles.

Let me say at once that but for the loudness and absolutely unqualified conceit with which the moral superiority of socialist production is tirelessly proclaimed, most of us would agree that the principle of 'one for all and all for one' is *prima facie* more likely to be realised in a collectivistic than in a capitalistic system, and that communism presents a moral image which is by definition unselfish, whereas capitalism rests four-square on what it likes to call 'enlightened self-interest'. Clearly there are moral advantages on the side of a collectivistic system on condition that it scrupulously safeguards the freedom of the individual. After all, if the comradeliness of the comrades were genuinely cultivated, they would have at least one advantage over the alienated workers of the west. But images such as these are misleading. The ritual of comradeliness is not enough, the *Volksgenossen* of the Nazis was an image with analogous emotional appeals to the need of comradeliness!

What is a novel development in communist writing is that nowadays, the affirmation of socialist allegiance and loyalty is often followed by a discourse on, or a report of, an empirical investigation which, in its objectivity and empiricism, does not fall below the level of discourses we expect from creditable Western sociologists. The comparisons are easy to make, for, after all, the problems which are discussed by the various specialists of American business schools are often no different from the problems of the socialist managers of factories and business organisations. These problems arise from corporate enterprise and they are not specifically confined to plaguing capitalist enterprise: they have been notoriously well known in socialist enterprise as well. The transmission of Western experimental procedures to the East of personnel management techniques, of organisational gambits, and so on, could be effected without much difficulty if ideological and doctrinal principles were not involved. When a procedure could be taken over *without* the sociological or psychological theory which was associated with it in the West, it would be taken over promptly and would be used. The trouble is that the theoretical strings remain attached and trail behind, in spite of all explicit denials. The so-called 'T-group' techniques, sometimes also called 'sensitivity-training' procedures, were adopted as 'round-table conferences of industrial leaders'.[128] When one examines the records of these conferences one sees that they operate in seeking to advance the insight and understanding of leaders in much the same way as the Western models do, but without reference to the psychological theories which gave rise to these in the West. That these groups are descendants of group-psychotherapeutic and largely psychoanalytic modes of thinking is certainly not realised by the participants and are carefully concealed by the importers.

Perhaps the best way to illustrate the intellectual gambit of the 'importers' is to take an example of communist management literature, and – by citing its theoretical observations – demonstrate that what is being taught to industrial management in communist countries today *is* the counselling ideology, but that it is 'adopted' by Marxism-Leninism, with its true parentage denied.

In a definitive volume on management studies[129] which emerged from a round-table conference of industrial leaders organised for them by the Hungarian communist state, one of the papers explicitly disclaims any relationship with what I call the counselling ideology. The author says that: 'A very significant result of Marxist psychology has been that it has deprived of its *raison d'être* the deep-psychological orientation, which believes in an unconscious influence on behaviour.'[130] Yet in surveying the psychological problematics of leadership and management he explains that workers and employees sometimes react to criticism with 'projection'. He writes: 'Often he (the worker) turns to the well-known psychodynamics of the defence of *projection* which consists in the defender not acknowledging his own fault and in attributing his own unpleasant and often unbearable psychological characteristic or condition to his fellowman, and this to achieve relief from tension'.[131] This is the type of interpretation which may illustrate the gambit of 'accept psychoanalytic insights but make sure that you reject the psychoanalytic theory, in so many words, affirming your loyalty to "Marxist-Leninist psychology", whatever that may mean'. The same writer also suggests that *regression (sic)* is a kind of escape mechanism 'into the past' or 'into illness'.[132] According to this writer, regression can be a response of a fellow worker in the face of a problem, and having explicitly denied the function of the unconscious he now openly recognises the importance of 'self-deception'[133] in the functioning of these very Freudian defence-mechanisms. And indeed he declares firmly that, ' . . . the management of men is work of great responsibility, demanding deep [*sic*] knowledge of men which must not be reduced to an administrative or mechanical procedure'.[134]

It is evident to those who read the management literature of communist countries that they have taken over the ideological orientation of counselling but they insist on calling this orientation by some name acceptable to the party. The philosophical idealism which dictates a condemnation of 'the administrative and mechanical handling of men' does not follow from historical materialism either, but, after all, this has been a very long-standing anomaly of communist inspirational writing and speaking, and this concerns issues which are partly outside the area of my present study.

The officially blessed new sociology of the communist régimes is the sociology of work[135] which, like a Trojan Horse, subverts the security of the doctrinal defenders. The Director of the Sociological Research Institute of the Hungarian Academy of Sciences, Andreas Hegedüs, in his introduction to a standard textbook reader,[136] writes:

There is often contradiction between the science of management and sociology, the former is inclined to regard as progressive all methods which lead to greater productivity without regard to the man! In the face of these excesses it is the role of sociology to protect the interests of man, even when this often incurs the charge of irresponsibility for economics! . . . In economic life the most important task of sociology is to fight off the kind of vulgar economic theory which fondly explains all phenomena in terms of material economic events.[137]

Hegedüs wants to use sociology as a 'humaniser' or 'rehumaniser' of the economic organisation of society. He says so explicitly. Naturally, to keep on the right side of providence, he has 'to say grace' and talk about 'vulgar' economic theory: if one is a communist one doesn't say that historical materialism is invalid; one says that those who believe that it is valid give it a 'vulgar' interpretation and that it is this 'vulgar' interpretation that is invalid. One is not supposed to proceed and confess that a so-called 'non-vulgar' interpretation is no longer historical materialism! One must retain one's good manners and pay one's respects to a materialistic theory, and proceed to use science, social science, in a moral-humanistic, economically costly and even hazardous manner. It is in this same textbook reader that three Russian sociologists report 'Half of the interviewed women workers in the Skorohod shoe factory said that their work's attraction is the collectivity of friendship', and at the same time the authors constantly refer to the 'moral incentive of work', which they locate mainly in 'the socialist production relations', 'the socialist political system and ideology'.[138] The reference to 'friendship', or 'fellowship', or 'comradeship' as an incentive to work is offered in the communist spirit and with the obvious reservation, that those who work under the banner of communism, find this spirit of comradeship ideologically guaranteed. But if so, why consult the Western textbooks for learning about the techniques of contriving an organisation which is favourable to the development of a spirit of comradeship? Why do communist writers talk about the 'humanisation' or the 'rehumanisation' of work-relationships with the help of modern industrial sociology, which is sometimes in conflict with 'conventional economic preconceptions' of communist management?[139] It is also here that a convergence of Western and Eastern thinking arrives at a similar conclusion from different premisses: didn't Hawthorne also attribute significance to 'fellowship' at work? Wasn't this fellowship effective even when there was no ideological support forthcoming to inspire it? And, above all, hasn't this 'fellowship', this semi-religious 'communion', been systematically subjected to group-analytical study, which is one of the fields in which the counselling ideology has been very active

indeed ? In the end, both West and East can be found using the theoretical and conceptual system of counselling to explain, as well as to
advance, 'fellowship' in the setting of work and employment, no
matter whether capitalist or communist.

In another Hungarian textbook on the management of industrial
enterprise the author says: 'It is very essential that the managers, in
handling their workers, each according to the speciality of his own
field, rely on the lessons of industrial sociology and industrial
psychology'.[140] In a paper by four Polish sociologists we find
similar memento: 'the personal, psychical relations are autonomous
welding factors of the plant society'. They further warn: 'In the
development of organisation consisting of human beings we must
not only take note of matters such as the programming of a machine
but we must also consider the human attitudes, motives, and subjectivity of those who take part in the operation.'[141] The study of
these 'attitudes, motives, and subjectivity' proceeds now with
increasing sophistication. Clearly, one cannot engage in a session of
'sensitivity training', and not discuss the most obvious barrier to
sensitivity: defences against truth. But a discipline of truth-seeking is
fatal to doctrine of any kind, and the long-term consequences of the
process of exploration are incalculable. The communist personal
service professionals may manage to keep up an appearance of ideological loyalty for a little while by the double-think device of 'saying
grace' in the preface, affirming all the proper creeds, and then ignoring
them in subsequent chapters, but this is not a device with a secure
future.

A Yugoslav testimonial has reached me through, of all people,
Barbara Wootton. Barbara Wootton regards the 'counselling' ideology
as a collection of pretentions and arrogant assumptions on the part of
professional workers. Lady Wootton herself speaks of the 'ideology of
modern casework',[142] and identifies one of its features as a deliberate
attempt to distract attention from financial, economic, and social
realities of human problems, and a preoccupation with their psychological and psychiatric features. The preoccupation with psychology
and personal relationships is, in her view, only too often a mere
vehicle to give the practitioners an air of self-importance and even of
omniscience or omipotence. Thus Lady Wootton's own reading of
the situation would confirm my conclusion that there *is* a counselling
ideology. Where she fails to follow through the implications of this

ideology is well disclosed by her own documentation: she quotes the Yugoslav (and therefore presumably communist) Pusic, a Professor of Zagreb University, as saying that social work 'endeavours systematically to understand motivation, to accept people as they are, to estimate and develop their capacities for self help'.[143] Lady Wootton quotes this as an example of the psychologistic bias in counselling. It is that, but is it not remarkable that such a bias should emerge in a communist country in which sociological formulas are by no means arrived at by the suppression of economic and financial considerations? Is this not, in fact, a document to show that Lady Wootton is less appreciative of the modern counselling technology in human relationship management than a communist thinker? The so-called personal 'enabling' attitude based on a study of the client's motivation is not one that was conspicuously enjoined by Marxism-Leninism.

I could go on with this documentation by producing weighty testimonies from the literature of management. It is surely not necessary to count the words, the paragraphs, the chapters, to speak of 'evidence'. It would seem to me hardly in doubt that the obvious regard for profit and status is powerfully countered by notions, propositions, and values of management which are inspired by, or even spelt out in the clinical literature of counselling. In our times, in the West, this seems to be a large part of the intellectual and moral regimen of the staff officers of business leadership, no less than it was shown to be a large part of the regimen of paedagogical facts and precepts for our teachers. In my previous book I laboured to show that this was certainly the guiding influence in the training of the counsellors themselves, and I also showed there that via psychological medicine, there were some significant over-spills into the area of general medical practice. And now, in this book, I am trying to show that the whole personnel of the personal service professions has been persuaded to observe certain standards of judgment about both facts and about values, standards which would not have evolved from earlier standards, Christian or scientific, standards of *practice* long respected for reasons entirely unrelated to the modern findings and tenets of a clinical and socio-psychological science. The outcome of all this is a momentous though incipient change in the quality of leadership in most types of modern society.

3. The Moral Reformation of Leadership in a Personal Service Society

A. ROLE-PLAYING AND PERSONALITY

The reader will have noticed that when I am relieved of the role 'social scientist' I seem to approve of the way I expect society to change, and I seem to believe that 'the momentous change', I mentioned just now – no matter how slow – will be to man's advantage. The disillusioned, the sceptical, or the merely tough-minded will, no doubt, express his distaste at the sight of my complacency. My relapse into some kind of a naive belief in progress – much like that entertained by our ancestors who were, of course, not so well informed as we have since become – will be viewed with much disapproval. At any rate, the sceptic will reject the idea that the professional workers have the necessary and unusual enough qualifications to effect a moral change in society. For the sceptic, professionalisation is a mere item in the broad changes which occur in the course of industrialisation. There is nothing seminal in professionalisation that could not be accounted for by the very context of industrialisation and affluence in which professionalisation occurs. Having settled for this indifferent explanation, the sceptic is content that nothing much more is to be said. I will maintain that he is mistaken; that professionalisation has become an autonomous process in the context of industrialisation; that professionalisation has become the contemporary carrier of man's desire to break through the confines of his brief episodic individuality; that professionalisation is a socially accepted secular occasion to depart from the rules of commonsense self-interest to which we are otherwise indoctrinated to conform; that professionalisation has created for us certain specific roles in which we can safely, and even comfortably, free ourselves from restrictions put on us by competitive self-seeking. Of course, the professional role does not void the self and its inviolable compact with itself: it merely makes the self serve itself in an entirely novel way by making it act selfishly *in an unselfish manner*. Moral progress – if such a thing is conceivable – must consist *not* in the reduction of selfishness, but in its transformation.

Of course, the professional worker's, the serving intellectual's knowledge and skill are obvious sources of reassurance to him about his strength, worth, and virtue. Naturally, he will find himself involved in using his knowledge and skill in, at least, two ways which may cause him some anxiety about his worth and virtue. *First,* he will be much prompted to enhance and display his knowledge and skill in competition with fellow professionals and also to excel in a world which honours and pays for professional knowledge and skill. *Secondly,* he will time and again be tempted to test his knowledge and skill, and through them his own worth, by applying them impersonally to those he is supposed to serve, by applying them impatiently, manipulatingly, and treating his clients as objects, and indeed trying to exercise power over them. The sceptics often remind us of the professional worker's desire for power and status. I feel that there are at least two reasons why this dichotomising into 'love' and 'power' need not sidetrack us. The *first* reason is this: if we are told that all men strive for power, say, social workers, nurses, and doctors, no less than cabinet ministers, generals, and business tycoons, then, at least we might conjecture that there is so great a difference in their respective behaviour when striving for power, and in the kind of power they strive for, as to warrant our regarding their respective acts, as well as their motives for acting as qualitatively different, and indeed essentially different. The *second* reason is that the very dichotomising itself might be invalid: following Nietzsche, we may try to construe all love and concern as gobbling-up and dominating. However, the manifest absurdity of this interpretation drives us back to the insight that if the will to power does not explain and envelop all, 'some autonomous other thing' must be drawn upon for explanations. Sure enough, in social change, power is more dramatic, shriller and, therefore, more conspicuous. Power is more public, and can be exercised over publics, whilst concern is suspect when not private and personal. 'And yet power is real', says James Baldwin, but adds, 'and many things, including love, cannot be achieved without it'.[1]

To clarify what seems for the moment paradoxical and insufferably obscurantist in this preliminary conclusion is the burden of this last section of my book.

Has professionalisation set in motion a moral transformation of leadership in society? And if it has, what is the nature of the change of heart? Is there, in fact, any justification for speaking about a 'change of heart', and are the overt changes in leadership roles – which are nowadays so often coextensive with professional roles – reflections of personality changes as well? Are the roles played *sincerely* enough to spell substantive changes in the human qualities of leadership or do they rarely go beyond merely empty formal changes?

Although my ensuing analysis of the problems in professional role-playing relate mainly to the personal service professions, these problems overflow into the other area too, and are present in the professional stance everywhere. Even if these problems are experienced much less severely and obviously by practitioners in the impersonal service professions they have a certain impact on their positions too, for these professions apply ethical codes to themselves, which they are wont to model on the ethical codes of the personal service professions. That this is so, must have been apparent from the last chapter.

It is mainly in the course of applying these ethical codes to their own professional conduct that the problems of role-playing take on some social significance, and are of some sociological interest. I have already reminded us that these ethical codes often enjoin the practitioner to put the interest of the client above his own; and these codes lay down that to act professionally is partly *to profess* that this is what one aspires to do, and indeed that this is what one is already doing.

'To profess' is to assert or utter or manifestly imply a set of propositions. In the personal service professions the set of propositions is bound to include some such items as these: 'I earnestly care that what I do for you will help you', which implies that, 'I care for your welfare', or that 'I am interested in exploring and understanding your condition', which implies that, 'I am interested in you', or that, 'I am trying to help you to realise your legitimate aspirations', which implies that 'I regard some of your aspirations as legitimate', or that 'I approve of some of your aspirations', or even that 'I approve of you', and, of course, in a number of cases, that 'I like you'.

With some mounting concern we now ask: does the professional worker mean these implications? And, above all, what does it mean that 'he *means* these implications'? To attempt to answer these questions is to attempt a study of *professional sincerity or insincerity*. I propose to approach this study by considering briefly the concept of 'role' in professional practice.

The role-concept is used in contemporary sociology as a 'buffer' between the individual organism and society. First, there is the organism which learns to play roles, and secondly, the roles played by several organisms knit together with other roles thus forming a social system of roles. Indeed, the two processes, the learning of roles by individual organisms and the entering of these organisms into social relationships, are simultaneous. Soon after birth, the very notion of a 'role-free' organism becomes not only an abstraction but an impossibility. A so-called existential wrenching-free from socially defined roles as described by Sartre[2] is beyond our strength. Sartre too often blurs the distinction between 'freedom from conventional roles' and 'freedom from roles'. What he does eloquently establish is an ideal that we, all role-players, should forever strive to scrutinise the conventional roles that are at hand, and while playing them we should constantly amend them, renew them, improve upon them, or reinterpret them, and above all, that we should feel free to change from one role to another. But even this, the discipline of role-revision, the discipline of living up to the ideal of self-renewal, is the playing of a role, and surely, by the same token, a cultivation of existential freedom too is a cultivation of a role.

'Whenever one chooses in an act of will to subject himself to the demands of a role, there is inauthenticity.'[3] This is an extreme view voiced by some existentialists, the view according to which the very act of 'playing a role', any role, is an act of insincerity. For example, Heidegger regards all the residues of social learning as 'inauthentic', as artificial accretions of the authentic self, and Sartre's notorious 'hell is the others' conveys the same sort of message for, if the others are hell, the only roles we can learn from them are those of the devil. (Of course, many a man has been able to play infernal roles with total sincerity! 'One can "spontaneously" commit murder and "authentically" press a guided missile button'.[4])

It is an implication of the 'all-the-world-is-a-stage' view, that the world is false, the world always prevaricates, and all is shamming. The existentialists tend to maintain that 'the authentic self' – whatever that may be – can and will rebel against this. Conformity to social norms is an enemy of authenticity for this entails violation of the central – though elusive – core of the individual. According to this conception conformity and sincerity do not go together, and the role-players who conform have resigned themselves to the role of a life-long confidence trickster.

In general, genuinely 'role-free organisms' are either gravely defective or totally unconscious and vegetating individuals who might be kept alive only by the gratuitous brilliance of modern medicine. A minimum of intelligent imagination is required if the individual wishes to assume a role. From the earliest childhood the organism plays roles: it learns to play any of a number when it is prompted by its own needs or by the demands of the environment. As it grows older, it builds up a repertoire of roles, and soon it has one for every occasion. If a new kind of occasion arises for which its wardrobe of roles hasn't the appropriate garment, the individual personality will soon cast about in its social environment, and having located a suitable model, copies it. The very notion of a *personality* may be defined as a system of roles learnt by an organism. It is, of course, understood that the way in which the learning occurs and the way in which the roles are played are powerfully and constantly influenced by the organism.

Existentialist psychiatrists and psychologists sometimes write of the 'personality' or of the 'self' as stratified or stratifiable into so-called 'inner division' on the one hand and 'false', outer, put-on divisions on the other.[5] The clinical picture they draw is vivid and appealing enough, and has achieved some popularity. But those who have assimilated its conceptualisation have either overlooked their blatant mysticism, or their intellectual obligation to relate it to their positivistic notions. Laing, for example, writes about this 'inner self', about this inner core of the personality, as if it was some holy of holies, originally impeccable, and corrupted only by the wrong kind of learning. Yet the more one studies Laing's clinical accounts the more one is made to depend on well-known Freudian assumptions about the self. Laing quotes Mallarmé's '*L'enfant abdique son extase*', and translates this as 'having lost our experience of the spirit'. It is not at all obvious that when we say the child abdicates his ecstasy we mean by this that he abdicates his spirituality![6] Nor has spirituality an obvious place in a positivistic-mechanistic universe, which Laing and other psychiatrists invariably postulate for the purposes of the everyday etiologies. Some people, anxious to keep out the cold, wear a white laboratory overall on top of their cassock. One should be charitable and not mind. I only wish that they would not go about with an air of wearing a casual lounge suit only. The truth is that the infant begins to learn primary roles in the simplest of social situations which is the mother-child relationship.

These primary roles of childhood form themselves into either a unitary or a divided system. The later secondary roles will be aligned, according to the Freudians and many other determinists, in a correspondingly unitary or divided manner. If the self is to be described poetically as 'divided' it is not obvious that the division is between a mystically 'authentic' or 'true' or 'essential' or 'genuine' *inner self and a self-imposed false self.* It would seem easier to surmise that the division is between roles and role-systems which are incongruously or incompatibly juxtaposed, and which are expected to function harmoniously in spite of their incompatibilities. I am certainly not averse from considering the possibility of some legitimately construed core concept of the personality in metaphysical and even mystical terms. In fact, the total orientation of this book is not discouraging to those who would like to move in such directions as these. But I find it somewhat tiresome to have to face *psychological* and *clinical* theories, put forward as *scientific* theories of the personality, theories which blithely enunciate mystical and metaphysical principles as their foundation, and to have to be content with a mere enunciation however passionate.

If I look beyond the 'learned role system', *science* does not allow me to see anything more than the organism. Perhaps the living and receptive organism waiting to absorb the complex and culturally construed roles is the carrier of a principle which is already superorganic. I don't know. Nor can a scientist of personality afford to assume that he knows.

Here I am not concerned with estimating the relative significance of the inherited and congenital organism as compared with what it acquires in the form of a system of learnt rules, or indeed with assessing the organism's power either to veto some roles or to foster others. The organism is a mere potentiality which grows into a 'personality' through the process of learning to play roles, and by the acquisition of a collection or system of roles, any one of which it is capable of assuming. This point of view is vividly – though somewhat naively – expressed by Peer Gynt, when he tries to find the soul of an onion by peeling off one layer after another. At length he is obliged to accept that there are only layers and nought else. One minor and one major reservation is called for here. The minor one is this: it may be claimed that we learn simple responses which do not attach to any one role, or attach to several at the same time, and that these too are constituents of what is called 'personality'. Whether this is so, I do not wish to argue here. What matters to us in the present context is that these responses are either embryonic roles or become integrated into existing roles anyway. The major reservation is this: whilst the architecture of the onion does not suggest a hierarchy the architecture of an individual's role-organisation may become dominated by a single central role – a cardinal role – of the personality.

Every time this 'role-system-carrying-organism' chooses to pivot itself on one particular role or, to put it simply, every time the individual chooses to play one of its roles, the network of the remaining roles stays in abeyance. Meanwhile the complex system of these roles accommodated by the organism watches over – controls even – the individual playing its chosen role. By now, the organism itself lies in the background, and the thick layers of roles have built an impenetrable barrier between it and the outside world. There is no such thing as a virgin organism continuing to act as a host, a guardian, let alone a controller of the role-system as a whole or of the playing of any one particular role. The role-player is controlled by the *totality of the roles* he has assimilated to date, or which he is in the process of assimilating, or indeed, even by those which he has just begun to assimilate with deliberate diligence.

As I have already suggested, the role-system is not a democracy of roles, a system in which the roles have an equal influence on the system, a kind of 'one role, one vote'. There are roles which dominate the role-system, and others which are either secondary or even marginal in their influence on the system as a whole. For example, the role of 'mother' usually presides over a role-system which may include such usually second-class citizens as 'neighbour', 'niece', 'graduate', 'secretary', 'member of the W.V.S.', and so on, as well as influential citizens such as 'Christian', 'daughter', 'professional woman', and others, last but not least, 'wife'. Of course, there is often a precarious co-chairmanship between 'mother' and 'wife', and other pairs of roles may co-exist in various measures of equally matched disharmony. Much has been written about the so-called role-conflicts already, and though professionalisation gives rise to some such conflicts, this theme does not lie near enough to the path I am about to follow here. But the other theme, that the role-system is hierarchical and that the presiding roles may 'expropriate' the personality is of first importance to me here. This is what I must now consider in some detail.

It is a commonplace observation that teachers can be painfully schoolmasterish when at home, that lawyers are sometimes insufferably legalistic on occasions which require no legal scrutiny whatsoever, that soldiers retain their military bearing when in mufti, and generally, that professionals find it difficult to come off duty. It would seem that the two subjects, the hierarchical arrangement of roles and the influence of roles on the personality as a whole, meet here: the dominant roles have a way of colouring or contaminating the cognate roles or even the role-system as a whole, and, in doing so, they tend to change the character of the whole personality. 'It is probable', writes Theodore Caplow, 'that professors are more absent-minded, reporters more cynical, chefs more excitable, and policemen more brutal, than an examination of their Rorschach scores would suggest.'[7] This is a more conservative appraisal of the depth to which the role-inspired change of personality can reach. There is no way of discovering whether, and to what degree, the Rorschach scores themselves may well change as a result of the playing of these occupational roles, and to what extent these roles were chosen *because* the erstwhile Rorschach scores differed, that is, *because* the erstwhile personality differed.

'The work life invades the after-work life, and the sharp demarcation between the work hours and the leisure hours disappears. To the professional person his work becomes his life. Hence the act of embarking upon a professional career is similar in some respects to entering a religious order. The same cannot be said of a nonprofessional occupation.'[8] The overspill of the professional concerns into the global life-structure of the individual is matched by the channelling of the global life resources into professional activities. This is not something which we have on sufferance. Most professionals wouldn't have it otherwise and are proud of their unity with the role. Dr Lydgate of George Eliot's *Middlemarch*, for example, reproves his wife for claiming to love him and maintaining about his medical profession at the same time that ' "I do *not* think it is a nice profession, dear". "It is the grandest profession in the world, Rosamund," said Lydgate gravely. "And to say that you love me without loving the medical man in me is the same sort of thing as to say that you like eating a peach but don't like its flavour. Don't say that again, dear, it pains me." '[9] A testimony of a professional which could not be bettered: his person has no substance which is not coloured by his avocation. It is not only that the person is 'contaminated' by the profession but also that the professional role absorbs much of the person's essential ways of expressing itself. This may seem to be a 'two-way process' but experimental psychology has so far concerned itself only with the influence of the role on personality.

The literature attesting to the extent and depth of this kind of influence has been much growing of late. We have now experimental evidence to show that the prolonged occupation of any role in a social system affects the individual's thinking, feeling, and behaviour.[10] Role enactment can be shown to produce changes in somatic processes, in performances, in attention deployment, and in cognitive dispositions.[11] One might bluntly say that role-playing can change, and even mend or destroy an organism. Just 'to speak the part' may change our attitude and opinion. 'Overt verbalisation induced through role-playing tends to augment the effectiveness of a persuasive communication. This outcome seems to bear out the notion that "saying is believing" .' In essence, we are often taken in by our own propaganda. The personal service professional may only 'go through the motions' and repeat certain verbal formulae which he has learnt to regard as appropriate in a person-to-person professional situation, but these near-automatic responses are cues not only to the client but also to the professional practitioner. When, on the other hand, he performs with some deliberate effort to succeed in achieving some professional objective, when, that is, he is not functioning absent-mindedly, or in a mere routine manner, but with a special effort, improvising and creating fresh ways in which he proceeds, the effects of this on his own opinions and attitudes are even more impressive: 'The "improvisation" hypothesis asserts that people tend to be especially impressed by their own persuasive efforts when they are stimulated to think up new arguments and appeals in order to do a good job of convincing others.'[12] The creative adaptation of a role or indeed the invention of a new role requires inspired efforts, the power of which automatically ensures the credibility of the role both to the role-player and to his audience. One of the clearest statements of the processes, which I think are of the greatest importance if we are to understand the social impact of professionalisation, is contained in a paper by Elms and Janis. They write:

> It has been observed that many people, when complying to role demands, express the prescribed attitudes and values even though they do not privately accept them. Less frequently observed has

L

been *the transformation from outer to inner compliance that seems to be a central feature of role adaptation* – a gradual change whereby a person comes to accept privately the beliefs and value judgments that he has expressed publicly while playing the expected social role[13] [my italics].

It is an especially compelling notion that 'inner compliance' is to be regarded as the condition of adaptation to a role! Elms and Janis were concerned to study the conditions which were favourable to this inner compliance – here I need not even consider their detailed analysis any further, and the controversies into which they and others have entered: for above the details and the controversies there is a unanimous agreement on the personality-moulding power of the role, and this alone is of significance to the present argument. Here we needn't seek to settle the dispute between those who think that 'self-persuasion' is prompted by incentives and bribes, or by sponsorship, or by reaction formations, or by dissonance reduction. What matters is that 'self-persuasion by role-playing' is the most powerful agent of lasting change in both the individual and in the cultural-moral texture of society as a whole. This self-engendered and volunteered contribution of the role-player to the stock of ideas, valuations, formal expressions, and the like, heightens his own involvement in the role which he is so strenuously trying to do justice to. The so-called 'Faustian man' resolves to seek values which are in the role, but not as yet in his person, and by sheer willing – be it even called autosuggestion – he hopes that the values will become personally binding and real. As Goethe put it, 'For a man to achieve all that is demanded of him, he must regard himself as greater than he is.' All attitudes begin with attitudinising. This may sound cynical but it isn't. Man's resolve to make reality out of fiction and his ability to achieve this do not encourage a cynical or sceptical view of man. The power of the role over the person is great and lasting enough to bring about changes in personality or in certain attitudes imprinted by other roles previously played.[14] Complementary to this resolve, to embrace and assimilate role-values, he must fight off tendencies against scepticism, against doubt of his own sincerity, and this fight is sustained by the resolve 'to suspend disbelief',[15] to set aside the incredulousness about one's capacity to change. The greater the incredulity that has to be overcome by a strong commitment to play the role the greater the likelihood that there will be almost an 'idolatry' of the role, or a perfectionist and obsessive striving for the realisation of a plausible role: but this is a marginal instance. Normally, roles are pace-setters and pace-makers and the rank and file of role players slowly and steadily almost absent-mindedly metamorphose into roles and transform their role-playing personalities gradually and undramatically.

Of course, this transformation of the personality is, in my parlance, a transformation of the individual's total role system. The collection of prominent roles, which constitute the 'leadership' of the personality-system strikes the observer as the 'profile of the personality'. The transformation of the personality is first affected along the lines of major dimensions such as, say, *ascendency*, in terms of supervisory, commanding, paedagogical, or judgmental role-features, or *submission*, in terms of self-denying, complying, accommodating, pleasing or flattering, role-features. There are indubitably certain generic qualities in the roles played which transfer themselves earlier and more effectively than others. These qualities become 'generalised into an "identity" or self-concept' of the individual.[16] It is not only that the whole role-system has now changed but, understandably, with it the individual's self-concept has changed as well. 'He has indeed changed since he became a Justice of the Peace', is not the impression only of his friends and acquaintances, but he himself feels that he has merged with the role, has got married to it, as it were. He does not seem to be able to play other roles in his repertoire without a self-sense of the fellow who is a Justice of the Peace. He will carry over some of the flavour of judgmentalness, or at least judiciousness. Often enough his self-assurance will appear magisterial and pompous. Of course, the role-system of the personality may not welcome the intrusion of an authoritative role and the countervailing influences brought on by, say, 'a man of humility', may result in all sorts of combinations and hues of playing the role of Justice of the Peace. The role reluctantly adopted may even fail outright – but this is an extreme case. In ideal circumstances a well-tempered stance of authority will evoke a pleasantly hybridised role. When, however, sharp or lumpy fragments of either the one thing or the other appear on their own, it would be idle to pretend that the alloy of the new role is homogeneously cast. Those who play any role which has had to be superimposed on an unaccommodating role-structure are all subject to experience any one of these outcomes or intermediate variations of them. There are some characteristic gambits of defence open to the role-player who is having difficulties. For example, the role-player may jokingly and self-deprecatingly confess to his fumbling attempts at concealment of uncertainty: but even here, there are difficulties in distinguishing the man who is spontaneously amused by his own gawkiness, and the one who has learnt to play the role of being spontaneously amused by his own gawkiness, and learnt it because laughing at one's own expense is rewarded in the culture in which he lives. In the ultimate resort it will depend on the credibility of his performance whether this gambit succeeds in solving his problems of role-playing. And as Goffman noticed too, credibility of performance depends on how credible the performance is to the performer. 'When an individual has no belief in his own act,' wrote Goffman, 'and no ultimate concern with the beliefs of his audience, we may call him cynical, reserving the term "sincere" for individuals who believe in the impression fostered by their own performance'.[17] This passage invites further clarification. Is 'belief in his own act' the same thing as 'belief in the impression fostered by his own performance'? The second of the two may include the first: one can have a belief in one's own act without believing in the impression fostered by the act. Rather like Oscar Wilde saying of one of his first nights, 'The play? it was a success, but the audience was a failure.' Also a virtuoso performer wearily addressing a naive and credulous audience may have belief in the impression fostered in the audience without having a belief in the act itself. Clearly, the two criteria will have to be telescoped somehow. Sometimes we play roles and pretend to be what we are not, because this seems to be the only way of finding out what it is like being in that role. We simulate a real life situation in order to study that situation. And even in a case like this we are enveloped by the fiction we have wilfully enacted. In simulated air defence experiments 'crew members become deeply involved with the organisation's goal and its successes and failures . . . crew members reported restless nights and bad dreams – attackers boring in without an interceptor available . . .'[18] In fact the method acting of war game players is a requisite to the accuracy of their lab-work! This is a good practical illustration of Pindar's 'become what you are!'

Unfortunately the terms 'belief' and 'concern' in Goffman's statement are hopelessly subjective and inaccessible, and therefore it would be necessary to separate these two concepts and see whether we could identify objective indicators for them. Let me, therefore, start afresh, having been thus alerted by the difficulties encountered by others.

'That man is insincere!' is an observation which is provoked on occasion when the behaviour of a man is judged by us as not truly reflecting the personality which we felt obliged to infer from his behaviour on other occasions. It is not that 'acting out of character' is acting insincerely: many an act which appears to be out of character is not truly 'out of character', for we have had small indications and unconsciously noted signs that an act of this sort might take place. And for this reason, though we may call an act 'out of character', we wouldn't necessarily deny its sincerity. Of course, we have never the advantage of a totally computed record of all the stimulus-response sequences of an individual's previous life. No empirical evidence can be more than a hopelessly remote approximation of a complete record. We normally rely on other indicators which are also in a way empirical and objective. The role the individual plays, and the way he plays it, require of him a display of sentiment, or at least an implication of sentiment; but the rest of his role-system, and especially its dominating roles, either preclude this or, at least, by virtue of their established strength, contaminate the current performance. The result is that what is being displayed is inescapably adulterated with what the role-player tried *not* to display. 'Not truly reflecting a man's sentiment' thus means that in all cases of insincerity we are conscious of observing a discrepancy between the role-player's total role-system (personality) and the concrete role he is playing in a specific instance. This discrepancy *is* the criterion of insincerity.

Yet we are still nowhere near a relatively concise definition of sincerity–insincerity. Perhaps it will temper our impatience if we remember the view – a plausible-sounding view – according to which the search for a definition of sincerity–insincerity is foredoomed to failure: as Sartre put it, the ideal of 'sincerity' is utterly nonsensical for 'to be sincere . . . is to be what one is', and 'that supposes that I am not originally what I am'.[19] Just the same, certain criteria of insincerity can be distilled and I shall try to discover whether they add up to a working definition.

Consider the following situation: we might be wrong in calling a medical man insincere who, believing himself unobserved, puts down an Agatha Christie thriller before finishing it, and picks up the current issue of the *Lancet* instead – even when from our personal knowledge of him we might be encouraged to conjecture that he would rather have continued with the former and would rather have indefinitely postponed perusing the latter. But, if we saw the doctor promptly exchanging his reading matter upon our entry into the room we might, in some instances, have cause to believe that he acted as he did to impress us, to conceal his preoccupation with the lighter pursuit.

The difference between the two situations is that in the latter case there is clearly an act of communication, a representation, in fact, *misrepresentation* of preference, a misrepresentation of sentiment. If our arrival merely coincided with the act, and if our presence did not motivate the switch, we would have no reason to construe the act as an act of communication or representation, and certainly not as one of misrepresentation. We might then conclude that where there is insincerity there must have been some form of communication or representation.

When we talk about the 'sincerity' or 'insincerity' of a communication we mean that a sentiment is being displayed and that this sentiment has a certain characteristic. In watching the display of sentiment we feel that there are objective signs from which we can assess this characteristic. Relying on these we may conclude that a sentiment is being displayed not because it is experienced but because it is socially valued. The communicator expects some advantage from making us believe that he feels in a certain way. Hypocrisy is not greatly different from ordinary insincerity: it is only a special case of it. One might call it 'high-principled insincerity', an insincerity which is more pretentious because it not only claims the sentiments but also the articulate belief in principles and values which is supposed to excite them.

It is a literary and philosophical commonplace that no experience, and for that matter, no sentiment can be totally and perfectly communicated. The poet, the artist, are capable of richly and powerfully evocative communication of sentiment, but it is also well known that the poet or the artist in general may be merely 'toying with' the sentiment himself, and that it is extremely difficult to decide what we mean when we say he actually *experiences* the sentiments, which he so effectively transmits. The artist is a professional evoker of sentiment, and the personal service professional, at his best, is an artist in evoking sentiment. In both, sincerity depends on skill, even virtuoso skill, which is inseparably bound up with single-mindedness. By single-mindedness I mean the resolve to make the point without any sign of reservations, without any detectable sign of distraction, or of a failing of attention, indeed, the resolve to give several objective signs that the communicator is personally involved in making the point effectively.

It is one of the contentions of this book that the playing of professional roles, especially the personal service ones, imposes a psychological discipline on the role-player, a discipline of guarding against reservations, distractions, and any lack of personal attention. It is unnecessary for my present purposes to intimate that this discipline is self-imposed because of some mystical vow of loyalty.

Nor is it necessary for me to prove that *all* personal service professionals comply with the discipline or that most of them comply completely. The usual gambit with which my propositions are countered is to put them in a sweeping form and then show how ridiculously sweeping my propositions are. For example, in his 'comment' on a paper of mine Professor Sol. L. Garfield wrote among others that he questioned 'whether *all* personal service professionals are *completely* sincere with their clients . . .'[20] Of course, the italics are mine but not the naive exaggerations. The professionally helping man is still recruited in a singularly unhelpful culture. Only few of our leaders were trained in the second half of this century in which the more marked features of what I am describing can be found. Though the growth in man's aspirations to help is slow and rhapsodic I claim to have plotted an initial rise in the curve of growth, a rise which is sociologically significant in many ways, but not as yet one which has rendered cynicism or, at least, scepticism intellectually dubious. The entirely prudential observation that the job cannot be done without a total application of the self, or that an absent-minded doing of it can become stressful or even painful will suffice to impose the discipline.

In the 'classical' personal service case, that of the counsellor, the transition from learning a professional skill to changing one's personality is engrossing to watch. In an account of this phase of the training of psychiatric residents in the Boston Psychoanalytic Institute we read, 'In the process of absorbing this therapeutic stance, the residents – new to the world of strong affective interchange with patients – often stand in awe of the emotional elasticity and range of response shown by some of their seniors. They now wish to identify rather with their senior figure's warmth or empathy than with his diagnostic brilliance or his command of the literature.'[21] And let there be no pleas that this is a marginal case in an 'esoteric' setting! There are important analogies in the training of all personal service professionals.

In answer to the question, 'Does the professional worker *mean* the implication of concern in personal service?' we will reply that he has certainly resolved to mean it when he resolved to play it. To play the role, he resolved to dismiss reservations, doubts, and inattentions which would have interfered with his total personal application to do the job. Naturally, the strength of his resolve, its inclusiveness, and its perseverance will be variables and the measure of his sincerity will be defined in their terms. Culture, which defines the professional role, will define the style and strength of this resolve in general and the individual variations will, on the whole, remain within the culturally fixed latitude. Of course, there will be individual innovations and plain deviance.

B. THE MAXIMISATION OF PROFESSIONAL VALUES

When the personal service professional works, he has to resolve to *perform* a role of empathic consideration, that is, a role of concern. In his experience and judgment this is necessary if he is to be professionally helpful to the client. While using his personality in a specifically instrumental way, he, not unlike the actor on the stage, makes a dedicated effort to *perform* according to his best judgment. Society, like the scenario and the stage director, defines the roles it expects us to play. It goes without saying that it wants the best possible performance it can get. And here stands an important signpost for us: in most definitions of the concept of 'role' we find that social psychologists call it a system of 'expectations', or of 'norms' of behaviour. These norms, more often than not, carry with them injunctions to realise as much of the role-values as possible. Now, complying with 'expectations' and 'norms' is not a simple 'task-completing' activity. It is not a simple matter of matching a certain number of finite measures or acts, which the role prescribes; it does not mean just doing so much and no more. Role-values imply the perfectionist notion of *ideals* towards which one is invited to strive, and to which one is expected to approximate, as much as possible. In the roles of personal service especially, the resulting 'aspirational behaviour' presupposes a kind of moral greed, an attitude which excludes complete satiety with what one has managed to achieve. At any rate, in the case of the personal service professions, there always seems to be at least some open-endedness about what the role-player has to do, though we often come across the phrase – even here – that 'I have done all that has been humanly possible', a plea which society accepts because it, like a *cri de coeur*, affirms that an aspiration to do the maximum has been at work. It is implicit in society's acceptance of this plea that the role-player should testify to having exerted himself to a maximum degree.

Originally, apart from working in the more mercenary types of medicine, to become a personal service professional has never been the best way to enhance one's income or status. On the contrary, to become a teacher or social worker has spelt in most countries a life-long frugality and shabby respectability. At the same time to choose the path of the personal service professions has been to will a kind of self-enhancement, which consists, to some extent, in the enhancement of the selves of others. Having so chosen the choice must be sustained with resolve and the resolve must be renewed from time to time. There is no guaranteed proportional increase in either money or status as incentives for this renewal.

Yet, in the comparative absence of adequate incentives of this kind, the resolve continues to press on the personal service professional. Perhaps it is a mere stubbornness to continue with what one has started, the compulsiveness of 'task-completion' of which the *Gestalt* psychologists have told us so much. This *Gestalt* answer is unconvincing because it tells us nothing about who or what does the completion. It simply postulates that gaps must be bridged, and that systems compulsively close gaps. 'Compulsively'? But why compulsively? The truth of the matter may be that the system which does this closing-up of gaps has an immanent conception of states 'without gaps', and an immanent anticipation of these states. It may be a criterion of a system that the image of 'closure' attracts it. For want of a better word I don't mind calling this conception and anticipation '*dynamic*', because it is a quality which drives the system on to a constant flow of responses in the direction of repairing a breech or completing a circle. Task-completion is not an empty or a colourless process and objective: it is of the very essence of the living process. Maximisation is merely a cultural recognition of the presence of this striving, and all kinds of perfectionism and idealism are merely cultural formulations of this process. The will to amplify our sense of living cannot be bribed into silence by large gains of money or status though in most known cultures, these clearly symbolise for many a success in this amplification of the self. In fact the will to force the pace or at least to sustain it continues, when no further rewards of money or status can be expected. This is a well-known, and even a commonplace, phenomenon in all walks of life – not only in the personal service professions – yet the sociological significance of this is consistently underestimated. When the middle-class or upper-class man gratuitously overworks, the effort is explained either with reference to status and prestige, or just inertia; work is done merely to avert boredom. It is little noticed that culture encourages this overwork by waving the flags of diligence, of giving and not counting the cost, of service, and the like. Culture defines the situation and the role idealistically and the role-players comply and aspire. The image is usually incorporated in perceptible symbols and the role-players respond to the symbols like the rodents of the psychological laboratory respond to the conditioned stimuli. 'The ideals' thus become 'the causes' of actions even when they are rationalisations and ideologies. The culture itself is the soil in which the ideals are generated and kept alive. Cultures, in this way, become the context in which maximisation, already provided for in the germ cell, is formalised and facilitated for us.

That in the beginning there was the word, might be viewed as a psychological proposition: the word is stimulus to which man's action is a response. The 'word' describes an ideal, and beckons to man, drawing him out of himself. Man, on his part, has a native desire to be so drawn out. The process which ensues is maximisation. I find that the term of *maximisation*, already used by economists, is a suitable one to describe this quality of role-playing behaviour in the professions and especially in the personal service professions. Most of the professional roles which people have assimilated comprise a dimension, a powerful dimension, a maximising urge, telling the role-player to amplify his role in some respect, to evolve it, perhaps to transform it in the direction either implicit in the role or, explicitly prescribed by the role.

The term 'maximisation', originally used by economists to refer to income and wealth, has undergone some curious changes in contemporary economics. The economists have been obliged to extend the notion of income to 'psychic incomes' and by talking about 'satisficing behaviour' they have appeared to be mistakenly abandoning the notion of maximisation altogether. Herbert Simon, for example, recently suggested that man was a satisficing animal rather than a maximising animal.[22] Certainly, 'maximisation of economic gain' does not explain everything, but this should not dispose of 'maximisation' as a decisive psychological principle. Maximisation of the values of the personality remains a central explanatory principle of behaviour. It was right for the economists to abandon 'economic maximisation' as a sole explanatory principle, but they would be wrong to abandon with it the principle of 'maximisation' altogether. The economists' lingering errors when using this term did not consist in postulating maximisation at all, but in restricting maximisation to material utilities. Man is indeed a maximising animal! At first sight this may seem the same as saying that all men are perfectionists. Clearly that is not true: too many men are evidently not perfectionists; too many of them are sluggish, unaspiring, and apathetic or worse. Yet the sociological student of human cultures, determined (with what is surely a maximising zeal) to get the normative qualities of culture clear, reaches one conclusion with comparative ease: human cultures are *not* created by the sluggish, the unaspiring, or the apathetic! Culture is made by the maximisers and the perfectionists or by any man during a maximising or perfectionist phase of his life. And as the roles are defined by culture, and the rules are laid down in the definitions, so the rules are perfectionist rules; they imply ideals *towards which* the compliers with the rules must strive. Sometimes man also maximises values other than material ones, at the expense of material values. 'Workers may turn down employment opportunities at better pay and with better living conditions, preferring to stay in the community and occupation to which they are accustomed, even if that means living on the "dole" in a "depressed area".'[23] It is tacitly admitted that by maximising our efforts when realising certain values we are merely halving the distance between ourselves and the ideal standard, we are not, in fact, accomplishing a realisation of an ideal standard.

This gives us the chance of conjuring up new ideals, and changing our course as the circumstances demand, when we will maximise our efforts in a new direction. It is strange that sociological theory has not identified and conceptualised the built-in idealism of all cultures. When the Marxist-Leninist state calls a man 'Hero of the Soviet Union' or 'Honoured Artist of the Soviet Union' the honour is functionally analogous to the O.M. or the K.C.B. or the *Légion d'Honneur*. No matter how explicitly anti-idealistic a culture, the very fact of its sustained and consistent functioning entails the constant proclamation of *ideals*. The ideals of anti-idealism do not differ in their psychology and in their socio-cultural trappings from the ideals of idealism. It is of the greatest possible importance that sociological theory recognise the endemic and ineradicable element of idealism in the quality of all cultures and in the creative activities of all men. To say this is not the same thing as affirming a doctrine of moral-philosophical idealism: it is merely stating a proposition about the facts of social life. Lord Simey put the case guardedly and wisely when he explained that a present task of sociology is 'to reconcile the superabundant realism of current social research with the need to make due allowance for the idealism of social policy and action, which are such prominent features of our age',[24] or, indeed of any age. No matter how *wertfrei* sociology is trying to be, the universal idealism of man is a social *fact* which sociology – because of its commitment to an old-fashioned kind of positivism – consistently underestimates. Whether social action is therapy, or reform, or revolution, it is spurred on by an advance image of a 'better' or a 'best' state of affairs, that is, it is spurred on by ideals.

Of course, there has been no dramatic and large scale displacement of the 'economic man' by a new species which has lost interest in economic maximisation, for assuredly, 'man *does* live by bread alone when there is no bread'![25] In these cases he is persuaded to funnel all his maximising effort in the direction of securing bread. And so long as large tracts of the world are inhabited by the hungry and the insecure, my concern and sociological propositions apply only to a small, though evergrowing, portion of humanity. But in our own industrial societies most professional workers, like other workers, are not entirely absorbed in the task of securing subsistence for themselves and their families. Naturally, they will still be determined to earn their living, support their family, and *maximise* their income. Professional-isation does not displace these motives for working and for making exceptional exertions. Yet we must recognise that the introduction of professional values and aspirations leads to a recolouring of these motives in a circuitous and possibly retroactive way: money will get mixed up with status, and status will get mixed up with the desire to be liked, and the desire to be liked by others will get mixed up with a desire for, and a liking of, others. There is also an insidious blurring of differences between the pursuit of personal advantage, which is almost unqualified and openly professed to be the sole or main purpose of work, and the pursuit of personal advantage which is accompanied by the professional's reiterated belief that his job is, and his personal advantage must be derived from, assisting others to secure *their* own personal advantage. His desire to be regarded as nothing less than frank and honest will begin to show itself with simple disclaimers: like the hardheaded business man's ostentatious 'I am in this for profit and nothing else!' The professional might add prestige, status, and the good of his own soul. Of course, even in these self-deprecatory exercises there is a manifest effort at self-purification and self-improvement. Unless he prefers to fancy himself as a cynic – and if he does, he is not likely to remain a personal service professional for long – he would need to believe that his personal contentment depended to some measure on the personal contentment of others. He would also want to believe in his own sincerity, in his resolve to play the role, otherwise he would have to resign himself to a loss of faith in the very thing he is doing.

Erving Goffman calls this effort 'idealisation' in the presentation of the self, that is to say, in role-playing. He quotes Charles Horton Cooley and thus reminds us of how well this effort has been understood for some time.

> If we never tried to seem a little better than we are, how could we improve or 'train ourselves from the outside inward?' And the same impulse to show the world a better or idealised aspect of ourselves finds an organised expression in the various professions and classes, each of which has to some extent a cant or pose, which its members assume unconsciously, for the most part, but which has the effect of a conspiracy to work upon the credulity of the world.[26]

The notion of 'maximisation' closely corresponds to the ideas expressed in this. In this maximisation there is a large dose of the enhancement of the self through what the existentialists call the realisation of our 'essence'. The 'essence' is to be brought into being by the 'deliberate character' of the existential decision which precedes it. In Mary Warnock's exposition of Sartre, ' . . . there is no essential human nature, given in advance. Men are stuck down in the world, and they become whatever they choose to become by doing and feeling what they choose to do and feel.'[27] And, 'a conscious being, on the other hand, is aware of his own possibilities, of what he is not, or is not yet. So it comes about that he can pretend to be whatever he likes, and try to be whatever he likes.'[28] Of course, this does no really break the determinist's closed circle, but it supplies an image of its possibility, and thus it adds the fantasy of indeterminacy to the determinacy of our existence. And one ought not to pause too long to consider whether a rich fantasy of freedom can at all establish a regimen in which we can deliberately and successfully fly in the face of established constraints of which we disapprove. For if culture fosters such a regimen so that we think, feel, and act, in an enterprising manner, then it would be merely a matter of taste whether or no we say that culture *determines* our so-called illusion of freedom or that culture has made us free.

It is, as it were, an essential part of the role-specifications spelt out in the ethical codes of the professions that one is supposed to work away at the role, and by cultivating certain aspects of it, refine it, or at least orient it in the 'ideal' direction dictated by the role itself. There are especially three values which the professional practitioner's role singles out for fostering and, therefore, for maximisation: First, the value attached to securing the maximal possible knowledge and skill for the performance of the task; this leads to the maximisation of *mastery*. Secondly, the value attached to a dispassionate yet maximally sensitive empathic consideration of the client's needs, personality, and circumstances; this leads to the maximisation of a *concerned empathy*, or, at least, of an untiring alertness and openness to experience this. Thirdly, the value attached to the subordination of the role-system to the professional role, an identification of the personality with that role, effected through a constantly perfected 'style' of performance, which credibly and plausibly impresses on the client that the first two values are being diligently and consistently advanced in his interest: this leads to the maximisation of professional *integrity*.

In the impersonal service professions the second of these three values (empathy) is far less in evidence (if at all) than the first (mastery) and, therefore, the efforts required to cultivate the third value (integrity) are correspondingly different. The inclusion of 'style' in the description of the third value does not suggest some empty formality: the value consists in that the style of authenticity shall discipline or suppress in the role system all that is incongruous with it. This alleged imperative to maximise values will be viewed with caution, if not with scepticism, by those who regard the idealising aspirations of the professional as hypocritical acts designed merely to defend and advance his status, power, and income. This is reflected by another practice: in trying to reduce the distance between the maximised role performance and society's sceptical assessment of it, the professional may well be described as one who is engaged merely in 'legitimising' his position. His efforts may well be conceived as efforts directed to squaring accounts, or as merely putting on a show and paying the market price for the advantages of status and income. Interpreted in this way, there would be no grounds for thinking in terms of a progressively sustained effort to 'maximise' values. Those who are set on the task of merely 'legitimising' their position, accomplish their task when the legitimisation is accomplished: but 'maximisation' is never accomplished, legitimation is a finite process; maximisation is interminable. McCall and Simmons take up the well-known concept of 'legitimation' and, when writing of role-playing, give an account of it which somewhat blurs this distinction:

> Because role-identities are idealised and rather idiosyncratic conceptions of oneself, the realities of life are constantly jarring them, raising difficulties and embarrassments for them. As a consequence of this jarring, we are always having to devise perspectives that allow us to *maintain* these views of ourselves, at some level, despite contradictory occurrences. As a creature of ideals, man's main concern is to maintain a tentative hold on these idealised conceptions of himself, to *legitimate* his role-identities.[29]

But to '*maintain*' is not the same thing as to '*maximise*'! Of course, McCall and Simmons did not intend to convey scepticism, but their concept of 'legitimation' lends itself to the concealment of the progressive-aspirational aspects of this kind of behaviour. The concept, 'to legitimise' has overtones of compromise, camouflage, of papering over telling cracks, or just marrying off the bastard's mother to the natural father – or anyone else willing. It amounts to doing what is required, and no more. Meanwhile maximisation, an interminable and cumulative process, exacts untiring efforts to pile up more and more of the cherished values, to build up a credit balance of mastery, of empathic understanding, and of integrity. Professional roles, especially in the personal services, stipulate a kind of compliance which fulfils itself only when it surpasses itself. Here 'overdrive' replaces 'drive', and an excess of both motivation and performance is the norm. Of course, no professional worker can sustain this excess all the time, and most of them will sustain it only episodically, deriving moral self-assurance in between from the highly motivated episodes. The personal service professional not only 'legitimises' his posture, he 'over-legitimises' it. *The role player in this case must keep running in order to stand still.* And even this will not suffice in the case of the maximiser, to whom the Red Queen's wisdom is applicable: 'it takes all the running you can do to stay in the same place. If you want to get somewhere else, you must run at least twice as fast as that.'

What should have been strikingly obvious from the definitions of role-theory has in fact been consistently overlooked. One representative definition will suffice to make this point: Shibutani, for example, writes, 'role-playing consists of *living up to the obligations* of the role that one assumes and insisting upon others "meeting his claims" '[30] [my italics]. But 'living up to' is not a finite process; the realisation of values and of ideals is interminable, not unlike the pursuit of the horizon. Also, to change the metaphor, the process has the odd characteristic that hitting the target one must invariably overshoot it. 'One feels more ardent by kissing, more humble by kneeling, more angry by shaking one's fist, that is, the kiss not only expresses ardour but manufactures it'.[31] Dante had something like this in mind about the deliberateness and wilfulness of sincerity, 'I am one who, when love inspires me, take note, and go setting it forth after the fashion which it dictates within me.'[32] This is the essence of it: one 'takes note' of what 'inspires' one and then one sets forth to enhance the inspiration with presumably no clear idea of an upper limit of rapture in mind. Writing of *The Spiritual Exercises* of Ignatius Loyola, Francis Ferguson says, ' . . . their purpose is to reveal through the techniques of make-believe, the potentialities of human nature and the realities of the human situation. . . .'[33] There is no doubt about the nature of the view put forward here: make-believe is a mere tool, even a tool for unearthing the truth about ourselves, which would have remained latent without the device of role-playing! And, in fact, this is the view adopted by Sartre, when he concluded that 'the desire to play is fundamentally the desire to be'.[34] Far from being an occasion for lessening our authenticity, role-playing is an enrichment of it. Another aspect of this was brilliantly caught sight of by Oscar Wilde, 'Insincerity', he wrote, 'is merely a method by which we can multiply our personalities', and 'multiplying' is extending the scope, the sensitivity and receptivity of the personality – not reducing its reliability. On this showing, all insincerity is embryonic sincerity, some get born and some get aborted. The fate and the outcome will depend on the application of the total personality to the task. And this is just the point, for if there is unreserved application, insincerity is much reduced or may liquidate itself altogether. The notion that the idealisation of role-performance and, therefore, the maximisation of role-values is an essential component of the professional task, is not offered naively. There must be a will, a single-mindedness to assert the minority of my nature in order that it may so amplify even the smaller part of my personality that it will grow to represent most, or all, of my personality, and do so credibly. For the time being, it would seem that the difference is merely this: *there is a determination to become that which I am not yet, but which I aspire to be, whereas in insincere behaviour there is a determination only to convince others that I am that which I am not.* And the paradox I am trying to reveal, a paradox of the greatest social significance, is that even this deception may dissolve, because to deceive others we must deceive ourselves as well in some ways, and if we succeed in achieving this we also succeed in changing ourselves!

Of course, one does not blindly ignore the fact that there are long spells of grey and cloudy functioning during which the personal service professional lives by light, for which he has contrived to store up the fuel between these spells. Or, to change the metaphor, in patches of fog the professional hands over to an automatic pilot: during uninspired times of low visibility automatic guidance is given by some terse slogan which embodies a principle. As a result, the professional can advance towards his goals and ideals with reasonable assurance, even when he is absent-minded, or weary, or sceptical. I have no desire to deceive myself into believing that *all* professional workers are *always* bent on progressively enhancing *all* the three values of mastery, empathy, and integrity. But I do assume that from time to time they do rededicate themselves to these values, and above all, that when they are aware of sluggishness, neglect, failure or even cynical indolence, they also become guiltily and uncomfortably aware of some deep inadequacy, and are strongly impelled to trace their steps to a renewed beginning towards a maximisation of values. I feel that a *cynical or even sceptical denial of being so impelled is a denial that a professional role is being played at all.* Admittedly, amidst the anonymous multitude of workers in the personal service professions there

M

are some who rarely seem to engage in more than repetitive responses to routine professional tasks, or whose maximisation of effort *appears to be* limited to the maximisation of income and status. My suspicion is that – even when aggressively all out for income and status – the role-playing of the personal service professional commits his personality and channels his maximising performance in the direction of other-regarding values. The case is the same no matter how anaemic, or absent-minded, or blasé his professional practice daily sets out to be. Even when he plays the role of service merely instrumentally – going through the motions, as it were – the initial indolence of his personality will be affected by the absent-mindedly assumed pose, gesture, and facial expression. As Martin Buber put it, 'Artifice has so much got the upper hand that the fictitious dares usurp the place of the real'.[35]

Of course, most of the time the role is not played merely absent-mindedly and the artifice is not put on without some resolve. The difficulty we experience is showing where this resolve comes from is undoubtedly great. We are obviously disinclined to believe that what Karl Jaspers calls, 'the will to authentic communication'[36] is capable of self-generation. In this age of science it is especially uncongenial to contemplate the possibility that this resolve can appear without a cause. We find an uncaused, or at least an immaculately conceived 'emergent' hard to accept. It seems to be the proper thing to believe that only an authentic self can will authentically. An inauthentic self simply cannot will authentically, and there's the end of it! Yet, again, the idea or the image of authenticity can be not only familiar but also desirable to the inauthentic, perhaps compellingly so. Slightly adapting La Rochefoucauld one would have to say, 'Nothing so much prevents our being authentic as the desire to seem so!' and authenticity is the only aspect of role-playing which we cannot will into existence. But by willing mastery, empathy, and integrity it may spontaneously arise.

Whether we so will or no, will depend on the heredity and life history of the personality. The sociologist is preoccupied with the fact that this heredity and especially this life history is embedded in a culture which forever moves and changes its models of mastery, empathy and integrity as well as the attractiveness of each of these three attributes. In evolving the institution of the professions culture has placed the life histories of our personalities in an environment in which they are persuaded to reach out for more and more of the three attributes. And this is true no matter whether our man is a doctor in

Chicago or a manager of personnel in Irkutsk, because irrespective of the variations in culture the compulsion 'to reach out' is a quintessentially human quality.

The commerce is then both ways: it is not only between culture and role-players as well as role playing and personality, but also from the basically human personality to the role-definition and from the role-definition to cultural renewal. Innovator role-players are able to change not only roles but also culture.

It is not too difficult to see how closely culture and its social institutions are linked with the roles which make up these institutions. Meanwhile though the power of the roles over the personality is unanimously accepted, it is a disappointing notion and is resisted. We are almost as distrustful of the personality-renewing power of roles as we are of the rejuvenating power of cosmetics or, for that matter, of the genuineness of wigs and falsies. Sidney Jourard puts this distrust aptly when he says, 'we may be fooling ourselves as well as others into believing that we *are* the kind of people we so expertly seem to be'.[37] But to plead that we succeed merely in 'fooling ourselves' is probably arbitrary, and possibly, itself a case of 'fooling ourselves'. To question or underestimate the appropriateness and truthfulness of 'being cast' or even of 'having cast ourselves' comes from regarding that which comes later as less real than that which came earlier. In our psychoanalytic age we shall continue to be tempted by the genetic fallacy: we shall continue to attribute more significance to where it all comes from than where it has come to, more significance to who plays the role, and why he plays it, than what the role does to the role-player. Being obsessed with the antecedents we are blind to the nature and behaviour of the consequents. R. D. Laing tells the story of the patient in a lie-detector who was asked if he was Napoleon. The patient's reply was 'no' and the lie-detector signified that the patient was lying.[38] The autohypnotic power and the self-educative power of the consciously held fantasy, the half or wholly accepted fiction, and also the roles played and identified with, will be ingrained so much as to register electro-neurologically! The mendacious role is so deeply entrenched that the lie becomes truth.

Of course, this is not to say that questions, 'who plays the role?' or 'why is he playing it?' are of no consequence. They are just not focal to my present business. The personal service professional is often one who was once attracted to the career by some impersonal interest in a scientific discipline, and by the prospect of having the intellectual's or the skilled craftsman's fun of being a virtuoso applier of that discipline. Such as these are eventually enticed by playing the role of personal service even when, at least initially, they were disinclined to apply anything but an impersonal science or skill and were indifferent to the attractions of a personal service. It is not that they come to scoff and remain to pray, but they often certainly come to be analytical, manipulative, and mechanical, and remain to be synthesising, global, and personal. The agent of this kind of transformation is not by any means the pure desire to maximise income and status, for inextricably mingled with this desire is the aspiration to maximise mastery, empathy and integrity. There is a kind of conscientiousness and care which surrounds the agent. You might, of course, deny this heroically; but just think of where the logic of this denial would take you and your heroic honesty! If T. H. Marshall is right, that the professional is one to whom the *caveat emptor* does not apply, this is because the principle that applies to him is the *caveat vendor*, which means that the one who renders the service is the one who *cares*.

Initially, in terms of career choice for example, the mixture of motives may betray little, if anything, of what will often have to evolve later. My point is that the professional worker changes the mixture while working, and he does so, often in spite of himself. The categorical 'must' of our value-maximising tendency may have selfish ulterior beginnings but not necessarily, not always, nor always entirely so, because the initial human desire to share, commune, and empathise sustains ethical commands which also strangely command their own self-regeneration.

Now, on the whole, professional attitudes range from cynicism to idealism and so they might not be expected to differ much, if at all, from human attitudes to life in general. One might say that the 'professional continuum' from cynicism to idealism is merely a special case of the continuum obtaining in the general and non-professional world. But whilst the general populace is relatively unhampered by the nature of their vocation when trying to take up their position somewhere between one extreme and the other in this continuum, it would seem to me that the professional surrenders much of his latitude when he becomes professional and is obliged to function in a much shorter continuum! No matter whether he is initially a sceptic or even a cynic, the professional worker is under the scrutiny of a society which demands of him that he consistently advances and maximises certain values. Society explicitly stipulates that the professional worker incorporates in his work the service of certain ideals as an essential part of what he gets paid for, and what he is respected for. Like the stage actor, he too is expected to perform plausibly, and when he fails to do this he is booed. In a free-market society – which may now be much less visible in the world of nationalised health, welfare, and education services – this will lose him clientele; but, of course, even in societies, in which *all* the personal service professionals are employees of the state or of institutions, the free market of prestige, of popularity, and so on, survive to sanction professional conduct.

Admittedly, society defines every citizen's role in idealistic terms; but there is an important difference: for the professional the enhancement of ethical values is an *occupational* task and goal, whilst for the rest of the citizenry it is not.

By having been trained for one of the personal service professions, and to have subscribed to one of the professional associations, the individual has committed himself to a stance, which he can now neglect only at the expense of a guilt-producing, anxiety-fostering, and, therefore, onerous, and even painful, awareness. Of course, not all, and perhaps not even most, would have this awareness: but more and more will be enticed by culture to have it. When one studies the curricula and general cultural orientation of the professional training courses for the personal service professions one cannot help reaching this conclusion. There is no doubt that much that is being taught, a good deal that is stated in the professional ethical codes, and reaffirmed by the practitioners, expresses aspirations or ideals. Meanwhile there are professional workers who manage to live through a wearying career of life-long scepticism – perhaps even putting on an hypocritical show of aspiration from time to time – whilst privately, consciously, and consistently belittling the aspiration and the ideal, and even cynically discounting it altogether. Yet such workers would have to endure the unwisdom of trying to discharge a professional task and at the same time demoralising the very professional role of personal service, without which it cannot be properly discharged.

There is a wide range of testimonies, if not evidence, that this is so. At one extreme, in clinical psychotherapy, we encounter authoritative reports[39] warning us that the therapist's insincerity is promptly spotted by the patient, and that his work can be all but entirely undone by a therapist's lack of genuine care for and interest in the patient. Analogous reports are available from the field of education, nursing, and social casework. At the other extreme, in the world of managerial style, in industry, we come across precisely the same kind of warning. The transparent managerial gambits, aimed at getting cooperation from personnel, expressed by guidelines such as 'Make them feel important, and they will do what you want', are usually recognised a mile off, and provoke not only an immediate negative reaction but also a lasting distrust. No one likes being 'manipulated' in this way, and the resentment created by this sort of lame deception is worse than what some authoritarian or arbitrary command would have elicited.[40] Paul Blumberg, whose concern is with issues of workers' alienation and participation, observes that the workers can't be conned with 'pseudo-participation'. This, he says, 'is merely a short step from being perceived as manipulation which will almost certainly backfire'.[41] In fact, it would not be far-fetched to claim that in the personal service professions insincerity is a sure way to inefficiency. The sceptic, who for ever doubts the professional worker's sincerity whilst continuing to pay his respects to a standard of professional efficiency, must perforce either resign himself to perpetual inefficiency of professional work or concede that he does not understand the things about which he is so sceptical. But the sceptic has never confessed to scepticism about the possibility of mechanical or technical efficiency: his scepticism is moral, and is reserved for the claims, the ideals and aspirations, and for their professed sincerity. The least we might be entitled to say about the sceptic is that a denial of the power of initially unmeant or half-meant affirmations to become fully meant is the repudiation of a verified social-psychological proposition about this power, and not the expression of a moral idiosyncrasy about moral postures! The sceptic says 'never mind that the service has in fact become authentic in the course of its practice. It was lacking authenticity at first, and therefore, scepticism must be maintained even when it has become manifestly untenable.' It is interesting to see the sceptic perpetrating the crime of the 'genetic fallacy' for there is no reason why he should be more sceptical about outcomes than causes! Another disadvantage, complementary to the disadvantage of inefficiency, is that under conditions of insincerity it is also very hard, if not impossible, to derive lasting gratifications from personal service work, the very essence of which is the realisation of personal values for others. There might not be evidence at hand to prove that prolonged and stressful personal service done entirely for money and status is less gratifying than when it is done, to some extent at least, for its own sake; but it does seem probable that an unbelieving and sceptical role-player has to work harder at his professional tasks, and that he must use up some badly needed attention and energy on the job of keeping up appearances, an extra exertion which is spared to the spontaneous performer. Moreover good liars not only require good memories and considerable histrionic talent, but must also pay for being good liars by enduring at least some constant anxiety about the humiliations of being found out.

There is, of course, a popular psychoanalytical explanation of why and how maximisation of attitudes, valuations, and so on, occurs at all. The Freudian defence mechanism of 'reaction formation' is said to be responsible for it all. For example, our fanatic approval of a social prohibition springs from our unconscious desire to transgress it. Here too the idea is the same: we must take out an insurance policy against the risk that the unconscious desire might present itself in consciousness, and to achieve this we maximise our loyalty to the prohibition. The consequent shouting from the roof-tops, or the whistling in the dark, are the outcome of anxiety and doubt about our ability to refrain from doing what we would dearly like to do. Similarly, what we would like to believe and don't, we assert with redoubled emphasis. The Adlerian 'overcompensation' is another version of the same type of explanation: the stuttering Demosthenes becomes Greece's greatest orator and the deaf Beethoven composes and conducts the Ninth Symphony. It is the obliteration of the very defect which creates its complementary excellence. Or as Santayana put it,

> We profess to live up to the fine sentiments we have uttered, as we try to believe in the religion we profess. The greater our difficulties, the greater our zeal. Under published principles and plighted language we must assiduously hide all the inequalities of our moods and conduct, and this without hypocrisy since our deliberate character is more truly ourselves than is the flux of our involuntary dreams.[42]

But there is also another and simpler way of arriving at the conclusion that insincerity in the personal service professions cannot be more than marginal and transitory. According to Leon Festinger it is a universal characteristic of our personalities that we are intolerant of 'dissonance' in our beliefs and desires, and that we are universally impelled to 'reduce dissonance'.[43] The disparity between the publicly professed and practised role and the privately believed role-image can be stressfully great: the 'dissonance' thus created is a burden, and our economising, ordering, and tidying nature compels us to cut down dissonance, and create consonance. 'The knowledge that one's public behaviour does not follow from his relevant private attitudes creates in him the motivational state of dissonance.'[44] And the writer of this adds that Festinger's theory reaches precisely this conclusion: 'attitude change occasioned by role-playing is a dissonance-reducing device, designed to make private attitudes consonant with public behaviour'.[45] According to this point of view one can do one of two things: one can either stop defining one's personal service professional role in 'aspirational' terms, in terms of the maximisation of 'values', or one can lift oneself up by one's bootstraps and try to live up to the aspirational values. The first of these two solutions amounts to a resignation from the personal service professional role, and, therefore, the second course is chosen, on which dissonance reduction is bound to occur. Consonance is approached by raising not only the practice but also the self-image to the level of aspiration, and to what is being professed.

The advantage of citing Leon Festinger's theoretical construction is that it forestalls a criticism: 'maximisation' may readily be taken as a spurious 'dynamic' or mystical notion whilst it is easy to see that in the theory of dissonance reduction there are no allusions to ineffable and ideal categories of thinking. Out of sober self-defence, we make it doubly sure that the reduction is effective and lasting, by strengthening the props of consonance far beyond what ensuring its stability might require.

Man does not like uncertainties nor have his ancestors ever failed to combat uncertainties. They would not have survived if they had not consistently devised defences against ambiguity. These defences have often appeared to be similar to some sort of insurance policy against being faced with uncertainty in the future: man has always tried to lay in stores of doctrine against the disturbing contingencies of cross-roads, conflicts, divided loyalties, contradictions, and all the other breeds of painful decision-demanding situations. Laying in stores of certainty is much more like laying in stores of food for a lean season. Maximisation of economic resources has often been initiated and even sustained by this sort of hoarding anticipation. Maximisation of the resources of need-satisfaction may well be regarded as having an evolutionary function. The concept of 'maximisation' does not therefore appear any more spurious than any of the other standard concepts of the evolutionary theory, such as for example, 'Survival of the Fittest' or 'Natural Selection'. One might say that a species which learns to maximise resources is more likely to survive than one which has failed to develop maximising tendencies. Naturally, a disfunctional or pathological maximisation is easy to imagine or indeed observe: the animal which gorges itself sick, the miser who encapsulates himself in possessions, and cuts himself off from humanity, are maximisers against themselves because they maximise values in meeting certain needs at the expense of other vital needs. The fact of life, that it maximises values, is an evolutionary product, and, in the case of man, also a product of culture. The fact itself is ultimately as much biological as it is social; it is, for all I know, as much moral as it is spiritual.[46]

The term 'maximisation' of values might be better understood in the light of some concrete examples of a relatively ordinary nature. These too are cases of self-generated amplification of valuation and sentiment, and they are not taken from professional life: a deliberate generation of righteous indignation on the political platform, 'working oneself up' to a pitch of frenzy, is one instance; a deliberate surrender to tears and sobs, and a joyful submergence in self-pity, is another; an outburst of hilarity far in excess of what the available mirth-producing cues might justify, is yet another. These, when the maximising effort is excessive, and thus incongruent with the personality's known nature, or indeed congruent with it, but is regarded as 'not seemly' by the culture in which it occurs – are often called 'hysterical' or 'manic' performances. But criticised and frowned upon though these instances are, they represent amplified samples of the general, and therefore usually socially approved, conduct. As a general psychological principle, we may state, that when we mildly – hesitatingly, or doubtingly – feel something, and we wish we meant it strongly and overpoweringly, the wish may be prompted by the need to experience the invigorating and pleasant flooding into us of a single-minded sentiment as a source of security and strength. At the same time, we may also cultivate this exercise as a method of self-transcendence. For all we know this enhancement may well have a straightforward and

raw organic base: the greed of the organism – especially under prolonged frustration – may command, even in animals, that they drive
themselves to excess. Whether this organismic greed is a component
of the progressive enhancement of sentiment, of the self-generated
exaggeration of a feeling, or of a 'moral greed', or a psychological
analogue of the lust for orgasm, I will not try to establish here; but
in man, in a creature of culture, it seems to be a universal mode of
response, especially in the face of uncertainty or ambiguity. The
ambiguity of the professional role is merely a special case of the general
and endemic ambiguity of man's social role. Of course, ordinary man
too has to balance his self-regarding and other-regarding tendencies to
function in society at all, but the professional man has to make this
equilibration an explicit part of his breadwinning activities.

As a matter of fact, all societies, and our competitive society is
hardly an exception, ordain that we maximise the values which the
roles are designed to serve. There is a built-in perfectionism in the
role-playing activity, and culture tirelessly encourages this: it is a
matter of common knowledge that society expects us to behave as if
we were better than we are. We always have to 'live up to' standards
and ideals. We also hold demanding views on morality, and on what
is seemly, and we require of ourselves – not only of others – renewed
efforts to keep in step with our standards and views. Incorporated in
the rituals, ceremonies, and formal proceedings of important social
organs and of institutions are the sentiments of respect, of obedience,
or its complementaries the dignity, the pomp, and the power. Even
garments, insignia, and uniforms are called in to help. 'The wearing
of a similar distinctive dress emphasises the solidarity of the group
and maintains morale. . . .'[47] Thus the uniform, the badges of rank,
and of valour, keep the soldier up to some idealised standard. We go
through the make-believe because we hope to make our aspirations
effect a change in us. It is as if we could will ourselves different from
what we know ourselves to be. The whole system of religious and
moral observances is influenced by this kind of intuitive and shrewd
psychologising. It is ardently hoped that the sentiments of the hymns,
liturgies, psalms, prayers, genuflections, and so on, will become our
spontaneously experienced sentiments. *Sacramentum non solum
significat sed causat gratiam.* The sacrament not only signifies but also
brings about grace.

To raise standards we frequently apply the techniques of forcibly willing and wanting to realise these higher standards. It is a common socio-cultural device to make social functions more effective by deliberately cultivating, savouring, and reflecting on the unselfish and service aspects of these functions. There are observances of respect towards elders, observances of protectiveness towards the so-called weaker sex or towards children; it is hoped that where there was no respect or not enough of it, the mechanical compliance with rules, and the psychological discipline of regarding these rules as good and their purposes noble, will generate the sentiments required. Surrender yourself to the playing of a noble role and the nobility of the role will insinuate itself into your personality. There are, to mention one example, elaborate measures taken to make the so-called 'open prison' do the job of a conventional closed one. As it were unrealistically, this prison pretends to be what it is not, a voluntary settlement or hostel. The purpose is to create a state of mind in the inmates that they are to be trusted, and it is hoped, indeed expected, that the prisoners' actual trustworthiness will actually approximate to the trustworthiness with which they appear to be credited. And – somewhat unfelicitously – this brings me back to my subject, the professional worker. Of course, he sells his professional personal service and receives a remuneration and even a status-recognition in exchange for what he sells. But are we dealing with a market-transaction only? These professionals engage in what I call 'maximising behaviour' or 'aspirational behaviour' by laying down observances and by reiterating declarations which say that the practice of the profession is a personal service, that doing that service is not only a breadwinning activity, and a status-creating activity, but also a meaningful use of the personality for its own sake. This extra, this gain, over and above the fees and the prestige, is enshrined in moral affirmations or assumptions about the fundamentally 'service' character of the professional activity. 'Despite the temptation to adopt C. Wright Mills' cynicism', wrote H. L. Wilensky, 'the norm of selflessness is more than lip-service. It is probably acted out in the established professions at a somewhat higher rate than in other occupations!'[48] Recently Dorothy Emmett aptly observed of the professional workers' morality, 'this may not be the deepest form of sacrificial morality nor in a largely competitive society is it one to be despised'.[49] In all these instances society makes provision for a slow change to take place. The aspirations which are enshrined in vows, in ethical affirmations, and the like, are themselves social facts even if people who voice them are not altogether and always sincere about them. When society elicits from its professional servants these protestations of fastidiousness about motives for work – which could be called 'loyalty oaths' to professional standards – and when these 'loyalty oaths' are publicly and repeatedly sworn, then, even the fact of their partial insincerity does not much weaken their socio-cultural and moral potency as a moulder of standards at large and for all. The professional claims and pretensions are not questioned by society radically because it is not in society's interest to liquidate these claims and pretensions. We intuitively understand that these claims and pretensions have an important social function today. In fact, the roles and functions which imply these claims and pretensions are institutionalised and thus the professional worker's aspirational behaviour is recognised to be, to some extent at any rate, realistic.[50] In the past the models were the saints, and the martial heroes, the holy men, and the brave. But these were too rare, and their performance too difficult to emulate. Now the culture heroes are the professional workers. Whether it is television's Dr Kildare or the suave consultants of Emergency Ward Ten and its all-too-human yet selfless nurses, or the wise social workers, the paternal teachers, the rough diamond police officers of other serials and documentaries, the agents of moral renewal in our society are increasingly, ubiquitously, and yet unob-trusively, the professional workers. We are also treated to their mildly portrayed selfishness, careerisms and jealousies so that the plausibility of their ultimate selflessness be confirmed for us. They are not presented as ascetically moral and therefore their eventual affirm-ation of the selfless professional standards is so much the more credible. And in real life too, when the first protestations and airs strike us as insincere or hypocritical we need not be misled: people will play the noble roles painstakingly until the nobility of the roles rubs off on their very motives. Those who are allowed to cultivate a stance of self-denying and of altruism may eventually progress genuinely in the direction of self-denying and altruism.

Yet there is no doubt that the professional role *is* ambiguous, and that many of us are healthily impatient when faced with the lofty ethical airs and claims of professionals. However, we must concede that the role-playing of being a professional is a *hard social fact*, and a potent behavioural model for the non-professionals, and thus for society at large.[51] If it is true that the personal service professions are engaged in an elaborate ritual of cant, and perhaps even in 'a conspiracy to work upon the credulity of the world', then the trumped-up roles would be discredited as soon as the world learnt the truth about this mammoth confidence trick. The strange thing is that the world cannot afford to dispense with being systematically conned! Of course, the truth is that the world is not being deceived: it demands the professing of values and their embodying in a culturally defined style and ritual, for these acts are vows and promises, they are expressions of intent, and, to a substantial extent, they are commitments which bind the performers of the roles sufficiently to matter not only to the world's comfort but also to its sheer survival. The sociologist's interest in these conclusions is briefly this:

(a) On the one hand, the maximising ethical quality of the commands built into the personal service roles is rooted in a given social reality. The culture which defines the role lays down standards of idealism in spite of its often vociferous protestations that idealism is discredited.

(b) On the other hand, the operation of the idealistic standards through the growth of professionalisation affects the total culture and moral climate of society and constitutes a momentous intervention in the process and nature of contemporary social change.

C. MAXIMISATION, SINCERITY AND SOCIAL CHANGE

Earlier the question presented itself to us with some force: what happens when the professional role does not occupy a dominant position, or at least one of the dominant positions, in the role-system, or when it is not influential enough to transfuse the whole system with its values, or generally when the values of the role-system (the personality) are, on the whole, at great variance with those of the professional role? We now know that the professional role is a maximising one and that it requires a supporting performance, a role-playing performance, which would be difficult to execute in face of a hostile or even of an indifferent role-system. To bridge the gap, constant exertion and vigilant effort is required. This is what Santayana called the 'deliberate character' of our application to the professional role which may energetically suppress the discrepancies, and working away at them over the years, actually reduce, or even eliminate, them.

At least those who are impatient of the notion of a seemingly un-caused 'deliberate character' – a will, that appears to spring from no cause – will agree that this existentialist 'free will' to wrench oneself away from one's origins is flagrantly outside the realm of science and, therefore, of social science. Whether the idea of an 'emergent', an utterly new development – unaccounted for by its antecedents – is logically defensible or no, is thankfully not my present task to explore. As a sociologist I shall be content with an entirely rationalist explana-tion of the origins of this seemingly abrupt 'deliberate character', and will take this resolve to emerge from a limiting and given context of knowledge, of skill, of ambition, of desire.

The practitioners of personal service work out the main lines of the role they have to play if they are to perform certain tasks which they set themselves. They then, however, conceptualise the goals, the ends, and the values, which they are to realise. They do this partly for the purposes of training in the skills and knowledge, partly to communi-cate with fellow workers, and partly to categorise for themselves the sense of what they continue to do throughout a life-time. No sooner have they conceptualised these ends and values than the concepts and the systems of concepts acquire a life of their own because concepts cannot survive in isolation, they must find a home in *theory*; they must be categorised, linked up, analytically explained and also synthesised. In the course of all this, concepts live a life which is not always and altogether at the mercy of social realities. In the long run, the conceptualised values, and the images attached to them, will begin to beckon the practitioners from outside the initially given social realities which originally gave rise to these values and images although they have, by now, acquired an existence to some degree independent of those realities.

Now the individual's experience of this is analogous to the exper-ience of society: what the practitioner picks up as skill, or information, or knowledge, orders itself under conceptual rubrics. Certain human values are going to be mentioned, named, conceptually identified. And soon these verbal flags will flutter in the wind without anybody waving them: they and the images these flags evoke will challenge and *cause* the professional worker to behave in certain ways far beyond the scope of forces which raised the flag erstwhile. It is not a bit illumin-ating to say that there would be no flag aloft without someone first ascending high enough to plant it in a conspicuous position, for the standard bearer does not command the wind and the elements.

It is from these elements, the upsurging humanity and its aspirations, which are – so far as we can know – unique in this universe, that the prompters of the deliberate character of sustained performance come.

This 'deliberate character' in our case is the will diffusing itself through the dominating professional role. This role has now taken charge of the total personality, and so, it can exact from the practitioner that he act in accordance with the idealised role-image even when it flagrantly opposes his almost equally strong and wilful inclination to brush the ideal aside. Even in the 'antiprofessional moods', a 'deliberate character' to play the professional role survives and this makes it possible for the role, as it were, to 'brainwash' the personality. Of course, so long as there are discrepancies between inclinations and resolve, there is a considerable hazard that not only are they perceived by those to whom the personal professional service is rendered, but they also prejudge the efficiency of this service. These discrepancies manifest themselves in professional performance which is sometimes dubbed as 'insincere', 'hypocritical', 'disingenuous', and so on.

'That man is insincere' is an observation which is provoked on occasions when the behaviour – with or without speech – is judged by us as suffering in some way from this sort of discrepancy. Yet the concept of insincerity is too complex to be settled in this cursory manner. There is, after all, an important type of discrepancy between the role played and the rest of the role-system where there is no insincerity; we must first identify this type.

A patient is announced to the consultant who remarks to his registrar, 'that old hypochondriac again!' Soon the patient is shown in. The consultant settles down to listening attentively to the patient's tale and responds to it with the 'deliberate character' of one who is single-mindedly ready to assist, assure, and relieve. Is he being insincere now or was he insincere earlier, when the *persona* he presented to a junior colleague was supposed to be ostentatiously unsentimental, sceptically perceptive, and hardened by experience? Of course, he may have said 'that old hypochondriac again', almost with an affectionate indulgence; then again, he may have said it with evident boredom or even disgust. It is especially in the latter case that the distance covered in a few minutes appears to bridge over a discrepancy. The image of professional perspicuity and discernment he wished to present to a colleague – with a dramatised posture of distaste for malingerers whom, with 'his immense experience', he could spot a mile off – is a role-image, which is promptly and unreservedly replaced by another, not bearing a single trace of the first. Naturally, it would be easy to dismiss the issue by exclaiming, 'good actor!' or, to use Erving Goffman's favoured term 'show', a 'good show!' Yet somehow we are disinclined to brand this performance as insincere unless, of course, the 'show' bears some elements of the previous and discrepant role – played for the benefit of the colleague – and thus fails to be a really 'good show'. Does this mean then that sincerity is a matter of dramaturgical talent, that is to say, those who have talent to act are sincere and those who have no such talent are insincere? And if so, what does this entail? Does it mean that in the ultimate resort, style is all, *for the sensitivity which shapes the authentic style provides the very testimony of its own authenticity?*

Let us concentrate on the transition that took place in the doctor when he switched from playing the role of doctor among doctors to the role of doctor among patients. In proceeding from the first role to the second *he had to resolve to perform* a role of mastery, of empathic consideration, and of integrity. This probably presented itself to him in the simple form, 'Now, let me see, what can I do for this patient?' In resolving to be professionally helpful to the patient, he started using his personality in a specific way, not unlike the actor on the stage, who too would make a deliberate effort to *perform* according to his best judgment. To understand the nature of what he, the doctor, was doing it is useful to take good care that we understand what the actor on the stage is called upon to do. Constantine Stanislawski's account of this runs as follows,

An actor can subject himself to the wishes and indications of a playwright or a director and execute them mechanically, but to experience his role he must use his own living desires, engendered and worked over by himself, and he must exercise his own will, not that of another. The director and the playwright can suggest their wishes to the actor, but these wishes must then be reincarnated in the actor's own nature so that he becomes completely possessed by them. For these desires to become living, creative desires on the stage, embodied in the actions of the actor, they must have become a part of his very self.[52]

Translated into the setting of the personal service professions Stanislawski's words might read something like this: 'The professional worker can subject himself to the institutionalised and codified ethics and etiquette of his professional association and conform to the principles of scientific objectivity, but to act on these rationally and logically he must use his own living desires and make the best use of his own personality.' It would be only too easy to quote Dr Johnson and weaken the force of this argument by saying, 'Sir, are you so grossly ignorant of human nature, as not to know that a man may be very sincere in good principles, without having good practice?' But the essence of professional role-playing *is* the incorporation of good principles in practice! The professional ethics as well as the professional aspirations and ideals must be reincarnated in the worker's own nature so that he becomes completely possessed by them. For the ethical principles to become living and creative principles in practice, they must be embodied in the actions of the personal service professional and must become a part of his very self.

Of course, this will read as an extravagant account, or to say the least, as an overstatement. The sober and staid professional would certainly view it with distaste, and, in fact, almost all professional workers would regard some terms of this account as all too dramaturgical and intensely histrionic. Meanwhile stage actors sense the underlying affinity without perplexity, and even with pride: 'I was brought up in a clergyman's household', said Dame Sybil Thorndike, 'so I am a first-class liar', for – without blurring differences between stage actor and professional – there is one thing certainly common to them both, and this is that the task of role-playing exacts a sustained, purposeful, and curiously progressive involvement of the total role-structure in the specific role which is being played. It is revealing that initially the actor was regarded as a perfectly sincere hypocrite and it is probable that the meaning we have for centuries attached to 'hypocrisy' was the outcome of a loss of wisdom. I am indebted to Mr David Holt for reminding me that 'the noun *Hypokrites* was used of the stage actor from about 500 BC. By the end of the 4th century BC in the speeches of Demosthenes, it was beginning to acquire a negative sense of "to play a false part, to deceive". It was this sense of the word which was picked up in the Greek translation of the New Testament when Christ was describing the Pharisees, and it is this sense with which we are familiar in our modern word hypocrite.'[53] I think that

N

the discovery of hypocrisy came from the discernment of bad acting and not the other way round.

All actors, on and off the stage, feel that they must search their own sensitivities and reject forms of behaviour, styles of performance, which might be a 'bad fit' between specific role and role-structure. Naturally, whereas the professional worker's total role-structure, his personality, is thus enveloped by the same role, the professional role, throughout his whole career, the stage actor commits the whole role-structure, his personality, only very provisionally, and to forever varying roles. For the actor, the only constant role is that he is a stage actor, and this in its colourful and varied way also involves his total role-structure. Both actor and professional may begin by insincerely pretending, but they are both taken in by their own propaganda, and, having maximised the values which they have initially, somewhat reluctantly, or even incredulously affirmed, they now find themselves believing in those values for all they are worth. This is by no means the most charitable account of what is going on in artistic or personal service performances. One could say, as R. G. Collingwood did, that the artist's expression of an emotion is always absolutely candid, and if it isn't, then it is not an artistic expression! According to Collingwood, there is no conscious resolve which precedes the act of creative expression, no resolve to express a certain kind of sentiment. 'For until that work is complete one does not know what emotions one feels,' and so, 'any kind of selection, any decision to express this emotion and not that, is inartistic. . . .'[54] Now just as the artist's sincerity is prejudged by the consciously contrived deliberateness to experience a certain sentiment, so is that of the professional worker. Here too, one might say, that 'until that work is complete one does not know what emotion one feels or, indeed, whether there is any emotion felt beyond pride in a redeeming craftsmanship. And thus the professional does not aim at sincerity of sentiments but at a maximisation of the values of personal service. The sincerity of the performance is an emergent by-product of the performance not its premeditated goal. So, according to this kindlier account, we do not begin with pretending or insincerity but with the resolve to perform competently. And what is most momentous for society, the 'method-acting-personal-service-professionals' are so plausible to themselves, and to others, that society has little cause to pronounce them insincere, which, of course, they are no longer, after the process of maximisation has taken hold of them.

Erving Goffman was able to reach a conclusion which, emerging as it did from his absorbing study,[55] amounts to an important corroboration and should be cited:

> While we could retain the common-sense notion that fostered appearances can be discredited by a discrepant reality, there is often no reason for claiming that the facts discrepant with the fostered impression are any more the real reality than is the fostered reality they embarrass. A cynical view of everyday performances can be as one-sided as the one that is sponsored by the performer.[56]

In the growing area of paedagogical and therapeutic role-playing we come across instances of 'as if', of 'pretending', which are thoroughly sincere, though in the initial resolve they may be contrived and willed. In psychodrama and sociodrama the roles are played experimentally, tentatively, searchingly, and with an honest desire for a better understanding of the roles themselves. There can be no question about the role-players' sincerity in desiring to learn to play the roles authentically, and oddly, they play the roles with their tongue in their cheek, as if they put insincerity in the service of sincerity: the roles are artificially enacted for the purpose that their habitual and ingrained insincerities be detected and disclosed. When role-playing is enlisted to help education, training, retraining, and rehabilitation, the same stratagem is used. When, for example, prisoners, about to be placed on parole, are invited to play the role of being free and, say, the role of trying to find a job, they are not only using 'let's pretend' to discover those instances in the past in which they were falsely behaving, and consequently failing, but they are also imaginatively anticipating the future role, defining this role, and bringing their total role-system in line with it.[57] The practice of paedagogy teems with examples of role-playing used as 'character-education'. In fact, the recourse to this technique in education is so common-place as to permit me to dispense with documentation. There are, however, other less conspicuous areas too in which this device is used. 'In the armed forces', writes Michael Banton, 'youths are often treated as men and respond by behaving as men. Often a role brings out in individuals qualities that might otherwise have gone unsuspected.'[58] One wonders whether a systematic and deliberate policy of treating all adolescents in this manner would not pay generous dividends in terms of a reduction of juvenile antisocial behaviour as well as in terms of an increase in youthfully vigorous additions to our social adaptability.

In all these instances role-playing is institutionalised explicitly to serve the social end of changing individuals in ways desired by society. Exigencies, situations, new turns of events are anticipated and responses to them are tried out in a planned and guided manner, under the supervision of professionals. At the same time we, unguided, solitary individuals too, prepare ourselves for contingencies in much the same manner. In fact, all our sub-vocal and private anticipatory thinking about what we will say to an antagonist when we meet him tomorrow, how we will parry his criticism, and how we will retaliate, or how we will assure him of our peaceful or perhaps even compassionate intentions, are rehearsals. Indeed, all projects in our contingency thinking are instances of rehearsing for role-playing. It wouldn't occur to us to brand this sort of forward-looking behaviour as insincere.

A well-known special case of this anticipatory pretending is the role-playing of the child. Writing of the play of primitive peoples and about their attitude to the mysterious forces of nature about them, George Herbert Mead explains that primitive man plays the roles of their gods and heroes 'going through certain rites which are the representation of what these individuals are supposed to be doing', and he goes on to explain that these have arisen 'out of situations similar to those in which little children play at being a parent, at being a teacher – vague personalities that are about them, and on which they depend. These are personalities which they take, roles they play, and so far control the development of their own personality.'[59] This theme of the anticipatory and progressive character of role-playing not only runs through man's life from infancy and barbarism to adulthood and civilisation, but is evident even in animal life. By now it is a trite hypothesis that the playing of kittens with a ball of wool is a preparation for the serious adult business of catching mice. But returning to the children, 'In play the child does definitely act the role which he himself has aroused in himself.'[60] Once again, this time with Mead's authority, we are reminded that the role-player with a kind of existential deliberateness 'arouses in himself' a role, generates in himself a new form. But even here one comes across the charge of insincerity, 'the child is typically hypocritical'[61] which is almost as much as saying that 'growing-up is hypocritical' or that 'maturation is hypocritical'. If so, one cannot help agreeing with Philip Rieff that, 'Hypocrisy is a precious thing in any culture.'[62]

There is yet another reason why the cynical and denigrating attitude to professional role-playing is wrong-headed. This consists in the naive 'black-and-white' disjunction of 'sincere-insincere'. There are surely all manner of intermediate positions which cannot be described by either of these two terms. Of course, the experiencing of the role may be 'put on' and yet, the very fact of the fine artistic craftsmanship coupled with the diligent and stubborn application to the task, transmit themselves to the beholders as devotedness, and sincerity: for who would describe the sentiments of a concert pianist as insincere just because the performance is prepared, practised, rehearsed, and contrived in every sense of the word? Or who would regard the conductor as one who merely shams the pathos and pretends the sentiments when gently stroking his adagios and petulantly whipping up his scherzos? How many of Winston Churchill's (and, indeed, of Hitler's) carefully prepared and rehearsed improvisations and elemental rhetorics could be fairly described as disingenuous? Is it not rather the case that the spectacle of sincerity will increase in proportion to the painstaking training and preparation that has gone into the final performance? Is it not that the integrity of the actor will be both moral and aesthetic and that his own idiosyncratic rejection of all that impinges on this integrity will keep it immaculate and, therefore, sincere? And doesn't this also convey a hint that perhaps the degrees of sincerity could even be expressed in sheer technical terms? Also, we are accustomed to look upon sincerity as an unqualified virtue; yet the devil is often sincere but his sincerity is infernal. Sincerity is a morally neutral attribute: though, of course, the sincerity which maximises the values of personal service will be morally appraised as distinct from the sincerity which maximises the values of political power.

Role-player artists, orators, psychodramatic patients, convicts, pupils and the like, systematically lift themselves up to the role they have resolved to play, and creatively call into being their emergent new selves. The product is one of aspiration, and what is achieved is real and true by the time it is achieved. What is displayed, really exists, and thus the performance established its sincerity.

Of course, the labour of defining 'sincerity' and 'insincerity' has presented philosophers with many intractable complexities. The sociologist might feel that he should avoid the making of distinctions which lie too far above or below his own level of analysis, and he should not burden himself with philosophical or psychological distinctions, which would only block insight into the larger social realities, no matter how valuable these distinctions might be in their proper place. For sociological and, therefore, limited purposes certain conclusions could be reached which might be helpful to contemporary role theory and which would assist in developing the central thesis of the present book.

1. The role-player's maximisation of the values of a dominant role in his role-system expresses itself in a role-performance which either effectively conceals, or recognisably fails to conceal, both from others and from himself, the influence of the values of other roles in his role system, roles that is, which are now in abeyance and are not now being played. When the role-performance fails in this concealment, the performance may legitimately be described as 'insincere' or 'hypocritical'. It is often assumed that in insincerity the relative social valuation attached to what is shown is higher than that which was intended to be concealed.

2. The greater the deliberate resolve and personal abandonment to the value-maximisation in a dominant role, the greater the chance of concealing and eventually suppressing discrepant values pertaining to other roles of the system which are not now being played.

3. The sustained, repeated, and one-pointed role-playing which characterises value-maximisation of the kind referred to in (2) results in a lasting change in the relative influence of the various dominant roles, on the role-organisation, and therefore, on the personality as a whole.

4. Professionalisation and especially a rapid growth in the number of those who are in the personal service professions entails a specific kind of lasting personality change in an increasing number of individuals and, *a fortiori*, a change in the culture and moral climate of the élite which these individuals are joining in growing numbers.

At its lowest estimate, 'the strength and tradition of the ideological legitimacy of the high-minded professions give them a peculiar source of inner security',[63] and as the number and influence of those who possess such attributes increases the moral quality of society's leadership becomes coloured with these attributes. At this lower estimate, one might even specifically observe that professionalisation of leadership widens the gap between it and the rest, and makes the harmonious democratic functioning of the whole more difficult. This is certainly a possibility not to be lightly dismissed.

The confluence of thinking about the process of 'professionalisation' and about 'role-theory' join here, and disclose the sociological importance of these considerations: by these considerations current social change is revealed to have certain interesting and promising directions.

It is a central notion of this book that the growing process of professionalisation is going to be slowly yet decisively responsible for the change in leadership ethics in our industrial societies. The maximisation of values which professional practice seems to entail, gives a new, though attenuated, charismatic character to professional leadership. Whereas in the Weberian scheme of things first comes the personal charisma, the dynamic crowd-converter qualities of unique personal leadership, and this is followed by the 'routinisation of the charisma', the dry spelling-out and codification of the great leader's values and aspirations, here we are faced with a strange reversal of the process. Being a practising member of a profession often involves the observance of ethical codes, and their rules, formulated to be adhered to. These codifications incorporate already routinised charisma which will be 'deroutinised' in professional practice. It is in practice that the abstract norms become concrete and the inert rules become living roles. In the personal service society a good deal of the charismatic, the inspirational, and the reforming initiative comes from the guerrilla activities of the multitude of dispersed professional workers. I wonder whether this concept, the 'deroutinisation of the charisma', is not a legitimate development, and indeed, an inevitable development from the Weberian notion? Until now, there has been no prompting, no perception of this in the social realities around us, but today, the social changes, mainly wrought by professionalisation, elicit this idea.

The professional codes embody the inspirational initiative of great Christian, Hippocratic, and humanistic leadership. In the industrial mass-societies some residues of this, some dehydrated packages of ideals can be found in the codes of professional ethics and conventions. In professional practice, one might say, the dehydrated matter is reconstituted. When the codes forbid the taking up of a calculating posture towards other people and enjoin the professional worker that he serves others, such codes give mere signs, by stating the rules: the signs are stationary and unmoving but those who take their direction from them will give the signs their meaning in practice.

In a recent paper,[64] D. J. Hickson and M. W. Thomas usefully summarised the principal criteria which appear in definitions of the 'professions' in the writings of twenty authoritative writers. There are altogether 14 criteria listed which seem to recur with varying frequency in these definitions, but no more than at an average of just under four only, in any one definition. I classified the 14 criteria into three groups: *'cognitive'* criteria, such as, 'skill-knowledge', 'education-training', 'competence'; *'institutional'* criteria, such as 'organised', 'licensed', 'fixed fee'; and *'normative'* criteria, such as 'code of conduct', 'altruistic service', 'applied to the affairs of others', 'indispensable public service', 'definite professional-client relationship', 'best impartial service given', and 'loyalty to colleagues'. So, of the 14 criteria – or 'elements', as the two authors call these – eight are *normative*, and of these at least six, or perhaps seven, explicitly prescribe conduct of an 'altruistic' or 'other-regarding' nature, as an essential 'element' of professional activity. The 20 definitions list the 14 elements altogether 79 times of which 33 are *normative*, 28 *cognitive*, and 17 are *institutional*. Out of a sample of 21 professional associations listed by Millerson, 18 forbid their members to seek to supplant a professional colleague, 16 forbid members to advertise themselves, except in prescribed ways, 14 forbid members to engage secretly in another occupation which may bring professional work or may compromise their position.[65] These are only three of a multitude of strictures. It may be said that in spite of these strictures professional people will find it possible to take up an unqualified mercenary stance whenever there is occasion for it. The sincerity of professional altruism is cynically questioned when we are exposed to the spectacle of a professional association's shameless bargaining for financial advantages for its members, or when we encounter gross mercenary behaviour displayed by members of a respected professional group. Not only the cynic but also the sober realist will refuse to be misled by sanctimonious and grandiloquent talk about professional ethics or by protestations of professional workers that their only aim in life is to render service to others. And yet it would be simply a misrepresentation of facts to omit from our account of professional behaviour the persevering seeking of other people's advantage and good, and the professional worker's evident gratification at the sight of realising that advantage and good in others. Clearly the professional activity is not only sustained by these, but without these – at any rate in the personal service professions – it would not succeed at all in discharging its tasks. In fact the professional worker realises his personality, at least partly, through realising certain professional goals which are other than the enhancement of his status or income. ' . . . Professionalism is an idea based on the real character of certain services', wrote Professor T. H. Marshall, and added, 'It is not a clever invention of selfish minds'.[66] It ought not to be necessary to draw sociological attention to the contribution made by professionalisation to cultural change. But the matter is grossly underestimated by the major ideological systems of social change. Of this Talcott Parsons writes, 'It is curious that . . . the ideologists . . . have almost completely overlooked the presence and strategic significance in our society of a set of occupational groups which are not either in their own opinion or by and large in the public estimation, devoted mainly to the goal of their own profit, but rather in some sense to "service". . . .'[67] There are, of course some who vigorously question this. Professor D. S. Lees is one of those who attacked professional pretensions to unselfishness and virtue. He put the claims and aspirations of the professional man in the following terms: The professional man's

> . . . activities are to be distinguished sharply from 'trade'. He is not engaged in 'selling' but in providing a service. He considers his client's (not 'customer's') welfare first; money-making is a secondary consideration. He is loyal to his group. He does not compete with his colleagues by price-cutting or advertising. He does not tout for business. He will not accept business offered to him 'which he knows, or in the ordinary case could have ascertained, is in the hands of another agent' in the same profession or, in some cases, allied professions. 'Thou shalt not covet thine colleague's client' is perhaps the first commandment of the professional creed. He does not associate with 'unqualified' persons. He conducts his personal as well as his business life in ways that reflect no discredit on his profession. He submits to disciplinary procedure which in extreme cases, may ruin him as a professional man.[68]

Professor Lees ends this description by declaring that 'to an economist schooled in the theory of competitive markets it seems at first blush suspiciously like mumbo jumbo.'[69] This is a good example of how a specialist outlook can become a distorted one for, 'schooled in the theory of competitive markets' might also read as 'steeped in and blinded by the theory of competitive markets'. For consider the two propositions: 'professional men sell their services' and 'dry cleaners sell their services'; both of these propositions are certainly true without justifying us in thinking that the motives for rendering the two services are entirely, or even mainly, the same. A table and an ass may both possess four legs and yet we should still hesitate to advance hypotheses which would proclaim their essential similarity.

Certainly, Professor Lees' strictures on the far-fetched claims advanced by professionals are salutary reminders. There is indeed often much hypocrisy in claims of this sort. I am entirely willing to accept the definition that 'the hypocrite is a man who sets a good example when he has an audience', and that professional workers are sometimes hypocrites. Of course, to the sociologist the audience reaction is – among other matters – of much interest, for the audience – that is to say society at large – may learn from the example and not from the hypocrisy. But irrespective of their actual influence on society, to maintain that the professional workers in general and especially in health, welfare, and education, serve entirely, or even mainly, their mercenary or power interests has remained an unproven hypothesis. Ralph Waldo Emerson said that a hero is an ordinary man who is brave five minutes longer. A personal service professional is an ordinary working man who gives that, say, five per cent extra service in excess of what could be formally expected of him. Of course, he does not go unrewarded for, as we know, the givers are well rewarded! *All that I am asking us to consider is that the cumulative and long-term social effect of this 'five per cent' extra, in societies, whose élites are totally professionalised, may turn out to be of substantial importance in terms of its influence on society and, therefore, in terms of cultural-moral change.* When British doctors, nurses and social workers go to the United States, for higher salaries or other personal advantage, and Pakistani or Indian doctors man some of the British National Health Service for similar motives, it readily comes to mind that these people are selling their services to the highest bidder. No one should underestimate this interpretation, though it is certainly not the only interpretation. But even so, what these people 'sell' is 'personal services', and selling personal services is different from selling anything else. There is no escaping the feeling – and possibly even the verifiable hypothesis – that the personal service professional 'would probably want to do the work even if fewer extrinsic rewards were available'[70] and that the work's rewards are either equal or superior to the best rewards life can offer in any station.

In our time when, in a number of countries at least, the medical profession is thought to have achieved a substantial though often well-deserved rise of income, and when British teachers go on strike for higher pay, my sociological diagnosis may appear to have much less the ring of truth about it than it could have had in other times. Certainly, sentimentalism about the professional man's alleged unconcern for financial advantage is not what I should wish to encourage. Yet, I would not allow a cynical account of professional motivation and aspiration to claim the monopoly of objectivity.

Of course, the professional worker sells his services, but he is also involved in a social performance which happens to be the carrier of moral idealism. *At its worst*, we have here a role-playing situation, an act of pretending, if you like. Yet it is a long enough sustained performance of make-believe to become what R. K. Merton called the 'self-fulfilling fallacy'.[71] One may say about the idealistic aspirations of professionals that many are well-meaning yet grey pedestrians, whilst some are born great, some achieve greatness, and some thrust greatness upon themselves.

But enough has been said: I have argued insistently and, I hope, not entirely unsuccessfully to show that when man plays a role he tends to maximise the values which the playing of the role is expected to activate. This, I have insisted, is a verifiable proposition about the nature of man. This characteristic of man is amplified and brought to striking prominence when the role played is in one of the personal service professions. But over and above the psychological propositions about the nature of man – that he is a maximiser of role-values – a sociological proposition is also advanced, according to which culture itself is so constituted that it defines roles in terms of ideals. Ideals are the maximisers of human performance and the cultural cues to human aspirations. Now, if these ideals are engendered and advanced by an élite group, constantly growing in numbers and influence, the materialistic, technocratic, and generally sceptical society will generate, in spite of itself, a culture of strong idealistic qualities. The Personal Service Society, a product of science and technology, an outcome of a rebellion against the old mendacious and hypocritical idealisms of the past, will become the carrier of an enlightened, objective and rationalistic idealism of the future.

These conclusions are about the past, as well as about the current, and the extrapolated future *facts* of the social process: they are not *prima facie* the affirmations of an idealistic moral philosophy. This book, the story it tells, the evidence it offers, is about social change. It does not offer a theory of social change which is to displace existing theories, either of the conflict-type or the functionalist harmony-type theories. It is offered as evidence for the pluralistic determination of social change, as an evidence for the need to qualify the predictions of both conflict – and harmony – theories.

The view has been expressed that self-assertion, competitiveness, and aggression are indelibly written into all forms of creativity, achievement, and personal autonomy. In fact, we are told by clinicians that dreaming about a thoroughly non-competitive society, a society without aggression, is foolish for such a society is incompatible with man's need to affirm his independence and ensure his adaptation in the face of a confining environment. Anthony Storr, in his recent book on *Human Aggression*,[72] takes Bertrand Russell to task because Russell looks forward to a world without war and want in which 'the liberation of the human spirit may be expected to lead to new splendours, new beauties and new sublimities impossible in the cramped and fierce world of the past.'[73] Storr thinks that Russell is naive in expecting an increase of creativity from peace, and plenty because 'a good deal of the world's great literature and music has been produced under the spur of economic necessity or political oppression'.[74] In one sense *all* the world's great literature and music has been produced either in misery or amidst misery: is any artist living even in the sophisticated luxury of the west unaware of what napalm does to Vietnamese children? Even if it be held disingenuous to say that contiguity and contemporaneity with the world's miseries make us all share it, the misery of our vulnerability and mortality we shall never escape and these will never cease to challenge us to resolve our anxieties creatively. It is certainly not the purpose of this book to conjure up naive images of an improbable future in which the state will consist of solicitous personal service professionals cultivating concern for all, and having lost God, satisfying the wildest fantasies of all about having arrived in some haven or refuge, under a parental umbrella of a personal service, provided for us all till the grave by a solicitous State. Of course, the personal service professionals will continue to be competitive, self-assertive, and aggressive, and so will everybody else, because it is our human nature to protect our personal integrity by energetically advancing it. But as culture changes, as the ideas informing our social institutions become clarified, as social institutions are made to serve our needs more efficiently and less painfully, so the mode, the manner, and the style of self-assertion and aggression of our leadership, and with it of our society, will change in the direction envisaged by Russell. The biopsychological endowments of man will not change for a very long time, if at all, but his institutions, his culture, his style of life and the climate of his moral order, still expressing the same biopsychological endowments, will change.

The actual process of change which will effect the necessary transmutation of an impersonal and disruptive society may not in fact rely on the personal service professions to the degree as this book suggested. I am sure that other factors too will play important parts, and that the sheer advance of science will always overshadow all other factors by the utterly unexpected influence it will exert. Yet in the wake of general scientific progress the personnel most closely in contact with its achievements and most intimately informed of its sociopsychological relevance will remain in the vanguard of moral change in society. And the members of the professions trained to render personal services to individuals and groups are likely to be the spearhead and main body of this vanguard, because they will, if anything, increasingly attend to needs that will never cease, or change no matter what surprises science may hold in store for us.

If, at times, my account appears to ignore elements in the social process which are discordant with the account it is not at all because it proposes to gloss over them. It passes over them because they have received a good deal more sociological attention than the ideas advanced by me, and because they are well entrenched in the minds of my readers already. The maximisation of role-values pertaining to the role-definition of concentration camp leaders, and of sundry other recently played notorious roles, would soon discourage us from blithely equating the theory of maximisation of values with a moral philosophical optimism and idealism, suggested by the spectacle of professional personal service. And yet we may be allowed to observe that there have been certain changes in industrial societies which have resulted in the growth of the number and influence of certain leadership roles, and in the corresponding decreases in the number and influence of some others, and that these changes have spelt the advance of certain role-values and the corresponding decline of certain others. Professionalisation constitutes a central part, the core, of the changes to which I am referring, and the growth of the personal service professions the central part, the core, of the process of professionalisation itself. The documentation of this process, the presentation of the evidence for its continuing occurrence was the task which I set myself in writing this book.

A series of hypotheses which represent my position and a summing up of this book may now be helpful:

1. Man's condition is constantly shaped and evolved not only through changes in his physical and social technology but also through the way this condition is henceforth more and more defined for him by those who are capable of perspicuous and discerning symbolic communication in the social sciences.

2. In the scientific-technological society of our times, and probably also in the future, most of those who are the 'appliers' of social science are the personal service professionals.

3. These professionals have institutionalised key-roles and increasingly prevalent roles, prevalent both in terms of numbers and in terms of social influence. The worthiest and, therefore, the most desirable social roles are to be those in which the gratification of the practising professional is to be realised in terms of the gratification of his clients. This type of *aspirational behaviour* becomes the dominant model to be emulated by others who are achievement-oriented in this society and it so happens that the ethos of the personal service professional becomes increasingly the ethos of the industrial society in which its constant growth has been made possible.

No doubt, these hypotheses about social change and cultural change suggest and even strongly encourage some value-judgments. Yet the aims of this book are hypotheses and their testing: the ethical overtones are those of humanity and of the subject-matter, not of the hypotheses themselves.

We have so often been misled by self-flattering interpretations of this kind that we have become insensitive to their potential reality and credibility. We must not allow this insensitivity to continue to conceal the possibility that the totally sceptical view may be, after all, a mischievously inaccurate one.

Notes and Sources

Preface

1. Berger, P. L., *Invitation to Sociology* (Harmondsworth, 1966), p. 66.
2. McClelland, D. C., *The Achieving Society* (London and New York, 1961).

1. The Personal Service Professions

1. Halmos, P., *The Faith of the Counsellors* (London, 1965; New York, 1966).
2. Szász, T., 'Psychiatry as a Social Institution', in *Psychiatry and Responsibility*, Ed. Schoeck, H., and Wiggins, T. W. (pp. 7 and 14–15. London, and New York, 1962).
3. Halmos, P., op. cit., pp. 74–90.
4. Rieff, P., *The Triumph of the Therapeutic* (London, 1966; New York, 1965).
5. Halmos, P., op. cit., pp. 11–26.
6. Halmos, P., 'The Personal Service Society', *British Journal of Sociology*, Vol. 18, No. 1 (1967), pp. 13–28.
7. Soddy, K., and Ahrenfeldt, R. H. (Eds.), *Mental Health and Contemporary Thought* (London 1955; New York, 1967).
8. Soddy, K., and Ahrenfeldt, R. H. (Eds.), op. cit., pp. 169–70.
9. Titmuss, R., *Commitment to Welfare* (London, 1968), p. 73.
10. Halmos, P., 'Interprofessional Tripos', *Times Educational Supplement*, London (5 December 1958), and 'A Link Between the Professions', *The Times*, London (15 February, 1960).
11. Goode, W., 'The Librarian: from Occupation to Profession?', *The Library Quarterly*, Vol. 31, No. 4, (October 1961), pp. 306–18.
12. Ibid.
13. Merton, R. K., *Social Theory and Social Structure* (Glencoe, Illinois, 1964), p. 221.
14. Millerson, G., *The Qualifying Associations* (London and New York, 1964).
15. Parsons, Talcott, *Essays in Sociological Theory* (Glencoe, Illinois, 1954), p. 42.
16. Wagner, H. A., 'Principles of Professional Conduct in Engineering',

The Annals of the American Academy of Political and Social Science, 297 (January 1955), pp. 46–52.

17. Roth, A., *Business Background of Members of Parliament (Parliamentary Profiles*, London, 1967), pp. xiv–xv.

18. Halmos, P., *The Faith of the Counsellors*, Chapter 1.

19. Ibid., pp. 177–8.

20. Masterman, C. F. G., *The Condition of England* (London, 1909), p. 83, and cf. Buch, P. W., *Amateurs and Professionals in British Politics 1918–1959* (Chicago, 1963), p. 63.

21. *Management of Local Government*, 'The Local Government Councillor' by L. Moss and S. R. Parker, Vol. II (H.M.S.O. London, 1967), p. 31.

22. Lee, J. M., *Social Leaders and Public Persons* (Oxford, 1963), p. 123.

23. Felton, N., 'Careers Incentive Plan for Higher Education of Non-Professionals' (New York University Plan, 1967, roneotyped).

24. *New Careers* Newsletter, Winter 1967. Vol. 1, No. 3. New York University.

25. Wiley, Martha, cf. 'Designing Jobs and Careers for Model Cities Program' (New York University, September 1967, roneotyped).

26. Elston, Patricia, 'New Careers in Welfare for Professionals and Non Professionals' (New York University, December 1967).

27. *The Indigenous Nonprofessional*, American National Institute of Labor Education Mental Health Program, Report No. 3 (November 1964).

28. Ibid.

29. Goldthorpe, J. H., 'Social Stratification in Industrial Society', *Sociological Review Monograph*, No. 8 (October 1964), pp. 97–122; Dunning, E. G., and Hopper, E. I., 'Industrialisation and the Problem of Convergence: A Critical Note', *The Sociological Review*, Vol. 14, No. 2 (July 1966), pp. 163–86; Goldthorpe, J. H., 'A Reply to Dunning and Hopper', *The Sociological Review*, Vol. 14. No. 2 (July 1966), pp. 187–96.

2. *Social Thought and Social Action*

1. Engels to Bloch, London, 21–22 September 1890, cf. *Engels*, ed. by W. O. Henderson (Harmondsworth, 1967), p. 333.

2. Op. cit. p. 335.

3. Marx, K., *Capital* (Moscow, 1961), p. 5.

4. Znaniecki, Florian, *The Social Role of the Man of Knowledge* (New York, 1940), p. 109; Gewirth, A.,' Can Men Change Laws of Social Science?'

5. *Philosophy of Science*, Vol. XXI, No. 3 (July 1954), pp. 229–41.

6. Marcuse, H., *Reason and Revolution* (New York, 1941), pp. 343–4.

7. Bowman, Claude C., 'Is Sociology Too Detached?', *American Sociological Review*, Vol. XXI, No. 5 (October 1956), pp. 563–8.

8. Davie, M. R. (Ed.), *Sumner Today* (New Haven, Conn., 1940), p. 109.

9. Ibid.

10. Myrdal, G., *An American Dilemma* (New York, 1944), pp. 1048–9.

11. Cf. also Rose, Arnold M., 'Sociology and the Study of Values', *British Journal of Sociology*, Vol. VII, No. 1 (March 1956), pp. 1–17.

12. Lynd, R., *Knowledge for What?* (Princeton, N. J., 1945).

13. Nettler, G., 'Toward a Definition of the Sociologist', *American Sociological Review*, Vol. XII, No. 5 (October, 1946), pp. 553–60.

14. Hovland, C. I. et al., *Communication and Persuasion* (New Haven, Conn., 1953), p. 12.

15. Cf. Gewirth, op. cit.

16. Leiserson, Avery, 'Problems of Methodology in Political Research', *Political Science Quarterly*, Vol. LXVIII (1953).

16A. Ellul, J., *The Technological Society* (London, 1965), pp. 158–9.

17. Marx, K., and Engels, F., *The German Ideology* (London, 1965). This version is printed in *Karl Marx, Selected Writings in Sociology and Social Philosophy*, edited by T. B. Bottomore and M. Rubel (London, 1963), p. 84.

18. Dollard, C., 'A Middleman Looks at Social Science', *American Sociological Review*, Vol. XV, No. 1 (February 1950).

19. *New Statesman* (London, 30 August 1968).

20. Riesman, D., *Individualism Reconsidered* (Glencoe, Ill. 1954), pp. 12–13.

21. Nietzsche, F., *Twilight of the Idols*, 'Maxims and Arrows', 24.

22. Popper, K. R., *The Poverty of Historicism* (London, 1963), pp. 13, 15–16.

23. Venn, J., *Principles of Empirical or Deductive Logic* (London, 1889).

24. Ibid., pp. 575–6.

25. Also cf. Lasswell, H. D., 'The Normative Impact of the Behavioural Sciences', *Ethics*, Vol. LXVII (April 1957), Part II, No. 3, pp. 1–42.

26. Venn, op. cit., pp. 577–8.

27. Moore, B., 'Sociological Theory and Contemporary Politics', *American Journal of Sociology*, Vol. LXI, No. 2 (September 1955), pp. 107–15.

28. Weber, M., *The Methodology of the Social Sciences* (Glencoe, Ill., 1949), p. 44.

29. Cf. Lynd, Robert S., *Knowledge for What?*

30. Halmos, Paul, *Towards a Measure of Man* (London, 1957), p. 216.

31. Shils's Foreword to Max Weber, op. cit., p. vi.

32. Bendix, Reinhard, 'Industrialisation, Ideologies and Social Structure', *American Sociological Review*, Vol. 24, No. 5 (October 1959), pp. 613–23.

33. Mannheim, Karl, 'The Ideological Uses of Sociology' in *The Uses of Sociology*, ed. by Lazarsfeld, P. F., Sewell, W. H., Wilensky, H. L. (London, 1968), pp. 63–77.

34. Glazer, Nathan, *Ideology and Utopia* (London, 1946), p. 37.

35. Jacobs, P., and Landau, S. (Eds.), *The New Radicals* (Harmondsworth, 1967), p. 100.

36. Skinner, B. F., 'Behaviourism at Fifty' in *Behaviourism and Phenomenology*, ed. by Wann, T. W. (Chicago, 1967), p. 91.

37. Ibid.

38. Ibid., p. 113.

39. Much of *The Faith of the Counsellors* is devoted to showing that this is so.

40. Soviet school children are enjoined to do this, cf.: G. C. F. Bereday, W. W. Brickman, and G. H. Read, *The Changing Soviet School* (London, 1960), p. 429.

41. Cf., Westwood, L. J., 'The Role of the Teacher', *Educational Research*, Vol. 10, No. 1 (November 1967), pp. 21–37.

42. Burt, Cyril, 'The Historical Development of the Guidance Movement in Education – England', *The Yearbook of Education* (London, 1955), pp. 80–99.

43. Ibid.

44. Morris, Ben, 'Guidance as a Concept in Educational Philosophy: United Kingdom', op. cit., pp. 121–40.

45. Cf. *Faith of the Counsellors*, pp. 156–75.

46. 'Curriculum and Promotion of Mental Health', *The Yearbook of Education* (London, 1958), pp. 242–58.

47. Butts, R. F., *A Cultural History of Western Education* (London, 1955), p. 391.

48. Wall, W. D., op. cit.

49. Moore, B. M., 'The Influence of the Promotion of Mental Health on the U.S. Secondary Curriculum', *The Education Yearbook* (London, 1958), pp. 259–71.

50. Ibid.

51. Cf. Burn, Michael, *Mr Lyward's Answer* (London, 1956).

52. Cf. Bandura, A., and Walters, R., *Adolescent Aggression* (New York, 1959).

53. Wheeler, O., Phillips, W., Spillane, S. P., *Mental Health and Education* (London, 1961), p. 165.

54. Peters, R. S., 'Mental Health as an Educational Aim' in *Aims in Education*, edited by T. H. B. Hollins (Manchester, 1964), pp. 71–90

55. Bantock, G. H., *Education and Values* (London, 1965), p. 97.

56. Brubacher, J. S., *Modern Philosophy of Education* (London, 1962), p. 319.

57. Niblett, W. R., *Education and the Modern Mind* (London, 1954), p. 83.

58. British Council of Churches, *Sex and Morality* (London, 1966).
59. Russell, Claude, 'Tradition and Change in the Concept of the Ideal Teacher', *Yearbook of Education 1963* (London, 1963), pp. 16–25.
60. Floud, Jean, 'Teaching in the Affluent Society', *Yearbook of Education 1963* (London, 1963), pp. 382–9.
61. Cf. *The Faith of the Counsellors*, pp. 68–73.
62. Judges, A. V. (Ed), *The Function of Teaching* (London, 1959), p. 129.
63. Cf. *Sociological Review Monographs*, University of Keele, Nos. 1–4, 1959–61.
64. Tibble, J. W., in *Linking Home and School*, ed. by Craft, M., Raynor, J., Cohen, L., (London, 1967), p. 222.
65. Craft, Maurice, *Education for Teaching*.
66. 'Supervising School-Practice Experiment in Use of Social Casework Technique', *New Era*, (June 1968), pp. 101–4.
67. Wright Mills, C., *White Collar* (New York, 1962), p. 32.
68. Bowen, H. R., *Social Responsibility of Businessmen* (New York, 1953), pp. 48–50.
69. Bendix, R., *Work and Authority in Industry* (London and New York, 1956).
70. Durkheim, E., *Professional Ethics and Civic Morals* (London, 1957).
71. Tawney, R. H., *Acquisitive Society* (London, 1921).
72. Carr Saunders, A. M., and Wilson, P. A., *The Professions* (Oxford, 1933), p. 493.
73. Cole, A. H., *Business Enterprise in the Social Setting* (1959), p. 15.
74. Hunter, G., *The Role of the Personnel Officer*, I.P.M. Occasional Papers, No. 12, p. 9.
75. Cole, A. H., op. cit., p. 74.
76. Selekman, B. M., *Moral Philosophy for Management* (London, 1959), p.5.
77. Ibid, p. 50.
78. Merton, R. K., *Social Theory and Social Structure* (Glencoe, Ill., 1964), cf. p. 212.
79. Galbraith, J. K., *The New Industrial State* (London, 1967), p. 141.
80. Ibid., p. 202.
81. Ibid., p. 141.
82. Ibid., p. 138.
83. Ibid., p. 265.
84. Katona, G., *Psychological Analysis of Economic Behaviour* (London and New York, 1951).
85. Ibid., p. 201.
86. Ibid., p. 196.
87. Ibid., p. 209.

88. Barber, R. B., 'Is American Business Becoming Professionalised?' in *Sociological Theory, Values, and Sociocultural Change*, ed. E. A. Tiryakian (London, 1963), p. 142.

89. Leeds, R., and Smith, T., *Using Social Science, Knowledge in Business and Industry* (Homewood, Ill. 1963), p. 52.

90. Vickers, G., *Towards a Sociology of Management* (London, 1967), p. 72.

91. Wright Mills, C., op. cit., p. 107.

92. McGregor, D., *The Professional Manager* (New York, 1967), p. 55.

93. Buber, M., *I and Thou* (Edinburgh, 1942; 2 edn. New York 1958.)

94. Lupton, T., *Industrial Behaviour and Personal Management* (London, 1946), p. 36.

95. Mullen, J. H., *Personality and Productivity in Management* (London, 1966), p. 41.

96. Greenwood, W. T., *Management and Organisational Behaviour Theories* (Cincinnati, 1965), p. 6.

97. Tannenbaum, R., Wechsler, I. R., and Massarik, F., *Leadership and Organisation* (London, 1961), p. ix.

98. Argyris, C., *Integrating the Individual and the Organisation* (London, 1964), p. 14.

99. Zaleznik, A., *Human Dilemmas of Leadership* (New York, 1966), p. 178.

100. Ibid., p. 207.

101. Levinson, H., Price, C. R., Munden, K. J., Mandle, H. J., Solley, C. M., *Man, Management, and Mental Health* (Harvard U.P., 1962), p. 169.

102. Ibid., p. 163.

103. Selekman, B. M., *A Moral Philosophy for Management* (London, 1959), p. 5.

104. Mills, A. E., and Edwards, J. P., *Management and Technologists* (London, 1968), p. 230.

105. Ibid.

106. Sofer, C., and Hutton G., *New Ways in Management Training* (London, 1958).

107. Warner, F. E., 'Education in Science and Technology', *The Political Quarterly*, Vol. 38, No. 1 (January–March 1967).

108. McNair, M. P., 'Thinking Ahead', *Harvard Business Review*, (March–April, 1957), pp. 15–39.

109. Jaques, E., *Changing Culture of a Factory* (London, 1951).

110. Sofer, C., and Hutton, G., op. cit.

111. Ibid., p. 87.

112. Ibid., p. 41.

113. Ibid., p. 55.

114. Ibid., p. 57.

115. Ibid., p. 71.
116. Ibid., p. 85.
117. Jahoda, M., *The Education of Technologists* (London, 1967), pp. 190–1.
118. Ibid.
119. Ibid., p. 89.
120. Ibid., p. 191.
121. Ibid., p. 35.
122. Ibid.
123. Brown, R. K., 'Research and Consultancy in Industrial Enterprise', *Sociology*, Vol. 1, No. 1 (January, 1967) pp. 33–60.
124. Ibid.
125. Ibid.
126. Chapman, Brian, *The Profession of Government* (London, 1966), pp. 110–111.
127. Ibid., p. 127.
128. Susanszky, J. (Ed.), *Veʒetési Ismeretek II, 'Management Studies II'* (Budapest, 1968).
129. Ibid.
130. In Ibid., Gábor, Horvath László: 'Aspects of Communication, Decision-making, Control, and Work Psychology in Management', pp. 127–74.
131. Ibid., p. 133.
132. Ibid., p. 134.
133. Ibid., p. 135.
134. Ibid., p. 135.
135. Fischer, G., in *Soviet Sociology*, ed. by Simirenko A. (Chicago, 1966), p. 341.
136. Hegedüs, A. (Ed.), *Munkasʒociologia, 'Sociology of Work'* (Budapest, 1968).
137. Ibid., pp. 11–12.
138. Yadov, Rozin, Zdravomislov, in Ibid., p. 348.
139. Ibid.
140. Varga, S. (Ed.), *Ipar-Vállalatok Veʒetése, Sʒerveʒése és Terveʒése, 'The Planning, Organisation, and Leadership of Industry'* (Budapest, 1968), p. 367.
141. Doctór, K., Hirsowicz, M., Matejko, A., and Kulpinska, J., in Hegedüs, op. cit., p. 376.
142. Wootton, Barbara, *Social Science and Social Pathology* (London, 1959), p. 278.
143. Ibid., p. 272, and Pusic, Eugen, *New Trends in European Social Work* (1954), p. 84. Dr Pusic, a signatory of the Report, *The Contribution of Social*

Sciences in Social Work Training. (Report of a United Nations (Unesco Meeting of Experts UNESCO, 1961), seemed to underwrite the recommendations along counselling lines in the psychological sections of this document.)

3. *The Moral Reformation of Leadership in a Personal Service Society*

1. Baldwin, James, *The Fire Next Time* (London, 1963), p. 81.

2. Sartre, J. P., *L'Être et le Néant*, English translation by Hazel E. Barnes *Being and Nothingness* (London, 1957).

3. Knudsen, R. D., *The Idea of Transcendence in the Philosophy of Karl Jaspers* (Amsterdam, 1958), p. 169, quoted by Tiryakian, E. A., *Sociologism and Existentialism* (New Jersey, 1962), p. 141.

4. Kenniston, K., 'Alienation and the Decline of Utopia', *American Scholar*, Vol. 29 (Spring, 1960).

5. Cf. Laing, R. D., *The Divided Self* (London, 1967).

6. Cf. Laing, R. D., *The Politics of Experience and The Bird of Paradise* (London, 1967).

7. Caplow, T., *The Sociology of Work* (London, 1954), p. 134.

8. Greenwood, E., 'Attributes of a Profession', *Social Work*, Vol. 2, No. 3 (July, 1957). Reprinted in *Professionalisation*, ed. by Vollmer, H. M., and Mills, D. L. (London, 1966), p. 17.

9. Eliot, G., *Middlemarch*, Vol. II (London, Everyman's, 1949), p. 26.

10. Sarbin, T. R., and Allen, V. L., 'Role Enactment, Audience Feedback, and Attitude Change', *Sociometry*, Vol. 27 (1964), pp. 183–93.

11. Sarbin, T. R., 'Role Theoretical Interpretation of Psychological Change' in *Personality Change*, ed. by Worchel, P., and Byrne, D., (New York, 1964).

12. Janis, I. L., and King, B. T., 'The Influence of Role Playing on Opinion Change', *Journal of Abnormal and Social Psychology*, Vol. 49 (1954), pp. 211–18. King, B. T., Janis, I. L., 'Comparison of Effectiveness of Improvised Versus Non-Improvised Role Playing in Producing Opinion Change', *Human Relations*, Vol. IX (1956), pp. 177–86. Culbertson, F. M., 'Modification of an Emotionally Held Attitude through Role-Playing', *Journal of Abnormal and Social Psychology*, Vol. 54 (1957), pp. 230–3.

13. Elms, A. C., and Janis, I. L., 'Counter-norm Attitudes Induced by Consonance versus Dissonance Conditions of Role-Playing', *Journal of Experimental Research in Personality*, Vol. I (1965), pp. 50–60. Janis, I. L., and Gilmore, J. B., 'The Influence of Incentive Conditions on the Success of Role Playing in Modifying Attitude', *Journal of Personality and Social Psychology*, Vol. 1 (1965), pp. 17–27. Elms, A. C., 'Role Playing, Incentive, and Dissonance', *Psychological Bulletin*, Vol. 68, No. 2 (1967), pp. 132–48.

14. Liebermann, S., 'The effects of Changes in Roles on the Attitudes of Role Occupants', Oran, P. G., 'Induction of Action and Attitude Change: the function of Role-Self Conflicts and Levels of Endorsement', *The Journal of Psychology*, Vol. 168 (1968), pp. 39–48.

15. Richards, I. A., adapted from Coleridge.

16. McCall, G., and Simmons, J. L., *Identities and Interactions* (London, 1966).

17. Goffman, E., *The Presentation of the Self in Everyday Life* (New York, 1959), p. 18.

18. Chapman, R. L., Kennedy, J. L., Newell, A., and Birch, W. C., 'The Systems Research Laboratory's Airdefense Experiment' in *Simulation in Social Science: Readings*, ed. by Guetzkow H. (New Jersey, 1962), p. 185.

19. Sartre, J. P., op. cit., p. 62.

20. Garfield, Sol. L., 'Some Comments on: "The Problem and Promise of Sincerity in the Personal Service Professions" by Paul Halmos'. Presented at the 7th International Congress of Mental Health, London, 1968.

21. Sharaf, M. R., and Levinson, D. J., 'The Quest for Omnipotence in Professional Training', *Psychiatry*, Vol. 27, No. 2 (May 1964), pp. 135–49.

22. Simon, H. A., 'Theories of Decision-Making in Economics and Behavioural Science' in *Surveys of Economic Theory*, Vol. III (London, 1966), pp. 1–28.

23. Hayes, S. P., 'Some Psychological Problems of Economics', *Psychological Bulletin*, Vol. 47, No. 4 (July 1950).

24. Simey, T. S., *Social Science and Social Purpose* (London, 1968; New York 1969), p. 49.

25. Haire, M., *Psychology in Management* (London, 1956), p. 35.

26. Goffman, E., op. cit., p. 35. Cooley, C. H., *Human Nature and the Social Order* (New York, 1922), pp. 352–3.

27. Warnock, M., *The Philosophy of Sartre* (London, 1965), pp. 53–4.

28. Ibid., p. 62.

29. McCall, G., and Simmons, J. L., *Identities and Interactions* (London, 1966), p. 71.

30. Shibutani, T., *Society and Personality* (New Jersey, 1961), pp. 47–8.

31. Berger, P., *Invitation to Sociology* (London, 1963), p. 113.

32. Dante, *Purgatorio*, XXIV.

33. Ferguson, F., *The Idea of a Theatre* (Princeton, 1949), p. 236.

34. Sartre, J. P., op. cit., p. 581.

35. Buber, M., *Pointing the Way* (London, 1957), p. 8.

36. Jaspers, Karl, *Way to Wisdom* (London, 1967), p. 26.

37. Cf. Jourard, Sidney, *Disclosing Man to Himself* (New York, 1968).

38. Laing, R. D., *The Divided Self*, p. 35.

39. Cf. Halmos, P., *The Faith of the Counsellors*, pp. 54–60.

40. McGregor, D., op. cit., pp. 74–5.

41. Blumberg, Paul, *Industrial Democracy: the Sociology of Participation* (London, 1968; New York 1969), p. 118.

42. Santayana, G., *Soliloquies in England and Later Soliloquies* (New York, 1922), pp. 133–4.

43. Festinger, L., *A Theory of Cognitive Dissonance* (London, 1959; Stanford, 1959).

44. Zimbardo, G. P., 'The Effect of Effort and Improvisation on Self-Persuasion Produced by Role-Playing', *Journal of Experimental Social Psychology* (1965), pp. 103–20.

45. Ibid.

46. The reference to a 'moral' or 'spiritual' fact must not pass without comment. All I intended to say is that if humanity is the bearer of an as yet inexplicable quality which raises it above the level of the material universe then it is that quality which I shall regard as a 'moral' or 'spiritual' 'fact'.

47. Wood, S. M., 'Uniform – It's Significance as a Factor in Role-Relationships', *Sociological Review*, Vol. 14, No. 2 (July 1966), pp. 139–51.

48. Wilensky, H. L., 'The Professionalisation of Everyone', *The American Journal of Sociology*, Vol. 70, No. 2 (1964), pp. 137–58.

49. Emmett, D., *Rules, Roles and Relations* (London, 1966), p. 163.

50. Etzioni, A., *A Comparative Analysis of Complex Organisations* (London, 1965), p. 221.

51. Thoenes, P., *The Elite in the Welfare State* (London, 1966), pp. 29–30.

52. Stanislawski, C., *Creating a Role* (London, 1963), p. 50.

53. Holt, David, *Hypokrites and Analyst*. The Guild of Pastoral Psychology Lecture, No. 145 (London, 1968).

54. Collingwood, R. G., *The Principles of Art* (Oxford, 1963), p. 115.

55. Goffman, E., op. cit.

56. Ibid.

57. Martin, R., Weeks, H. A., 'Role-Playing as Preparation for Release from a Correctional Institute', *Journal of Criminal Law, Criminology and Police Science*, Vol. 50, No. 5 (1960), pp. 134–7 (Reprinted in *Sociology in Use*, ed. by Valdes, D. M., and Dean, D. G., London, pp. 110–20.)

58. Banton, M., *Roles* (London, 1965), p. 100.

59. Mead, G. H., *Mind, Self, and Society* (Chicago, 1959), p. 153.

60. Ibid.

61. Ibid.

62. Rieff, Philip, *The Triumph of the Therapeutic*.

63. Bensman, J., *Dollars and Sense* (London, 1967), p. 74.

64. Hickson, D. J., and Thomas, M. W., 'Professionalisation in Britain:

A Preliminary Measurement', *Sociology*, Vol. 3, No. 1 (January 1969), pp. 27–53.

65. Millerson, G., *The Qualifying Associations* (London, 1964), p. 167.

66. Marshall, T. H., *Class, Citizenship, and Social Development* (New York, 1964), p. 159.

67. Parsons, Talcott, *Essays in Sociological Theory* (New York, 1964), pp. 370–1.

68. Lees, D., *Economic Consequences of the Professions* (I.E.A., London, 1966), pp. 7 and 32.

69. Ibid.

70. Hall, R. H., 'Professionalisation and Bureaucratisation', *American Sociological Review* (1968), pp. 92–104.

71. Halmos, P., 'Social Science and Social Change', *Ethics*, Vol. 69, No. 2 (1959), pp. 102–19. Cf. the famous dictum of W. I. Thomas, 'If men define situations as real, they are real in their consequences'. See Merton, R. K., *Social Theory and Social Structure* (Glencoe, 1964), pp. 421–36.

72. Storr, A., *Human Aggression* (London and New York, 1968).

73. Russell, Bertrand, *Has Man a Future?* (London, 1961), p. 125.

74. Storr, A., op. cit., p. 53.

Index